Stitched Up

Counterfire

Series Editor: Neil Faulkner

Counterfire is a socialist organisation which campaigns against capitalism, war, and injustice. It organises nationally, locally, and through its website and print publications, operating as part of broader mass movements, for a society based on democracy, equality, and human need.

Counterfire stands in the revolutionary Marxist tradition, believing that radical change can come only through the mass action of ordinary people. To find out more, visit www.counterfire.org

This series aims to present radical perspectives on history, society, and current affairs to trade unionists, students, activists and everyone concerned about the state of the world. The best measure of its success will be the degree to which it inspires readers to be active in the struggle to change the world.

Also available:

A Marxist History of the World:
From Neanderthals to Neoliberals
Neil Faulkner

How a Century of War Changed the Lives of Women
Lindsey German

Forthcoming:

The Second World War:
A Marxist History
Chris Bambery

Stitched Up

The Anti-Capitalist
Book of Fashion

Tansy E. Hoskins

PlutoPress
www.plutobooks.com

Fernwood Publishing
HALIFAX & WINNIPEG
www.fernwoodpublishing.ca

First published 2014 by Pluto Press
345 Archway Road, London N6 5AA
www.plutobooks.com

Distributed in the United States of America exclusively by
Palgrave Macmillan, a division of St. Martin's Press LLC,
175 Fifth Avenue, New York, NY 10010

Published in Canada by Fernwood Publishing, 32 Oceanvista Lane, Black Point,
Nova Scotia, B0J 1B0 and 748 Broadway Avenue, Winnipeg, Manitoba, R3G 0X3
www.fernwoodpublishing.ca

Fernwood Publishing Company Limited gratefully acknowledges the financial
support of the Government of Canada through the Canada Book Fund and the
Canada Council for the Arts, the Nova Scotia Department of Communities, Culture
and Heritage, the Manitoba Department of Culture, Heritage and Tourism under the
Manitoba Publishers Marketing Assistance Program and the Province of Manitoba,
through the Book Publishing Tax Credit, for our publishing program.

Library and Archives Canada Cataloguing in Publication
Hopkins, Tansy E., 1981-, author
    Stitched up : the anti-capitalist book of fashion / Tansy E. Hopkins.
Includes bibliographical references. ISBN 978-1-55266-663-0 (pbk.)
    1. Clothing trade–Social aspects. 2. Clothing trade– Political aspects. 3. Clothing
trade–Environmental aspects. 4. Fashion–Social aspects. 5. Fashion–Political aspects.
6. Consumption (Economics)–Social aspects. I. Title.
HD9940.A2H66 2014   338.4'774692   C2013-907529-1

Copyright © Tansy E. Hoskins 2014

British Library Cataloguing in Publication Data
A catalogue record for this book is available from the British Library

ISBN   978 0 7453 3290 1   Hardback
ISBN   978 0 7453 3456 1   Paperback (Pluto Press)
ISBN   978 1 55266 663 0   Fernwood
ISBN   978 1 7837 1006 5   PDF eBook
ISBN   978 1 7837 1008 9   Kindle eBook
ISBN   978 1 7837 1007 2   EPUB eBook

Library of Congress Cataloging in Publication Data applied for

This book is printed on paper suitable for recycling and made from fully managed
and sustained forest sources. Logging, pulping and manufacturing processes are
expected to conform to the environmental standards of the country of origin.

10   9   8   7   6   5   4   3   2   1

Typeset from disk by Stanford DTP Services, Northampton, England
Text design by Melanie Patrick
Simultaneously printed digitally by CPI Antony Rowe, Chippenham, UK and
Edwards Bros in the United States of America

To my parents, Kay and Gareth,
with love and affection

Contents

It is because being oppressed sometimes brings with it some slim bonuses that we are occasionally prepared to put up with it. The most efficient oppressor is the one who persuades his underlings to love, desire and identify with his power; and any practice of political emancipation thus involves that most difficult of all forms of liberation, freeing ourselves from ourselves.

The other side of the story, however, is equally important. For if such dominion fails to yield its victims sufficient gratification over an extended period of time, then it is certain that they will finally revolt against it. If it is rational to settle for an ambiguous mixture of misery and marginal pleasure when the political alternatives appear perilous and obscure, it is equally rational to rebel when the miseries clearly outweigh the gratifications, and when it seems likely that there is more to be gained than to be lost by such action.

Terry Eagleton, *Ideology: An Introduction*

Seeing nothing is as political an act as seeing something.

Arundhati Roy

Introduction

There is no difference between a knight
and any other man except what he wears.[1]
Robin Hood

Bobae Tower in Bangkok, houses the largest wholesale market in Thailand. It is an underground maze of booths piled high with clothes. When I visited it in early 2013, my friend and I got lost in the labyrinth and ended up – unintentionally – back at the entrance. Instructions were shouted over the phone: '*leo sai, leo sai*' (turn left, and turn left), then '*leo qua*' (turn right). Weaving our way through the low-ceilinged, rabbit warren of clothes we eventually found Beam Design.

Beam Design has been in business for a decade, run by husband and wife duo Mr and Mrs Nin. Their booth is piled high with bundles of formal trousers waiting to be collected – smart office wear, tuxedo and harem pants in black, navy, taupe and grey. When I asked Mrs Nin how business was going, she responded with the familiar story that since 2008 business had fallen by about 40 per cent. Demand at Beam Design – and countless other companies, began to fall as the entire fashion industry slowed during the economic crisis. As demand fell, competition with other suppliers increased. *Kuu kang gan* (competition) came up time and again as we talked. In the labyrinth of Bobae Tower there are over 1,000 suppliers, and buyers can simply wander from booth to booth until they get the lowest possible price. If they do not get a price they like at one booth, they just move down the row. This constant downward pressure on the Bobae suppliers from buyers is what characterises the fashion industry.

Downward pressure drives companies, both large and small, to seek cheaper labour markets, to cut wages and to evade environmental standards in search of cheaper materials. Trousers made by Beam Design are no longer stitched in Bangkok; instead it is cheaper for the fabric to be cut in the capital and then be driven up and back to Isăn – a poor province in the north of Thailand. In Isăn the trousers are sewn by homeworkers, and it is they who have borne the brunt of the 40 per cent drop in orders. As she talked, Mrs Nin snipped loose threads from the cuffs and buttonholes of finished trousers. They could not afford, she said, to scale back much further.

* * *

There exists a conceptual impurity to the word 'fashion',[2] an impurity that some may accuse this book of contributing to. This book includes discussions of companies ranging from Chanel to Walmart, Louboutin to Tesco. I have not written separate books on 'high' fashion and 'high street' fashion, but have placed the two together. I have taken this approach for several reasons. First, there is a shrinking distinction between high fashion and high street fashion. In the Spring of 2013 River Island joined Topshop and Whistles as a contributor to London Fashion Week. Similarly J.Crew showed in New York and in Paris H&M held a show at the Musée Rodin.

Versace, Marni, Stella McCartney, Lanvin and Maison Martin Margiela have all done collections for H&M. Isaac Mizrahi, Missoni and Prabal Gurung have designed for Target in the United States, and Jean Paul Gaultier and Karl Lagerfeld both spent time as creative director for Coca-Cola. Famous couture houses rely more on sales of perfume and bath oils for their profits rather than $50,000 dresses.[3] Mass-produced sunglasses, 'It bags', boxer shorts, cosmetics, designer t-shirts and jeans with the word 'couture' printed on the label make up the majority of profits for the 'high fashion' industry. So why discuss only the pollution caused by high street brands in China when 'It bags' are being made in the factory next door?[4] Why discuss only the issues of body image and race representation on the catwalks of Paris and Milan when Topshop and H&M display the same exclusive aesthetic? Why pretend over-consumption is a problem only with regards to the cheapest brands?

Fashion is a social production. All of the materials and skills that give rise to great works are socially produced. Just as the greatest pianist needs a socially produced piano to play on, so the most lauded designer needs socially produced pencils and paper, materials, a set of skills learned from teachers and a history to both follow and rebel against, not to mention huge assistance in the form of design teams, administrators, financiers and, often, domestic staff.[5] Numerous copyright lawsuits against brands like Zara show just how much inspiration the high street takes from high fashion. Yet high fashion houses also rely on the high street to popularise their ideas and their brand (as well as continually doing their own thieving).[6] Ignoring social production leads to the mystification of fashion. The point of this book is to unpick and demystify the fashion industry and its ideology, not add to its carefully cultivated mystique. Therefore 'high fashion' gets no special pedestal. Instead, this book uses a simple, workable definition of fashion: 'changing styles of dress and appearance adopted by groups of people'.[7] This is an immediately controversial position, one that some accuse of being Procrustean[8] (after the legend of Procrustes who chopped people's legs off to make them into an arbitrary size). Fashion, it is claimed, is purely a European concept indistinguishable from capitalism, with Burgundy in the 1400s named as the 'cradle of fashion'.[9] Whilst I do not dispute this analysis of the origins of fashion, I do take issue with the way this definition has allowed 'fashion' to be historically guarded for a demographic that is rich and white.

There is a prevalent myth that those outside this demographic do not 'do fashion'. That what Paris/Milan/London/New York produce is fashion but what everyone else produces is just clothing or apparel. Everybody else – the vast majority of the world – has been relegated to being 'people without fashion', which translates to 'people without history'.[10] Julius Nyerere, the first president of Tanzania, stated: 'Of the crimes of colonialism there is none worse than the attempt to make us believe we had no indigenous culture of our own; or that what we did have was worthless.' This racist approach allows for the dehumanisation, and therefore guiltless exploitation, of the so-called third world. As the Marxist art critic John Berger has written: 'The last need of imperialism is not for raw materials, exploited labour and controlled markets, it is for a mankind that counts for nothing.'[11]

Defining fashion as Western also looks woefully out of date with regard to design and production as it is today. Countries as diverse as China, Colombia, India and Nigeria have vibrant industries, while neoliberalism and austerity have downgraded European wages to the point where corporations are scrabbling for the attention of Chinese consumers who may soon have more purchasing power than their European counterparts. For all of these reasons I have chosen a definition that is deliberately open and inclusive, material not ethereal, and which does not mystify the fashion industry.

The reality is far from mystical. In 2008 I went on a research trip to Dharavi, Mumbai's infamous city-within-a-city slum which houses over a million people. We walked through overhung alleyways lined with workshops filled with child workers losing their eyesight as they stitched clothes. A lot of the workshops were live–work units with rooms housing entire families perched on top. We climbed a rickety ladder to speak to a line of children working at a loom. Other children sat on the hard wooden planks of the floor sewing beads onto luxury shawls. 'Small fingers for difficult little beads,' our guide said shaking his head sadly.[12]

Later, turning a corner, the smell of goat skins hung up to dry in the searing sun hit the back of my throat and made me gag – to the amusement of the tannery workers. Skins dripped onto the dusty floor as around the courtyard people in workshops sewed bags and wove strips of leather into belts and jewellery.

'Do you make things for international clients?' I asked one of the workshop owners.

'Yes, of course,' he laughed and pointed at me. 'For you.'

He was pointing at my belt, bought the evening before. Woven leather sprayed blue and gold by people I now knew worked without protective equipment or masks. Their work, their lungs filling with paint fumes, their children going without an education, all to provide shops with accessories that are worn once or twice before being replaced. Victorian England's slum factories, staffed by children as young as seven, have not been banished to the history books as examples of cruelty: they still exist.

This book will not mystify the fashion industry because, above all, *Stitched Up* takes the position that whilst items from the fashion industry can be viewed as signs of the times or products of social consciousness, they should also be seen as products of industry. A dress is not just a structure of meaning, it is also a commodity produced by a corporation and sold on the market for a profit at huge environmental cost. The designer is a worker, whose work exists to enrich their company and earn them a wage – no matter how extravagant.[13] Paris Fashion Week is just an expensive sales pitch.[14]

By analysing the fashion industry as an industry, *Stitched Up* aims to keep the discussion of fashion firmly in the material world and to recognise that there is nothing academic about the struggles of those women and men seeking to free themselves from exploitation and oppression.

* * *

Early on in this process, I was abruptly asked what right I had to write about an industry I had not worked in (other than the inevitable stints on various shopfloors). My reply was that I *had* to write this book, that no one had adequately explained this omnipresent element of my life, that there was no single book on fashion that dealt with everything I wanted an end to: the terrible working conditions, the environmental destruction, the eating disorders I have watched friends fight, the racism that fashion promotes, the self-loathing and the black hole of wanting that exists and cannot be filled no matter how much you buy. I also reject the idea that only people who work in the upper echelons of the fashion industry should write about it. Fashion corporations purposefully work to have an effect on all of us – their ideas must be answered and, where necessary, rejected. The obligation to endure gives us the right to know,[15] but it also gives us the right – and the urgent need – to protest. Not working in fashion has blessed me with the freedom to write without worrying about future job prospects – a serious issue in an industry so devoid of criticism. As the photographer Nick Knight said: 'An art medium without a critical forum is not a healthy art medium.'[16]

I have not, however, written this book simply in order to criticise. Writing *Stitched Up* was possible only because I believe fashion truly is glorious and enthralling, as well as exasperating and terrible. The fashion industry's creations are inspiring and breathtaking. It is an incredibly skilled and demanding artform: 'In a society that expects from its authors and playwrights one or two great works in a lifetime, we take it in our stride when a designer does a magnificent collection each season.'[17] For every critical word in this book there exists a beautifully handcrafted item that captures the spirit of its time. But who made these clothes, and why did they not get to wear them?

Currently, the dreams and escape proffered in fashion are available only to the few, not the many. We suffer from 'possessive compulsive disorder'[18] rather than enjoyment, and fashion is, like the rest of art, tangled in a web of commerce and competition. Because I find fashion glorious as well as terrible, I write in the hope that it will one day be free from commerce and be experienced by everyone at unimaginable heights of creativity.

Finally, I write about fashion from an anti-capitalist perspective because for me there is no way of separating the issues in this book. There is no way to write about fashion's environmental impact without writing about the factories' impact on the people that staff them. Discussing the treatment of people necessitates an examination of racism and body issues, which also necessitates discussion of both alienation and consumption, and the impact of the monopolised ownership of the industry and the media brands that support it. To divide up these issues would be an artificial act, which would ignore the overarching role of capitalism. As the feminist academic Audre Lorde said: 'There is no such thing as a single-issue struggle because we do not live single-issue lives.'

* * *

Populations of vulnerable poor workers like those found in Isăan in Thailand are replicated the world over, a historically recent phenomenon created by colonialism and neoliberalism.[19] Neoliberalism refers to an economic model championed by Margaret Thatcher and Ronald Reagan in the 1980s, and Bill Clinton and Tony Blair in the 1990s. It emphasises the liberalisation of trade, the global integration of markets, the deregulation of state power and the privatisation of public services, all of which are portrayed as inevitable, like gravity.[20] Neoliberalism drives down wages and pits workers in different countries and companies against each other in the so-called race to the bottom. To fill the spending gaps produced by falling wages, neoliberalism pushes personal credit – an issue particularly pertinent to fashion.

Neoliberalism has gone hand in hand with globalisation ('a polite term for big companies setting up in places free from environmental restrictions or pesky unions') and fiscal reform ('tax cuts for the rich balanced for the sake of fairness with welfare cuts for the poor').[21] As a result, we live in a global society where malnutrition causes a third of all child deaths, yet world-wide, sales of luxury goods stand at approximately $150 billion, 60 per cent of this $150 billion goes to just 35 brands, most of which are owned by just a few conglomerates.[22]

The financial crisis that began in 2008 was the result of neoliberal strategies privileging deregulated financial services over manufacturing in Europe and the United States. This strategy saw the creation of a real-estate bubble built on sub-prime mortgages. The bursting of this bubble brought bank bailouts – a forced transfer of wealth from the poor to the rich – on a scale never been seen before.[23]

The disarray and uncertainty resulting from neoliberalism and the financial crisis has led many people to look for answers elsewhere. The anti-capitalist movement sprang into the news in 1999 when protestors in Seattle disrupted a World Trade Organisation summit. This was followed by mass demonstrations in Genoa in 2001, World Social Forums in Brazil and India, global anti-war campaigns, mass social movements across Latin America, and #Occupy, amongst many others. The Arab and African Uprisings of 2011 were largely a revolt against neoliberal conditions, and strikes and protests continue to flower across Europe. Here in London, UK Uncut stage occupations at Fortnum & Mason, Vodafone and Topshop. Anti-capitalism as a movement is vibrant and dynamic, but not always cohesive.

The lack of a single anti-capitalist manifesto does not negate the need to work towards an alternative to capitalism. In *Stitched Up* anti-capitalist means the rejection of the capitalist system as a whole because it is the systemic cause of sweatshops, child labour, environmental devastation and alienation. The problem is not simply one of bad companies or bad people at the top of society (though these exist), but of a bad system that produces destructive imperatives. The financial crisis has shone a spotlight on the work of anti-capitalism's most seminal thinker: Karl Marx. His work, and the work of those he influenced, plays a primary role in each of the chapters in this book.

But what does Karl Marx have to do with Karl Lagerfeld? What does neoliberalism or economic crisis have to do with the fashion industry? They are inextricably linked. Despite fashion being 'capitalism's favourite child',[24] the industry has been hit hard by the economic crisis. The impact on production was not just ten million jobless Chinese workers, but shock waves through the upper reaches of the industry, with the fashion designer Giorgio Armani saying: 'We are all feeling the crisis. It touches us all. Stores are buying less than last year. We cannot ignore it.'[25] The precarious nature of the fashion market has led one fashion CEO to state: 'I feel like I'm having a black tie dinner on top of a volcano.'[26]

The fashion industry lays out in sharp relief all the ins and outs of capitalism – the drive for profit and its resulting exploitation, the power that comes from owning society's means of production and the very real need to overhaul the unstable system we are currently living in.

Despite being unstable and unfair, capitalism is protected because it is often 'too close to the eyeball to be objectified'.[27] Like the traditional saying *the fish do not talk about the water*,[28] few people (up until the financial crisis) ever talked about capitalism as a system. Instead, life just seemed like life, not life under capitalism. *Stitched Up* is not an attempt to write a definitive book of fashion, but an attempt to make capitalism visible by discussing its very real impact on the fashion industry and by showing how the very concept of fashion is part of the social process of capitalism. Along the way, some fundamental characteristics of capitalism are illuminated and explored.

Ideology

Trying to make sense of the world that we live in, means looking at the world around us. What people see when they look is not implicit; rather, it can be determined through the use of ideology – the ideas, values and feelings that determine how people experience their societies at different times, how they see the very world around them.[29]

Take, for example, the coronation dress worn by Queen Victoria in 1837. Is this dress the symbol of the divine right of one family to rule all others; the legitimately accumulated wealth of a civilising empire, and of a national, racial, and class hierarchy that brought order and allowed trade and exquisite fashion design to flourish? Or does this dress represent tens of millions dead in famines across India in the late Victorian holocausts that created the so called third world?[30] Does it represent impoverished seamstresses going blind as they stitch by candlelight, and mercantile capitalism siphoning off wealth to wrap racist, unelected, inbred figureheads in organza, pearls and gold thread? Controlling which of these viewpoints is the accepted one is a powerful thing. It has allowed, throughout history, small groups to defend their property and their power without daily resort to armed suppression.[31] The essence of ideology is its ability to legitimate the power of the social class that is in charge.[32]

Imagine for a moment how it feels to walk around the National Gallery, surrounded by giant paintings of monarchs and aristocracy. From the oil paint to the gilt frames and surrounding building, everything exudes authority, all pointing towards the divine right of the rich to rule as if it were 'inevitable' (as Brad Pitt says in his Chanel advert). This authority is also exuded by the fashion industry.

Fashion is a solid gold picture frame for its wearer. It also requires its own solid gold frame because, after all, we are talking here only about bits of cloth, no matter how artfully sewn. It is everything that *goes around* clothes that makes them fashion. Catwalks, media prestige and hype, and elaborate shops combine to produce a false religiosity.[33] The National Gallery feeling occurs in fashion museums and branches of Louis Vuitton or Chanel, where the buildings and clothes ooze with a sense of righteous power: no one but Chanel could produce such wonders, so Chanel *belongs* at the top. The role of ideology is to ensure that this power structure either feels natural – or is simply not felt at all.[34]

Fashion is key to ideology. It so legitimates power that the mere fact of switching clothes can bestow a person with ruling-class prestige. Think, for example, of what occurs when poor clothes are swapped for rich ones in the films *The Prince and the Pauper*, *Aladdin*, *Pretty Woman*, *Maid in Manhattan*, *A Knight's Tale*, *The Count of Monte Cristo, Cinderella* or Ridley Scott's *Robin Hood*. Suddenly the protagonist is imbued with all the privileges of the ruling class. They have not changed, only their clothes have changed, causing 'Robin Hood' to declare that 'There is no difference between a knight and any other man except what he wears.' The role of clothes is made clear in these films: they legitimate power and cement the idea that those in charge of society are *supposed* to be in charge. Does class make fashion? Certainly, it is a key way for the rich to signal and reproduce their power.[35] Once the masses gain access to a certain fashion (or close approximation of it) the ruling classes move on, to leave everyone else behind.

As an artform, fashion plays a complicated role within ideology. Fashion can be both oppressive and emancipating, glorious and terrible, revolutionary and reactionary at the same time. It is inherently contradictory, as is all culture, and indeed all social reality.[36] Dominant culture's ability to smooth over, and hide, the vast contradictions contained in this book is a key reason why people are not in continual revolt. Therefore, whilst fashion can be inspiring and prompt us to dream of a brighter future, it can also be deeply oppressive. If fashion resists power, it is also a compelling form of it.[37]

Fashion is capable of summing up any given epoch, of bringing together time, society and art. In his work on this subject, the Marxist theoretician Louis Althusser described how art is held within ideology at the same time as maintaining a distance from it. This means that art is one medium whereby the ideology that gives birth to art can be perceived.[38] In short, art does not simply reflect ideology. The experience of art – including fashion – gives you the experience of the situation it represents. This does not mean looking at fashion provides a literal interpretation of a given period. The playwright Bertolt Brecht described art as reflecting life with special mirrors, when it reflects it at all. Fashion distorts what it reflects, and often what is not shown tells us as much as what is.[39] If we can understand ideologies, we can understand both the past and the present more deeply – an understanding that is needed to achieve liberation.[40]

* * *

Stitched Up unfolds as follows. Chapter 1 examines the monopolised ownership of fashion brands. It takes a historical look at the advent of fashion for the masses and examines the sums of money being made. It also explores the impact of the economic crisis on old and new fashion markets. Chapter 2 explores the monopolised nature of the fashion media and the impact this has on our common cultural heritage. It examines the impact of the internet on fashion reporting, dissects fashion blogging, explains the lack of criticism in the fashion industry and lifts the veil on the trend-forecasting industry.

Chapter 3 discusses the idea that the consumer is king and that the ills of the fashion industry are the fault of consumers. It puts into context the role of consumers by examining questions of class, debt and credit, recession, advertising, alienation and commodity fetishism. Chapter 4 is the flip side to this question – a look at the people who make fashion. It is an examination of the different forms of fashion production, of the impact on fashion of losing of the Multi Fibre Arrangement and of the economic crisis. It examines historical and present-day industrial struggles for change and critiques pro-sweatshop arguments by revealing who really benefits from exploitation.

The fashion industry's ill-treatment of people is linked irrevocably to its ill-treatment of the planet. Chapter 5 therefore concerns the environment. In examining case studies – water shortages, pollution, animal skins and chemical explosions – this chapter explains why environmental destruction is taking place under capitalism. There is also an examination of the shortfalls of proffered solutions – consuming differently, corporate social responsibility and technology.

Chapter 6 looks at the links between the fashion industry and body image, eating disorders and women's rights. It shows the impact of fashion on women employed by the industry as models and on the general public. It explores why such a narrow version of beauty is propagated and how the use of digital enhancement makes reality unpalatable. Chapter 7 answers the question: Is fashion racist? First, it examines the premise the industry is based on – that Paris makes fashion whilst everyone else makes 'apparel'. It looks at the representation of people of colour in the industry, critiques the habit of cultural appropriation, and discusses why such racism exists and its particular characteristics during this time of neoliberalism and economic crisis.

Chapters 8–10 examine attempts to change the fashion system. Chapter 8 looks at resisting the fashion industry. What happens when people use their clothing and appearance to defy fashion? Can fashion be reversed or refused? If you dress differently, does this count as rebellion? Is it possible to shock an industry that loves to shock? And is it possible to avoid co-option? Chapter 9 looks at both historical and present-day attempts to reform the fashion industry. Why do green fashion books suggest an ethical calculus to solve ethical dilemmas? Can corporations ever be green? Are trade unions or legislation the answer? And is there such a thing as just capitalism? Finally, Chapter 10 explores how we might dress in an ideal society. Who would design and make clothes? What would the world of fashion look like without class, race or gender? Would it even exist?

I agree with the activist economist Michael Albert who wrote: 'Our negative or critical messages don't generate anger and action but only pile up more evidence that the enemy is beyond reach.'[41] Whilst it is vital to expose the machinations of the fashion industry, I hope I have avoided the trap that Albert notes by writing about struggles that are seeking to change the fashion industry for the better. In addition, the last three chapters culminate in ideas for a brighter future. To combat hopelessness, I would like to reiterate that the fashion industry must be seen as part of capitalism. Capitalism is not a natural state of affairs; it is an economic system with a history, and what can be born can also die.[42] I hope that *Stitched Up* will bring capitalism into focus again instead of it being too close to the eyeball to be seen. My aim is to unpick one thread of the capitalist system and reveal what lies behind the clothes we wear. Hopefully, by the end of it, you will want to pull on the thread until the whole system unravels and we can re-stitch it into something new and beautiful.

CHAPTER ONE

Owning It

Linkenholt is a Hampshire village of meandering lanes lined by banks of daisies. Turkeys strut on manicured lawns and the village shop is run from the front room of a house. A bus only comes to the village if it is booked. The blacksmith can work for days without seeing another person and the story is still told of two sisters, now in their eighties, who cycled down the hill to a village dance where they met the two brothers who became their husbands.

In 2009, Linkenholt and its surrounding 2,000 acres were put up for sale. It was an unusual event that drew international attention – entire English villages do not often come on the market. The financial crisis cut Linkenholt's price tag to £25 million – far less than its actual worth. The sale passed the destiny of the land and the people who live and work on it into the hands of one man. The villagers met their new 'squire' the day after the sale was completed. He held a pit roast, shook hands with everyone and, by all accounts, gave a good impression of himself. He has not, however, been seen there since and neither lives nearby nor drops in to shoot pheasant on the estate. The nearest clue to the wealth of this distant figure lies 11 miles away in Newbury – a large, glass-fronted shop with a red sign, which sells leggings, cheap jeans, sweatshirts and sequinned dresses. The shop is always busy. So are the other 2,500 branches of this chain that encircle the planet.

Stefan Persson inherited H&M from his father. The budget clothing chain has made him the eighth richest person in the world. Forbes.com has a 'Real Time Billionaires' calculator. Refreshing itself every five minutes, it calculates which of the world's billionaires have just become even richer, based on the cost of a single share. It makes for compulsive viewing and, the last time I checked, Persson's fortune stood at $26 billion. No one I met in Linkenholt shopped at H&M. They were, however, all aware that they paid rent to one of the world's richest people and wryly acknowledged that he had probably bought Linkenholt with the 'change from his back pocket'. That is not to say that anyone spoke badly of him – the village narrative was one of gratitude that Persson had, so far, preserved Linkenholt's way of life.

There is a tension in Persson's ownership of Linkenholt – the romanticised preservation of English village life by a man made rich as Croesus from selling disposable fashion. H&M clothes are made in factories from Tunisia to China. They are mass-produced, using valuable water and crop resources and cause appalling pollution. The company produces up to 50 collections every year and advertises them using faked photographs of perfect bodies. In 2010 21 Bangladeshi factory workers were killed in a fire whilst making H&M clothes.[1] It seems that nothing could link the peaceful lanes of Linkenholt with this globalised chaos, but it does. Both are part of a business plan, devised within a capitalist system that allows vast resources to be concentrated in the hands of one person. This concentration of wealth and power recurs throughout the fashion world. The creativity and beauty of fashion is time and again channelled into the pockets of billionaire shareholders. But just how did selling t-shirts and hair clips make so many Forbes top-twenty billionaires?

The New Mrs Jones

Mass-market fashion is a new concept. While clothes have long been the playthings of the rich, the working classes lived for centuries with only the bare minimum on their backs. In 1844 Friedrich Engels, co-author of *The Communist Manifesto*, observed at first-hand the poverty in Britain's slums: 'the prevailing clothing consists of perfect rags often beyond all mending, or so patched that the original colour can no longer be detected. They wear . . . a suit of tatters.'[2] The Industrial Revolution introduced the factory production of materials such as cotton. Yet clothes continued to be made in unsanitary cottage industry workshops, characterised by very low wages and unsafe working conditions which resulted in high accident and death rates. By 1900 the clothing industry in Britain employed 1.25 million people and was the second largest employer of women and the fifth largest employer of men.[3]

A pioneer of moving clothing production from home workshops to large, purpose-built factories was Meshe David Osinsky, a 'not quite penniless' Russian Jew who emigrated to Leeds in 1900 to escape the anti-Semitism of Tsarist Russia. Starting out as a door-to-door pedlar of shoe laces, Meshe David Osinsky became Montague Burton, owner of a shop selling ready-to-wear men's suits for a just about affordable 11s. 9d. By 1909 Burton had four shops and owned a factory – Progress Mill in Leeds.

Five years later, at the outbreak of the First World War, Burton owned 14 shops. Men's clothing production had been geared towards the mass production of limited styles and colours, which amounted to uniforms for working-class men.[4] This converged with the need for actual uniforms when 5.5 million men were called up to fight.

Women were also put in uniform for the war effort and the women's branch of the Board of Agriculture sold cheap clothes such as dungarees to women agricultural workers. In 1918 four million demobilised troops were given either a 'demob.' suit or a small clothing allowance. As a result, by 1925 Burton owned the largest clothing factory in Europe. In the 1920s working-class women could save up and buy ready-made clothes from chain stores, but most made their dresses from cheap materials using Paris-inspired patterns found in magazines like *Mabs Fashions*.

The Great Depression of the 1930s saw two million people out of work. The poor of Britain survived without coats and with holes in their shoes. Having just one set of clothing was commonplace. 'How amazing,' wrote the journalist H. V. Morton in 1933, 'that in an age of electricity, of chromium, of trans-Atlantic flight and worldwide radio, the poor were still living like Saxon peasants'.[5] At the same time, Hollywood was in its influential Golden Age and the resulting fashions caused J. B. Priestley to tut that among the better-off urban populations there were 'factory girls looking like actresses'.[6]

By 1939, Montague Burton owned 595 shops, including five on Oxford Street.[7] The Second World War demanded more uniforms, but like a 'giant tapeworm'[8] it also brought rationing, sent factory workers off to fight on the front-line and reduced clothing consumption. The clothing trade was given a wartime boost (and Burton's was saved) by the government's Utility scheme between 1941 and 1952.

A drop in living standards and news of the 1917 Russian Revolution had caused a wave of agitation and dissent. Fear of an uprising was intensified by the Second World War. As Britain's allies fell one by one to the German army, the need to inspire people to fight for their country meant they had to be given a stake in society – in the

Tory politician Quentin Hogg's words: 'We must give them reforms or they will give us revolution.' The government, led by Neville Chamberlain, hoped the Utility scheme's provision of good quality, cheap clothing would keep up morale. The reluctant Chamberlain, a believer in leaving markets to themselves, set out to control raw materials. By May 1940, the government was the sole importer of nearly 90 per cent of all raw materials, including wool.[9]

Measures included the introduction of minimum production standards but also limited material use by restricting skirt lengths, sleeve widths, trouser turn-ups, and the use of elastic.[10] The Board of Trade insisted it was not looking to become a 'fashion dictator' but only wanted to ensure that the best possible use was made of supplies.[11] British *Vogue* approved and called Utility a mode of dressing 'well suited to these times'.[12]

In war-torn countries women were once again employed as munitions workers, bus conductors, front-line medical staff and labourers. They wore trousers and jumpers and tied their hair up in scarves. At the Californian Radio Plane Company, David Conover, a photo-journalist, met a worker named Norma Jean Baker. The resulting photographs for *Yank Magazine* were Marilyn Monroe's first step towards stardom.

The war ended in 1945, but the hard times and rationing rumbled on. Central planning of cloth production ended, but price and quality controls continued. Utility clothing led commentators to write that the workers looked well dressed.[13] One writer declared that 'for the first time in history fashion (such as it was) derived from the proletariat, not from the privileged'.[14]

This was a big change. Paris had traditionally been the fashion centre of the world. Styles started there, and then trickled down. The war had caused the loss of this sartorial guidance.[15] When the Nazis occupied France, their plan was to move the entire Parisian fashion industry to Berlin or Vienna. Although they decided against this, they did almost completely destroy the ready-to-wear sector, which had been a largely Jewish industry. The loss of French exports had given manufactures in New York a window to establish themselves as an alternative centre for fashion creation. For much of the fashion industry, the war's levelling of both the creation and wearing of fashion was disastrous. Where was the money in fashions that could not quickly be made unfashionable? How were the rich to be superior if egalitarianism eclipsed exclusivity?

The economic importance of the Paris fashion industry was summed up by Jean-Baptiste Colbert, an advisor to Louis XIV, who said: 'Fashion is to Paris what the gold mines of Peru are to Spain.' Determined to keep their goldmine open, in 1945 the Chambre Syndicale de la Couture Parisienne organised a tour of the latest Paris-designed fashions through Copenhagen, Barcelona, London and New York entitled *Le Théâtre de la Mode*. To avoid causing offence to war-ravaged cities by showing off the luxurious designs, they were sold as a form of resistance – beautiful clothes made 'with frozen fingers in their famished city'.[16]

The endeavours of Paris to regain its dominance were embodied by a man who had spent the war designing clothes for the wives of Nazi officers and French collaborators – Christian Dior.[17] He now turned his talent towards reinserting rigid hierarchies into fashion. In February 1947, Dior presented a collection which the media dubbed the 'New Look'. In Dior's words: 'We were emerging from a period of war, of uniforms, of women soldiers built like boxers. I drew women-flowers, soft shoulders, flowering busts, fine waists like liana and wide skirts like corolla.'[18] Essentially, the New Look replaced ease of movement and physical strength with an ultra-conservative vision of femininity complete with corsets. The look matched the political agenda of returning women to home and hearth, the style's forward thrust of the hips a sign that women were designed for child-bearing.[19] As 1.25 million women left industry,[20] the message was clear: women no longer needed work wear.

Dozens of books and articles have been written on how this was what women wanted and how ultimately the women of the world *chose* to adopt the New Look.[21] But to claim this is to ignore both the political climate of the era and the role of the powerful fashion system. In the tradition of fashion promotion, the styles received heavy coverage through a sophisticated network of media, including magazines like *Vogue* and *Harper's Bazaar, Mademoiselle, Seventeen* and *Women's Wear Daily*. The New Look had its own newspaper advertisements, publicists sent free clothes to influential women to wear and be photographed in, and department stores and shops promoted the style to encourage women to buy entire new wardrobes.

Dior and the New Look were funded by France's richest and most influential industrialist, Marcel Boussac. Known as the 'King of Cotton', Boussac backed Dior with an unprecedented 60 million French francs. It is no coincidence that the skirts of the New Look required 16 yards of fabric, a huge amount compared to the resourceful styles of the early 1940s. Boussac was determined that the fabric-heavy skirts of Dior's New Look would revitalise not just the Paris fashion industry but also the textile market.[22]

After a decade of death and deprivation, the desire to go from Cinders to Cinderella[23] was real. Amongst people without food, jobs or housing, however, the New Look was not popular. '40,000 francs for a dress, and our children have no milk' was one shout that went up when Dior's creations made their début in French shops.[24] It was not just that the style depended on reams of luxurious, expensive fabrics; there was also an emphasis on ornate accessories and jewellery which aimed at marking out the haves from the have-nots. There were organised protests against the style across North America, and in Britain the Labour government was asked to legislate against the long, wasteful skirts. 'I don't know whether to try to scrounge a lot of [clothing] coupons and sell off my clothes or just appear dowdy,' wrote one working-class woman in 1947.[25]

In Britain, the New Look and Utility clothing coexisted for several years, with the Paris style pared down to fit rationing requirements. After the war, British retailers and manufactures lobbied for the abolition of the Utility scheme, while trade unions campaigned for its retention. This difference of opinion over the provision of cheap, good quality clothing showed the disintegration of the wartime alliance between government, capital and labour. The war over, society was once again polarising.[26] Crudely put, Utility versus the New Look represents a political crossroads: For whose benefit should society be run?

In 1937, George Orwell had written of the mass production of clothing toning down the surface differences between classes.[27] But while rationing had reduced the worst ravages of poverty, the New Look reversed this trend and put working-class women back at the bottom of the fashion pile. As the New Look took over, sartorial post-war class lines were firmly redrawn. Big business and the rich benefited while women and working people lost out.

By the 1950s, Britain's Apparel & Fashion Industry Association (AFIA) was monitoring an industry transformed. Planned mass production worked at maximum speed using minimum labour; it was scientific, mechanised and employed trained managers and technicians.[28] The capability now existed to mass-produce fashion not just for men but also for women. All that was needed was for women to have the money to shop and the possibilities would be endless.

The post-war capitalist boom, which lasted from 1948 to 1970, was the result of continuing Cold War high arms expenditure and consensus amongst governments that the state must play a firm economic role in industry and social welfare.[29] As the unemployment rate fell to 3 per cent in the United States and 1.5 per cent in Britain, women were drawn back into work.[30] The number of married working women rose dramatically and overtook the number of working single women. This figure rose steadily until, by the 1980s, more than half of married women were in paid work.[31]

From the start of the twentieth century, Britain saw the advent of an independent 'teenage culture'. In the 1950s this had developed into distinct youth cultures in Britain and the United States, but not in France. As a result, the 1960s 'Youth Quake' (a term coined by *Vogue*'s editor, Diana Vreeland) saw the centre of fashion gravity shift temporarily from Paris to London. Brigitte Bardot told Chanel that couture was 'for grannies';[32] and the mini-skirt arrived. Although the 'Swinging Sixties' challenged the old guard, the infamous decade did not bring about fashion democracy. Rather than becoming egalitarian, fashion changed its currency. Previously the *grandes dames* with their money and social standing had been the focus of the fashion industry, now it was the turn of the mass youth.[33]

It was a case of fashion following the wealth line. This was the opinion of the influential fashion commentator Tobé Coller Davis. She pointed out that in 1929 the top 1 per cent of families in the United States had controlled 20 per cent of the country's wealth, but by 1953 this had dropped to less than 8 per cent.[34] Other senior figures in American department stores took the same view: 'I'd rather sell 5,000 units of something for $10 than one thing for $500,' stated a buyer who left the high-end store Saks Fifth Avenue to work at the more downmarket Sears. Stanley Marcus, owner of the Neiman Marcus department store, summed up the shift: 'We are geared to sell to the oilman, but even more, to the oilman's secretary.'[35]

The realisation that there was money to be made by selling clothes to more than just the top income bracket changed the industry's game plan. Manufacturing had been transformed, people had more disposable income than ever before and women were working in unprecedented numbers. Coller Davis called this challenge the New Mrs Jones: 'a flock numbering over 30 million women; she doesn't command one income of, say, $4000, but a Niagara of incomes of nearly one hundred billion dollars. If ever there were was a market, this is it.'[36]

Owning the Mass Market

In 1966 Paco Rabanne designed a paper dress as a publicity stunt for the Scott Paper Company. In a prophetic statement Rabanne said: 'It's very cheap and the woman will only wear it once or twice. For me it's the future of fashion.'[37] Fifty years later the market is characterised by throw-away 'fast-fashion', the result of competition having driven suppliers into shorter and shorter supply times. The market is also characterised by large international corporations owning clusters of brands and operating them internationally.

The Forbes 2013 Rich List read as follows: at number 1, Carlos Slim Helu the telecoms billionaire; at number 2, Bill Gates of Microsoft; then, at number 3, Amancio Ortega, purveyor of cheap shirts, dresses, shoes and blazers via the company Zara. Telecoms, computers and fast-fashion.

Ortega co-founded Inditex in 1963.[38] Comprising 100 companies, it is the world's biggest fashion company. These companies design, produce and distribute clothes to Inditex brands Zara, Massimo Dutti and others. Zara's storage and logistics warehouse is five million square feet, the equivalent of 90 football pitches.[39] In 2011, sales stood at approximately $18,236 million, of which $2,554 million was profit. By 2013 Ortega's personal fortune was $57 billion – rising by tens of billions over the course of the financial crisis.[40] At the time of her death in 2013, Ortega's former wife and Inditex business partner, Rosalia Mera, also had a personal fortune of $6.1 billion. In 2013 Inditex operated 6,058 stores in 82 countries and employed 120,000 people.

Ortega (and, of course, Stefan Persson) are far from the only billionaires in mass-market fashion. The Spanish company Mango is privately owned by its Turkish billionaire founders the Andic brothers. Bringing in $2 billion a year, Mango operates 1,200 stores in countries as diverse as Belarus and Iraq. In Japan, Uniqlo's founder, Tadashi Yanai, is the 88th richest person in the world with a personal fortune of $15.5 billion. Brazilian Nevaldo Rocha made $3 billion from co-founding Guararapes Confeccoes, the Brazillian equivalent of Zara.

Iceland's 2009 financial meltdown had an improbable impact on British mass-market fashion when Mosaic Fashions, owner of Oasis, Warehouse, Coast, Karen Millen and Principles, collapsed, owing £450 million to Iceland's Kaupthing Bank HF. To replace Mosaic, Aurora Fashions was established, with Kaupthing owning 90 per cent. Aurora now owns 766 shops in the United Kingdom, and has 6,900 employees and a turnover of £500 million.

No round-up of mass-market fashion would be complete without mentioning Primark, a company which for many has come to signify the evils of fast-fashion. In the first ten days of trading, Primark's flagship Oxford Circus store sold one million garments.[41] Primark is owned by Associated British Foods, a publicly traded company that is 54 per cent controlled by the Weston family's Wittington Investments.

Clothing is also big business for supermarkets, with 19 per cent of the UK fashion market controlled by supermarkets in 2005. Asda's George brand was worth £2 billion a year in 2011 and Tesco's stated aim is to become the world's largest fashion brand.[42] As a result of the recession, in 2012 supermarket clothing sales grew 6.2 per cent, while the fashion market as a whole saw a rise of just 2.7 per cent.[43]

The last decade has also seen the rise of online mass-market fashion. ASOS, for example, forecasts that it will be making a £1 billion in sales by 2015. Whilst the financial crisis has had an impact on UK sales, ASOS profits remain high because 'Fortunately we sell to 20-somethings all over the world.'[44]

The mass-market is also characterised by corporations owning multiple brands that appear to be competitors. In the United States, for example, in the casual clothes sector VF operates as a '$9 billion apparel and footwear power house'.[45] It owns dozens of 'competing' brands, including Lee, Wrangler, 7 for all mankind, Jansport, Eastpak, Reef, Vans off the Wall, The North Face and Timberland. Similarly, Gap Inc. owns Gap, Banana Republic, Old Navy, Piperlime and Athleta.

Another North American giant is PVH which owns Tommy Hilfiger and Calvin Klein. Calvin Klein's retail sales reached $6.7 billion in 2010. Most of these profits come from licensing agreements. Licensing involves a designer selling the rights to their name so that a third party can produce and sell named products. Calvin Klein has licensing arrangements with over 40 third partners. Everything from sportswear to suits are produced by licensees. Another heavily licensed company is publicly listed brand Ralph Lauren. The corporation includes the dozens of Ralph Lauren brands as well as Club Monaco. It had a net revenue of over $5,660 million in 2011.

Burton did not die with its founder in 1952. By 1987, the Burton Group had expanded to include 15 retail brands including Topshop. Sales of women's and children's clothes were higher than men's and it had a turnover of £1,338,600,000.[46] The Burton Group was renamed the Arcadia Group in 1997, and in 2002 Arcadia was acquired by Taveta Investments, which delisted it from the London Stock Exchange. Taveta Investments is controlled by the British billionaire Philip Green, who in 2005 received the biggest ever British corporate pay cheque: $1.2 billion. Conveniently, the company is registered with Tina Green, Philip's wife who is a resident of Monaco, a principality of 35,000 people and 350,000 bank accounts.[47] This exempts the Greens from paying tax on their $5 billion fortune. The use of tax havens is rife in the fashion industry. New Look, Monsoon, Matalan and River Island are all owned by companies based in tax havens, and John Lewis, Mango, Uniqlo, H&M, M&S, Primark, Gap and many others also utilise tax havens.[48]

The Treasure of Indigo Island

Mass-market fashion is an industry awash with billionaires. This is also true for mass-market's older and more glamorous sibling, high fashion. Indigo Island, in the Bahamas, has tropical beaches, a 133-acre estate with its own marina and hilltop villas that can be rented from Stellar Villas for $182,000–$322,000 a week. Indigo Island was bought by fashion billionaire Bernard Arnault for $35 million.

Arnault is the CEO of LVMH and its major shareholder. This is a result of Arnault being the chair and majority shareholder of the luxury goods group Christian Dior which is the main holding company of LVMH. Above all other companies, LVMH (Moët Hennessy – Louis Vuitton) dominates luxury fashion. A monopoly of primarily French heritage brands, LVMH's key brand is its namesake, Louis Vuitton. Louis Vuitton has been called the 'luxury Microsoft'[49] and also the McDonald's of the luxury industry: 'It's far and away the leader, brags of millions sold, has stores at all the top tourist sites – usually a step away from McD's – and has a logo as recognisable as the Golden Arches.'[50]

In 2012 Arnault was Europe's richest man and the fourth richest person on the planet, with a net worth of $41 billion. In 2013, he was listed as Forbes' tenth richest person, despite LVMH stock rising 6 per cent in this period.[51] A French businessman, Arnault made his money in property development and then spent two decades vacuuming up vast quantities of luxury companies. A close friend of former French President Nicolas Sarkozy, Arnault became the butt of anti-rich sentiment in France, with one newspaper running the headline 'Get Lost Rich Idiot'.[52] At the same time, he received a knighthood in the United Kingdom for services to business and the wider community.[53]

Arnault's acquisition tactics have been infamously ruthless. They heralded a new era for the world of fashion, ending the 'old boys' club. LVMH caused outrage and legal disputes by secretly buying up 22 per cent of Hermès in 2011. The Hermès family has now locked its 50 per cent share into a protected holding company. Hermès, along with Chanel (privately owned by Alain and Gerard Wertheimer, whose net worth was $19.2 billion in 2013), are hoped to be 'better guarded than Fort Knox'[54] against acquisition.

Amongst LVMH's main rivals is another conglomerate owned by another multi-billionaire. François-Henri Pinault is the major shareholder of Kering and has a net worth of $13 billion; he also owns the auction house Christie's. Kering was originally known as PPR, and before that Pinault-Printemps-Redoute, a company founded in 1963 to deal in woodcraft and building supplies. Kering's key brand is Gucci, Italy's biggest selling brand. Founded in 1921 Gucci was slowly bought up by PPR between 1999 and 2004. Employing 47,000 people, Kering's turnover in 2011 was about $16.1 billion.

The privately owned Labelux was set up in 2007 to be a significant contender in the luxury goods market. Labelux is a division of Joh A. Benckiser SE, which is owned by the reclusive Reiman family, whose chemical–factory fortune was valued at €8 billion in 2011. The Reimans also own Reckitt Benckiser, a cleaning products and skin care company, and Coty, the world's largest producer of mass-market perfumes, including fragrances by Beyoncé and Kate Moss. The Spanish conglomerate Puig owns four luxury fashion brands, including Jean Paul Gaultier, and controls 7 per cent of the world's premium perfume market. Puig made profits of €130 million in 2011.

A number of brands remain independent. Historically there has been a trend amongst Italian luxury fashion houses for remaining independent, family-owned businesses. Family capitalism is a trademark of the Italian economy and the patterns in fashion are repeated in other sectors like manufacturing and engineering. By 2013, however, this had begun to shift. The Prada Group was floated on the stock market in 2012,[55] and Versace and Marni are no longer private, family-owned businesses. For now the Max Mara Group remains private as does Dolce & Gabbana. In 2013 Domenico Dolce and Stefano Gabbana, were found guilty in the Italian courts of colossal tax evasion.

Giorgio Armani remains the sole shareholder for Giorgio Armani S.p.A. Since 1978 Armani has been backed by GFT (Gruppo Finanziario Tessile), Italy's largest textile manufacturer. With no

Table 1.1 Corporate ownership of major luxury fashion brands

LVMH	Kering	Richemont	Puig	Labelux	OTB SpA (Only the Brave)
Christian Dior*	Gucci	Chloé	Nina Ricci	Bally	Maison Martin Margiela
Louis Vuitton	Bottega Veneta	Azzedine Alaïa	Jean Paul Gaultier	Belstaff	Marni
Céline	Saint Laurent	Shanghai Tang	Paco Rabanne	Jimmy Choo	Viktor & Rolf
Loewe	Alexander McQueen	Alfred Dunhill	Carolina Herrera	Zagliani	Diesel
Berluti	Balenciaga	Lancel			
Kenzo	Brioni				Staff International:
Givenchy	Christopher Kane	NET-A-PORTER.COM			manufacturer and distributor
Marc Jacobs	Stella McCartney				for –
Fendi	Sergio Rossi	Plus:			
Thomas Pink		Cartier			DSquared2
Emilio Pucci	Plus:	Van Cleef & Arpels			Just Cavalli
DKNY	Boucheron	Peter Millar			Vivienne Westwood Red
Edun	Dodo	Purdey			Label
	Girard-Perregaux	Vacheron Constantin			Marc Jacobs Men
Plus:	JeanRichard	Montblanc			
NOWNESS	Pomellato	Piaget			
Bulgari	Qeelin				
De Beers	Puma				
TAG Heuer	Volcom				
Sephora					
Benefit Cosmetics					
Hennessy					
Moët & Chandon					
Belvedere Vodka					
Dom Pérignon					

* Luxury goods group Christian Dior is
the main holding company of LVMH.
Bernard Arnault is the majority
shareholder of Dior, chairman of both
companies and CEO of LVMH.

heir, he is thought to be establishing a trust that will take control of his company after his death.

One household name has been less fortunate. Despite critical acclaim and celebrity status, the French designer Christian Lacroix presided over a brand that never made a profit in 22 years of business. The company finally went bankrupt in 2009 and was bought by the North American conglomerate Falic Fashion Group. When he left, Lacroix lost the rights to his own name. He now designs interiors and uniforms for train companies and collaborates with high-street chains. This Faustian name loss has also happened to Martin Margiela, Jil Sander (three times), Karen Millen and Jimmy Choo.[56]

Inside Luxury

Conglomerates spend millions on their brands. When Puig bought Jean Paul Gaultier, it fought off competition to take on €14 million worth of debt. Another example is the remuneration received by Rose Marie Bravo, CEO of the Burberry Group from 1997 to 2005. Bravo's pay packet consisted of the following: a basic salary of £838,000 a year, with bonuses sometimes of the same amount; a rent-free flat in London, a chauffeur-driven car and a clothing allowance all valued at £250,000; £2.75 million in shares and ownership of an unprecedented 1 per cent of the entire company, worth £18 million in 2004.[57] Great Universal Stores, which owned 66 per cent of Burberry at the time, considered Bravo an indispensable asset.

These vast sums of money are considered good investments because even the financial crisis has not stopped the luxury sector making huge profits. Whilst there have been luxury casualties, like Escada, and whilst profits have fluctuated, overall the industry has not suffered in comparison to construction, farming or property. Globally, fashion remains a $1.5 trillion dollar industry.[58] Industry theories about luxury's recession-proof nature range from people wanting established brands during periods of uncertainty to people viewing designer bags as investments in hard times.

The continuing sales of luxury goods are best taken as proof of the unequal impact of the crisis. In Europe and North America the worst impact has been on the poor. The rich are still rich – and getting richer. In 2012 the *Sunday Times* found that the combined wealth of Britain's 1,000 richest people had risen by 4.7 per cent to £414 billion in one year.[59] The wealthy are still able to buy what they have always bought. They buy luxury brands to assure their status and to demarcate their position in society: 'The simplest and most obvious manner of displaying wealth is to take the greatest possible number of valuable objects and attach them to the wearer's person.'[60]

Another reason why profits have remained high is because the luxury fashion sector does not rely exclusively on the sale of very expensive clothes to make its profits. Instead, it employs a strategy known as the pyramid model: a small number of luxury products like luggage and couture are sold to extremely wealthy customers, but the biggest profits are generated through the sale of 'mass-market' goods (which are still very much overpriced). Perfume and cosmetics are estimated to make up 55 per cent of revenue at Chanel.[61]

Going back to the 1950s licences have been a huge source of income for the luxury sector. While Cristóbal Balenciaga refused to allow his name to be put on licensed goods,[62] Christian Dior licensed everything from handbags to hats. Perfume remains a heavily licensed, mass-produced commodity without which the luxury sector would not survive. Most perfumes are not created by design houses but by licensed multinational corporations like Procter & Gamble and Coty. There are huge profits to be made from perfume. Laboratories sell the liquid for two and a half times more than the cost to the licensee, who retails it for between two and four times the cost again, making a 30–40 per cent profit.[63]

The mass-produced 'It Bag' is typical of this pyramid strategy. The 'It' in 'It Bag' seemingly comes from Miuccia Prada's comment on the subject: 'It's so easy to make money'.[64] The It Bag phenomenon of must-have bags seemed to reach the height of absurdity in 2006 when Louis Vuitton released a laminated chequered bag of the sort bought on market stalls and used to carry laundry, except the Vuitton bag retailed for £1,200. Jil Sander also produced a brown paper bag purse made of brown paper which retailed at $290. The creative director at Bottega Veneta called the It Bag process: 'totally marketed bullshit crap. You make a bag, you send it out to a couple of celebrities, you get the paparazzi to shoot just as they walk out of their house. You sell that to the tabloids, and you say in a magazine that there is a waiting list.'[65]

The sale of handbags and leather goods made $11.7 billion for luxury companies in 2004.[66] The mark-up on these products is huge – bags are sold for 10–12 times what it costs to produce them. At Louis Vuitton they are sold for 13 times more;[67] any unsold bags are destroyed rather than ever being marked down to a sale price.

Some luxury items are made by artisans who labour for months on a single pair of shoes. Yet one of the reasons why the mark-up on bags is so high is that many 'Made in Italy' goods are actually 'Made in China'. Labels reading 'Made in China' are placed somewhere inconspicuous, for example the bottom seam of the inside pocket, or the back of the 'luxury' brands own label. Products are also made in China and then 'finished' in Italy, a tactic which allows its origins to be disguised.[68]

Along with bags, designer companies market items like belts, key rings, scarves and wallets to women *and men* who dream of buying 'luxury'. For the TV series *Secrets of the Superbrands* the BBC visited the Luxatica sunglasses factory in Italy where 55 million pairs of sunglasses are made each year for brands like Chanel, Prada, Bulgari, Ralph Lauren and Paul Smith. Not only are the 'designer' sunglasses made in this factory, but many are also designed there too. A pair of sunglasses from one of these brands retails for several hundred pounds, yet they are trifles light as air, nothing more than a few grams of plastic and glass shrouded in an illusion of luxury.

East meets West

The great capitalist boom in the West came to a shuddering halt in 1973. After the Second World War, those countries with high levels of arms expenditure sacrificed their competitiveness. In contrast, the 'losers', Germany and Japan, boomed in terms of economic development.[69] By spending just 1 per cent of its GDP on armaments, Japan mastered new technologies and experienced an economic boom of its own. This laid the foundations for Japan to become a prosperous and avid consumer of luxury goods.

There was, of course, another key Eastern market about to flourish. By the first half of 2009, LVMH was reporting that sales to Chinese consumers (in China itself and abroad) accounted for 18 per cent of Louis Vuitton's revenue. In 2010 Chinese consumers bolstered the luxury market by spending $15.6 billion on luxury goods. This market is set to increase, with the proportion of people in China earning between $17,000 and $35,000 a year predicted to rise from just 6 per cent in 2010 to 51 per cent in 2020.[70] As a result, financial experts are urging companies to adopt strategies to attract the Chinese middle class.[71]

The importance of the Chinese market to luxury is such that: 'If China has a cold, luxury goods get pneumonia.'[72] The precarious nature of the Chinese market and the sense that many brands are now overexposed to China led the CEO of Richemont to state:

> I feel like I'm having a black tie dinner on top of a volcano. In the morning we put on our ties and our watches, and the food's better, and the wine's better, and the weather is great, but let's not kid ourselves. There is a volcano somewhere, whether it's this year, in ten years' time, or in twenty years' time. We are exposed to China.[73]

European companies have begun to buy up Asian brands. For example, Hermès has collaborated with a new Chinese company, Shang Xia. Predictably, LVMH has begun an aggressive pursuit of non-European brands backed by huge amounts of capital. Its subsidiary, L Capital Asia, is scouting for strategic investments across Asia and has bought brands in India (where there is a huge market for fashion and very few brands), Taiwan, Hong Kong and Singapore. In China, L Capital Asia has purchased a 10 per cent stake in the Trendy International Group, a mass-market clothing company similar to Zara. LVMH's move from European luxury to the Chinese mass-market represents the saturated nature of the Chinese luxury market and the burgeoning spending power of China's middleclass shoppers.

Old Western capitalism is, however, unstoppably giving way to the new capitalism of the East. A key example of this is the way that China, as well as India and the Middle East, are now established as amongst the biggest consumers not just of luxury fashion but of entire luxury fashion houses. For example, Li & Fung is a gigantic corporation whose founders, Victor and William Fung, had a combined fortune of $6.2 billion in 2012. Li & Fung subsidiaries have bought Cerruti 1881, Gieves and Hawkes, and 80 per cent of Sonia Rykiel, one of the last remaining independent French luxury brands. Li & Fung's aim is to buy up failing but quintessentially European brands and use them as a springboard for expansion, particularly across Asia.[74] Similarly, when Gianfranco Ferré faced ruin after the collapse of its parent company IT Holdings in 2008, it was bought up by The Paris Group, a Dubai-based retail and restaurant empire owned by the Sankari family. For the *Financial Times*, the sale embodied luxury's shifting centre of gravity, brought about by the financial crisis.[75] Other examples of Eastern buyouts include the purchase of Escada by Megha Mittal, a member of the Lakshmi Mittal steel family; Sportswear Holdings acquiring stakes in Michael Kors, Karl Lagerfeld and Pepe Jeans; ownership of Pringle by Hong Kong-based S C. Fang & Sons; the South Korean firm EXR buying Jean-Charles de Castelbajac in 2011; and the acquisition of the failing British heritage brand Aquascutum by Hong Kong-based YGM in 2012. In 2013 the Qatari royal family bought the Valentino Fashion Group from Permira for £556 million.

* * *

Fashion's centre of gravity may be shifting but its key principle – monopolised ownership remains the same. Fashion shows, brand mythology and designer cults sustain an appearance of creativity and consumer choice.[76] Brands act as advertisements for these mass-produced products, covering up the fact that much of what is sold as luxury is little more than 'Made in China' bric-a-brac. To ensure that this illusion continues, the fashion industry needs a showcase to elevate their products to the stuff of legend. This showcase – the fashion media – is the subject of Chapter 2.

CHAPTER TWO

The Fashion Media

From 300-year-old magazines to media internet brands, personal style blogs and trend companies, the purpose of the fashion media is to act as a communication tool for the rest of the industry. As an intermediary between brands and consumers, the fashion media remain hugely influential in determining what is fashion. They showcase clothes that most people will never come into contact with and elevate clothes to 'fashion'. The media are also respected brands in themselves with coveted powers of endorsement. As one magazine executive told me, advertisers love fashion magazines 'because of the stardust that we scatter on their brand'.[1]

The internet has changed the whole of the fashion industry, but in particular the fashion media. The flow and availability of information is faster than ever. There is unprecedented access to the tools of communication, and brands have taken a step closer to consumers by being in direct contact with them online. People are no longer willing to wait months for clothes or trends to arrive and brands are no longer willing to have just a few seasons a year. As one trend forecaster explained: 'Everyone wants to try and get ahead of their competitors. Everyone wants to be seen to be doing the newest, latest thing. So no one waits. There is no waiting any more.'[2]

Fashion Magazines

The fashion magazine industry has come a long way since the publication of the first women's journal, *The Ladies' Mercury*, in 1693.[3] It is now a multi-billion-pound web of media brands monopolised by a few giant multinational corporations. Today's fashion magazine caters to two sets of customers who bring in two streams of revenue. The first are its readers; the second, its advertisers.[4]

Condé Montrose Nast worked his way up the American publishing industry in the early 1900s, before identifying an elitist women's journal with a small circulation that he decided to make the vessel for his theory for getting maximum profits from magazines. The Nast strategy was to drop any pretence of mass-market appeal and focus instead on attracting a wealthy minority who would attract advertisers. In his words: 'If you had a tray with 2,000,000 needles on it, and only 150,000 of these had gold tips, the 1,850,000 which were not gold-tipped would be no use to you. But if you could get a magnet that would draw out only the gold ones, what a saving!'[5] Nast acquired *Vogue* in 1909 and instructed his staff not only to 'get all their readers from the one particular class to which the magazine is dedicated, <u>but rigorously to exclude all others</u>'.[6]

A British edition of *Vogue* was launched in 1916, at the height of the First World War, when imports of magazines from the United States ceased. A French version was launched four years later. As a result of the Wall Street Crash of 1929 Nast lost control of his company and incurred business debts of $5 million. His namesake publishing empire, however, grew to formidable heights and became the hallmark of luxury chic. In 1959 the company was bought by the media mogul S. I. Newhouse's Advance Publications. Advance is still owned by the Newhouse family and is ranked as the 46th largest private company in the United States. In 2012 there were 19 different editions of *Vogue* with a collective readership of 24.8 million.[7]

In 2010, Jonathan Newhouse, chair of Condé Nast International, point-blank refused to consider an Arabic edition of *Vogue*: 'Our company has no wish to impose its values on a society which does not fully share them. And we do not wish to provoke a strongly negative, even violent reaction. It isn't even worth it for a few million in licensing fees.' He added that whilst there might be plenty of people in the Middle East who would like to read *Vogue*, 'unfortunately they live in the same general region as some of the most militant and violent elements. It is a problem I don't have to have. So I will simply avoid it by never entering the market. And I will sleep better at night.'[8]

The Condé Nast portfolio of media brands also includes *Teen Vogue*, *Glamour* ('read by 1 in 10 women in the US'), *GQ*, *Condé Nast Traveller*, *Allure*, *W*, *Vanity Fair*, *LOVE* and *Tatler*.[9] Condé Nast also publishes the industry insider journal *Women's Wear Daily* (*WWD*), whose influence with buyers and ability to make or break brands makes it the most powerful journal in the world.[10]

Condé Nast's contemporary and rival was William Hearst, the businessman who inspired *Citizen Kane*. Hearst regularly used his media ownership to support his various campaigns for public office, including an abortive run for the US presidency.[11] In 2012 the Hearst

Corporation was the world's largest magazine publisher. Hearst Magazines International distributes 300 magazines in 80 countries. Its fashion media brands include *Elle, Harper's Bazaar* (published in 43 countries) and the US edition of *Marie Claire*.[12]

Europe's largest private publishing group is Bauer Media, a division of the Bauer Media Group. They publish 300 magazines in 15 countries and, having bought EMAP's magazine and radio divisions in 2007, control 25 per cent of the UK magazine market. Among Bauer-owned media brands are *Grazia, Heat* (including *Heat Radio*) and *Closer*.

IPC Media claim to reach almost two-thirds of UK women. IPC Southbank is the corporation's 'upmarket' women's magazine wing and publishes UK versions of *Marie Claire* and *InStyle*. IPC Connect publishes the 'mass-market' magazines *Look, Now, Chat* and *Woman*. IPC also owns the controversial men's magazine *Nuts*.

In 2001 AOL Time Warner, the world's biggest media corporation, bought IPC Media from the private equity group Cinven for £1.15 billion. AOL Time Warner owns companies from CNN to New Line Cinema.

From her office overlooking Tate Modern, Jackie Newcombe, managing director at IPC Southbank, explained that publishers no longer see themselves as just magazine publishers; rather, this is publishing in the broadest sense of the term. Competing on the market now includes devising websites, digital editions of magazines, apps and daily emails (purposefully sent out just before lunchtime to attract bored office workers).

Component parts of companies also work in unison using vast sums of capital. For example, AOL Time Warner can publish a book, turn it into a TV show followed by a film, and produce every conceivable type of themed merchandise. Meanwhile these products can be publicised in their media outlets like IPC's magazines and the websites IPC Southbank currently runs with Diet Coke.[13] Describing this increasing cross-platform collaboration, Jackie Newcombe explained: 'We use everything that we do to promote everything that we do.'[14] Condé Nast has launched the Condé Nast School of Fashion, themed restaurants and the Vogue Festival aimed to appeal to a new generation of readers who expect brand participation.

Other than a shrinking handful of independent magazines like *Dazed & Confused*, the entire traditional fashion media is owned by just a few companies. These companies (and their media brands) are hugely important to the fashion industry because between them they reach 'pretty much all women who are interested in fashion'.[15] What does this ever-increasing concentration of fashion media ownership mean for choice and democracy? Big business monopolies dominate other sectors of the economy such as tobacco, oil and computer technology. Unhealthy concentrations of ownership leave industries vulnerable to the failure of big firms, market fluctuations and unfair domination by a single corporation. Whilst monopolies in other sectors can cause prices to rise and standards to drop, what happens when our received ideas, culture and information are dominated by just a few companies?[16]

Fashion is an industry that sells itself as providing choice and variety, yet its press is controlled by a few huge companies. There appears to be a choice between *Glamour* and *Vogue* or *Elle* and *Harper's Bazaar* but it is merely a choice between two media brands espousing the same values and owned by the same giant corporations.

Complimentary Copy

The reporting of fashion is skewed by magazines' symbiotic relationship with brands via the advertising industry. In 1893 Frank A Munsey cut the price of *Munsey's Magazine* from $3 a year to $1, choosing to sell the magazine for less than the cost of production and make his profits from advertising. The gamble worked and readership rose from 40,000 to 500,000 – a circulation that was only possible due to advances in print and distribution technology.[17] Magazines today are still sold at far less than the cost of their production, with advertising making up the difference and providing the profits. When I asked Jackie Newcombe how much the cover price of magazines would have to increase by if the advertisements were removed she answered: 'It would almost double, just to cover the revenue.'[18]

According to Newcombe, the removal of adverts would not be an popular move because it would make magazines thinner. Although 'the perception of value is clearly driven by the editorial, actually the adverts are an important part of giving value for money.'[19] Adverts, however, are not carried in magazines for the benefit of readers. They are there to sell products and to increase the parent company's and stockholders' profits.

The British *Vogue* editor Alexandra Shulman believes the allure of her magazine to advertisers is that 'things that appear in the magazine have an immediate connect sales-wise. Vogue has been around for so long, it does have an authority that people believe in. If you endorse something, people believe that endorsement.'[20] The British *Glamour* editor, Jo Elvin, agrees: she calls magazine editorial a badge of honour for brands.[21] Dallas Smyth developed the theory that the purpose of the mass media is to produce an audience that can be sold to advertisers, something that is done through the provision of a 'free lunch' of editorial content.[22] The job of a fashion journalist is arguably to deliver readers so that advertisers will buy space.[23]

Because brands are magazines' second set of customers, editors must take care to cultivate an environment which advertisers want to be associated with.[24] Chrysler once issued the following statement to magazines: 'Each and every issue that carries Chrysler advertising requires a written summary outlining major themes/articles appearing in upcoming issues.'[25] They insisted on being alerted ahead of any content that covered a sexual, social or political issue. This has serious consequences. Studies show a direct correlation between advertising and the exclusion of issues from magazines. Lung cancer from smoking and skin cancer from sunbathing are just two issues that magazines notably avoided talking about to avoid upsetting advertisers.[26]

Which issues are now being excluded? The risk of cancer from mobile phones or the dangers of using paraben chemical compounds in make-up? It is particularly worrying because magazines sell themselves as fulfilling a public health role and offering advice and guidance in the style of a trusted friend. As Dallas Smythe noted, the media do not just affirm the status quo, they actively prevent the raising of serious questions about our society.[27]

As well as creating a supportive editorial atmosphere, editors must also maintain what the former editor Gloria Steinham called 'complimentary copy'[28] – writing articles about 'beauty secrets', for example, in order to attract adverts for cosmetics. This restricts the content of magazines primarily to fashion and beauty issues, rather than what readers might actually like to read. 'Complimentary copy' is guilty of spawning endless articles describing perfumes, which are usually reduced to describing the bottle and its packaging once journalists run out of adjectives for fragrance.

Between pure editorial and pure display advertising is 'advertorial'. Advertorial occurs when magazines use a template based on their design style to create an advert for a brand. These are supposed to be clearly flagged as promotions, but more often than not they blend in with editorial content. It might be more accurate to describe everything in fashion magazines as advertorial. As one former *Vogue* publisher stated: 'The cold hard facts of magazine publishing mean that those who advertise get editorial coverage.'[29]

One informal survey showed a direct correlation between the number of adverts placed in a magazine and the number of editorial mentions in the text of a magazine that a brand received. Across the September 2002 US editions of *Vogue, Harper's Bazaar, InStyle, W* and *Elle* the following happened: Prada 52 adverts, 58 editorial mentions; Dior 44 adverts, 50 mentions; YSL 59 adverts, 58 mentions; Louis Vuitton 34 adverts, 31 mentions.[30] Is it possible to maintain journalistic independence when you are courted with freebies (like lunches, trips and clothes) or when you know a major brand will pull its advertising if you do not showcase its designs?[31]

Don't Upset the Emperor

The desire not to offend advertisers also partly accounts for the distinct lack of criticism to be found in fashion magazines. The fashion industry is rightly renowned as a spiteful place with insults hurled between individuals and design houses.[32] Occasionally, an unwelcome addition like Kanye West is publicly humiliated, but the aim of these displays is to increase fashion's elitism, not to challenge it. And yet for such a venomous industry, where is the rigorous press criticism?

Unlike other cultural publications, fashion magazines are utterly obsequious about the products they display. The response that criticism occurs through the selection of clothes for display seems unjustified in the light of the direct correlations between advertising budgets and magazine appearances. The effect of brand advertising seems hidden by its very obviousness. The fashion photographer Nick Knight described the search for people to appear on panels critiquing catwalk shows: 'Some people would not appear . . . magazine editors and stylists . . . because they were too frightened of losing advertisers. And, that's a bad situation for any art form to be in.'[33]

There was a time when fashion writers were serious powerbrokers in the industry. Able to make or break a collection, they travelled the world 'bulldozing their way through an effete world of air kisses and crinolines'.[34] With some notable exceptions, the vast majority of fashion journalism is now tediously sycophantic. The lack of criticism is compounded by fashion being the only creative field that bans the media for misbehaving. Whilst a film critic can simply buy a cinema ticket, or a restaurant critic can don a false moustache and dine incognito, a fashion critic must receive a personal invitation to a performance that will occur only once.[35]

As a result, well-known fashion critics come not from fashion magazines but from newspapers that are not solely dependent on fashion reportage or advertising. The Pulitzer Prize-winning journalist Cathy Horyn of *The New York Times* has been barred from numerous shows, including those of Dolce & Gabbana and Giorgio Armani. The *Guardian* journalist Hadley Freeman was banned from Jean Paul Gaultier shows for life after accusing him of gleeful savagery for his use of fur: 'Rarely can an animal have died in vain as sadly as the fox whose top half, head to tail, was splayed across an evening gown.'[36] The monopolisation of fashion means that critics can receive multiple bans – Suzy Menkes, fashion editor at the *International Herald Tribune*, received a one-day ban from *all* LVMH-owned shows.

The live streaming of fashion shows means that basic catwalk information is now widely available. Yet catwalk shows, as well as generating vast amounts of publicity, solidify what Horyn calls a 'rigid caste system'.[37] An invitation to a fashion show is more than seeing clothes at first-hand; it is also about being included (with the threat of exclusion if you misbehave).

Another reason why fashion media brands do not criticise is because they have a vested interest in maintaining the myth and glitz of the fashion industry. If they do damage with criticism they would be damaging themselves. To expose the emperor as naked would be to reveal the fashion media at the same time. Instead, all parts of the fashion industry must perpetuate the myth that the industry is the sole source of beautiful clothing. Rather than just being the victim of advertisers, the fashion media is a complicit and integral myth-maker.

Blogging Fashion

The internet brought the advent of 'the fashion blog', which for the traditional fashion press started as something of a nightmare. Blogs were an explosion of unauthorised reportage whose ingredients appeared horrifyingly simple: 'a blog, a camera, and a healthy dose of personal style'.[38] For the proponents of fashion blogging, this was nothing less than the long-awaited democratisation of fashion. Gone were the class barriers of attending the right school, wearing expensive clothes and working for free at internships secured by influential relatives. Instead, you could be from anywhere and distinctly unmodel-like in appearance. It was an information reformation, the rise of a second super-power,[39] the American Dream come true in a blaze of digital glory.

As advertisers followed consumers onto smart-phones and tablets, monthly publications faced the challenge of surviving in a climate where fashion news is tweeted. A backlash against bloggers by established journalists occurred. They accused bloggers of being dazzled by celebrity culture, offering uninformed commentary and only stating the obvious about clothes: 'It's got to be more than just "I loved it" or "I hated it". Criticism is not personal opinion.'[40]

Fashion blogs and style sites, however, showed a startling ability to garner huge numbers of readers, which in turn made a select few hugely popular with designers and corporations. For the designer

Mary Katranzou, bloggers provided 'a new way of getting in touch with people and finding out what they feel about your clothes'. They circumvented the hold of buyers and shops and gave direct access to customers.[41] The economic downturn also helped bloggers fill traditional areas of fashion debate. As newspapers sought to cut costs, fashion critics, with their international flight and hotel expenses, were some of the first to have their budgets reduced. Most newspapers then rushed to set up fashion blogs of their own.

Fashion magazines are now all online. Vogue.co.uk, launched in 1995, is an internet pioneer, with over one million visitors a month. Style.com, its US counterpart, gets on average 2.6 million visitors a month. The IPC executive Sylvia Auton believes the internet means magazines will only be around for another ten years.[42] It is worth remembering, however, that everything, from the car to the radio, was thought to be the invention that signalled the demise of the magazine. Also, new fashion magazines like *CR Fashion Book* by former *Vogue* editor Carine Roitfeld are still being launched.

The fashion industry, meanwhile, swiftly picked its favourite bloggers. They became front-row guests at fashion shows, had bags named after them, got magazine jobs and book deals, charged tens of thousands of dollars for appearances, sold advertising space on their pages, held conferences and branded Twitter parties, became brand ambassadors, sparked concerns over child and unpaid labour, and got modelling contracts and Hollywood agents.

In 2012 there were over 80 million blogs,[43] millions of them devoted to fashion. Fashion blogging proves that creativity and cultural production are not the preserve of an exclusive elite, as more people than ever have access to the tools for creating media. Although there is more interconnectedness and idea-sharing than ever, do fashion blogs really represent the democratisation of fashion? Bloggers can influence what styles of clothing are produced for sale by corporations – having drawn inspiration from society, they feed into the industry as an often unpaid 'look book'. Bloggers can also increase the sale of clothes they promote. But this is not the same as saying that bloggers have power over the industry. The power to influence the industry is not the same as the power to control the industry.

A closer look at the basic requirements for creating a successful fashion blog also sheds light on the demographic of people able to make a living from their blog or website. These basics are: a camera, a computer, the ability to write and read English, access to lots and lots of clothes, a network that includes contacts interested in the fashion and popular culture industries, a great deal of spare time, the ability to travel, a studied personal appearance that conforms to accepted beauty standards, no objections to selling products for multinationals and no objections to creating an editorial environment that is attractive to multinational corporations.

As a result it is unsurprising that out of the top 99 blogs as ranked by *Signature 9* (a 'lifestyle intelligence' website), 70 are from the United States, 21 from Britain and Europe, and just eight from the rest of the world.[44] Of course, just meeting these requirements is not enough to *Blog Your Way to the Front Row*.[45] What the American Dream fails to mention is that there is only space for a few at the top – 100 out of 80 million.

It is often argued that the internet makes everyone equal, that platforms like Twitter and Tumblr are democracy in action: 'A blogger from Croatia is just as important as Prabal on Tumblr,' according to Valentine Uhovski of Tumblr.[46] When *Business Insider* ranked the websites of the top American fashion magazines and inserted them into its ratings alongside fashion blogs and websites, it found that top brands with editorial boards often ranked lower than blogs written by one person.[47] But these statistics conceal a web of corporate power.

The Sartorialist (a street photography site started by Scott Schuman) took the top spot on the *Business Insider* rankings and is regularly listed as the world's most popular fashion blog. However, far from being independent, the site is heavily promoted by Condé Nast, which manages the site's advertising sales.[48] Condé Nast hired Schuman to photograph fashion shows and propelled the blog to the head of the pack. Schuman himself has said: 'The only stream coming in the beginning was working with GQ and Style.com.'[49] *The Business of Fashion* website calculated that *The Sartorialist* generates over $100,000 a month in income for Schuman based on his cost per thousand impressions (CPM) sales at his current traffic levels. In

2012 Condé Nast also bought *Nowmanifest*, a promotional network of top fashion blogs. The *Nowmanifest* bloggers were not told that their platform was being sold until 24 hours before the sale was announced.[50] Similarly 23 of the top 100 fashion blogs, including *Stylebubble*, 'collaborate' with *Glamour*, a Condé Nast publication. In 2011 Glamour founded the *Young & Posh Blogger Network*: '23 Chic Bloggers, All in One Super-Stylish Place'. Another network is *Style Coalition*, founded by the blogger Yuli Ziv. *Style Coalition* is a network of 40 top bloggers who collaborate with brands. *Style Coalition* first collaborated with *Elle* and then the entire Hearst Digital Media network. They have created custom advertising campaigns for brands including Microsoft, jcpenney, Lancôme, D&G, Gap and Maybelline.

The homespun nature of fashion blogs is extremely alluring to both readers and advertisers. Nonetheless, as with magazine journalism, independence ends when a writer is paid in cash or free gifts to write promotional copy. The defence 'they didn't tell us how to write it' is simply naïve. The required opinion is implicit in the acceptance of the pay cheque or gift. This is also the case for blogs that claim they only collaborate with brands whose 'aesthetic aligns with our aesthetic'.[51]

Fashion blogs can therefore be seen as corporate PR disguised as fresh young opinions.[52] Bloggers are flown first-class to fashion shows, given clothes and paid tens of thousands of dollars precisely because fashion corporations receive a far larger payback in terms of zealously promotional blog posts which sell products.[53]

This situation is not particularly the fault of fashion bloggers. Without an internet tax on advertising revenue or state funds for cultural producers like bloggers,[54] subsistence means selling out and selling advertising space. As a result, successful fashion bloggers have been incorporated into the same mutually beneficial fashion system as fashion magazines and cannot challenge it. Most bloggers form part of the unpaid labour force that has made billions for sites like Blogger, Tumblr and Facebook by producing endless free content. The glorifying of a few bloggers and the promises of riches and free clothes sometimes seems to function primarily as an advertisement for signing up even more people to such sites.

For those with access to it, the internet provides unprecedented knowledge of the world. Yet real democracy would mean democratic control of information – in this case of the internet. Currently, fashion magazines do not decide democratically what fashion consists of. Nor do blogs. Blogs are the opinions of a single person or a small team of people: there are no votes and no means of producing something different on a national or world scale. Corporations remain in control of multi-million online advertising budgets and established brands. They still have the ability to fight and win copyright and domain name battles, to direct traffic, to secure readers for their online platforms and to gather information about those readers to use as they please. And corporations still have the money to try to co-opt anything and anyone they please.

By the early 1990s major British magazine houses no longer recognised unions for either production or editorial staff. In the sphere of fashion blogging, the threat to the status quo has been subsumed as blogs have been co-opted by corporations mirroring capitalism's constant drive to privatise public spaces. In this way the internet both threatens and reproduces private property and class relations.[55] Ultimately, the battle for control of the internet that is being waged by and against corporations will decide who has strategic control over the fashion media. In a sense, as William Gibson, the writer who coined the term 'cyberspace', allegedly noted: 'The future is already here. It's just not evenly distributed yet.'

The Future Laboratory[56]

Trend companies are information hubs that suck in huge amounts of data from across the globe in order to calculate fashion trends up to two years in advance. This information is then sold to corporations who use it to stock their shops with billions of pieces of clothing.

Trend forecasting is not new. Tobé and Associates Inc. is considered the fashion industry's first trend forecasting company. It was founded in 1927 in New York by Tobé Coller Davis, whose weekly merchandising newsletter was distributed to department stores in Manhattan,[57] and who wrote a syndicated style column in the *New York Herald Tribune* until her death in 1962. In 1928 a group of women, including *Vogue* editor Edna Woolman Chase, Eleanor Roosevelt, Elizabeth Arden and Tobé Coller Davis, founded The Fashion Group to promote the American fashion business. They instigated trends by issuing trend reports and advice to multiple fashion businesses. Trends, it was discovered, increased sales of 'must-have' items and were good for business.[58]

Almost a century later trends are more important than ever, described as profits waiting to happen.[59] Trends help magazines produce streamlined editorials with simple recommendations; they allow for clothes to be mass-produced and let shops use their space efficiently to stock set colours and styles in numerous sizes. But above all trends get people shopping. According to Natalie Singh, Head of Denim & Street at WGSN (Worth Global Style Network):

> Trends are what drive the fashion industry. It's what makes people have to buy something new every few months. Without the trend part of it, without telling people: 'that bits over, scrap that bit of your wardrobe, you need this now,' it wouldn't be the industry it is. The purpose is to make you feel that what you've currently got is not quite right.[60]

Despite the overwhelming evidence, it has been argued that the fashion industry is no longer trend-driven. Yet clothes that are not on-trend are not available and insiders at the retail level describe an 'obsessional' emphasis on trends and of being sent home if their work clothes are not 'trend-based enough'.[61]

Corporations no longer produce two collections a year; they produce up to 50. Clothes must fit into the accepted trends of the moment with just enough individuality and innovation to make them stand out. Determining what will be on-trend is vital, so vital that despite a corporate subscription costing £16,500, WGSN has 3,000 corporate users and 38,000 individual users. WGSN's annual revenue is £40 million, prompting new forecasting companies like Stylesight to compete for the trend forecasting market.

Customers are lining up to buy knowledge about the future: 'Becoming a global brand without the WGSN trend report has become almost impossible.'[62] But how do trend forecasters (also known as 'futurologists' or 'cool hunters') predict what people will be wearing in two years' time? This impressive skill is grounded in the principle that while trends appear instantaneous, in fact they always start somewhere and build up. 'Identify the thread and you can identify a trend,' says Frank Bober, CEO of Stylesight.[63]

Finding the thread includes monitoring the state of the textile industry and the industrial futures of fabrics and dyes. This is a two-way process, however, as textile manufactures look to trend forecasters for confirmation of colours and styles. Future cultural events are also monitored – films, music albums or art movements, anything that might spark a craze or revival. Trend companies also watch the street by employing networks of observers who monitor youth movements, underground music scenes, skate parks, estates and bloggers in key cities like London, New York and Tokyo. Successful colours or styles on the mass market are also monitored. Whilst *haute couture* is traditionally listed as an inspiration for trend forecasting, the trend forecasters I interviewed told me it was of very little importance to their work.

The information is filtered and distilled into macro- or micro-trends. Macro-trends cover large political, economic or technological events that can produce long-term trends. Micro-trends cover key concepts like colours, shapes and fabrics, so that forecasters can tell brands: 'These are the colours that you need to do, these are the fabrics that you need to do, these are the prints that you need to do, these are the shapes, etc.'[64]

With the information being this specific, it is little wonder that even in the boardroom of WGSN, the debate occurs as to which comes first – the chicken or the trend forecast? Some forecasters, like Jaana Jatyri, founder of Trendstop, believe that ultimately the industry 'works in the direction dictated by consumer demand' and that trends are increasingly demanded by consumers.[65] Other forecasters see their role as assisting rather than dictating; they do not expect their reports to be copied wholesale.

Isham Sardouk at Stylesight previously worked as a designer at Victoria Secret. When I spoke to him he described Victoria Secret receiving reports from three companies, from which he would create his own trend report based on a panoramic of their work: 'We really hope that every person adapts the information to their own needs. They're not supposed to take it as is. They're supposed to look at it, watch it, absorb it and then do their own thing with it.'[66] The opposing view is best summed up by another top trend analyst at Stylesight: 'If you tell clients something is going to be big, you will probably make it so.'[67]

Natalie Singh at WGSN does not see the customer as being in the driving seat. When I asked her whether it was consumers or the industry that prompted trends she replied: 'I would come down more on the side of the industry. Ultimately, it is a fashion business and people have to keep continually selling things. To do that you've got to make people understand that you have something new that they haven't got, and which they need.'[68] Consumer power is the subject of Chapter 3, but it is worth noting here that the primary beneficiary of trends is the corporation not the consumer. The industry is geared around making maximum profits and that means organised, ratified trends that can be stocked in bulk.

Trend companies have some surprising clients. Prada, a brand known for its innovation, is a Stylesight client. Isham Sardouk describes the guidance Stylesight gives Prada as 'competitive intelligence'. But if even the innovators are buying trend forecasts, who has creative control within the industry? Who really decides what ends up in the shops?

Fast-fashion companies have become some of the trend industry's biggest customers. Catering to this section of the market is seen in some quarters as having lowered the tone of trend research by speeding it up and making it less specialised. In theory, trend forecasting could offer a solution to one of fashion's biggest issues – exploitative fast-fashion supply chains. Since trend forecasters can predict trends two years ahead, the industry could place orders further in advance and allow factories to work to more humane schedules. In a market economy this has no chance of success. As soon as forecasting reports are received, they are utilised by companies as Natalie Singh explains:

> Companies are driven to keep selling, selling, selling! Bring the buyers! New things! New things! More things! Try things! So the

minute WGSN puts a report out about emerging trends and what is coming in 18 months, they jump on it. They're not prepared to wait, so they act on it. The industry keeps getting faster and faster. It is like a big hungry baby that is gobbling everything up. It has got to explode at some point because it can't get any quicker, so what happens then?

The growing influence of blogs and style websites acting as free 'look books' leads some forecasters to wonder how much longer their industry will exist: 'We're basically an online magazine, another information source but not the only piece of information that they'll act on. Any company would be silly to only have one service and rely solely on it.' Expanding on this point, Natalie Singh explained why companies like Levi's hire in-house forecasters: 'It's an expensive service that we charge people for. At what point are companies going to realise that they could employ someone to sit and do this for them and get a much more personalised view out of it?'[69]

For now, however, trend companies are still the biggest monitoring networks for corporations, which use trends to increase the profitability of their business. As long as trends are key to profitability and trend forecasters retain their ability to predict the future – possibly because they are *making* the future – they will continue to be a central part of the fashion industry.

CHAPTER THREE

Buyology

To the women who cannot afford my clothes,
especially those who buy them.[1]
Hardy Amies

Dresses are like political opinion. There's always a newer, more exciting
idea on the horizon especially when conflicting parties are involved.[2]
The Art of Being a Well Dressed Wife

A dark, rainy Paris street. A woman driven to criminality by desire. *'There it was. Staring at me. I had to have it.'* Sarah Jessica Parker kicks in a shop window and tries to grab a bottle of perfume before being handcuffed and led away. Begging a police officer for just one little spritz of the scent, she is last seen wild-eyed and unrepentant behind prison bars repeating the mantra 'I had to have it'.

The advertisement for Sarah Jessica Parker's fragrance *Covet* is exceptionally similar to an earlier one for Dior's *Addict* perfume, in which Liberty Ross is on the run from the police through rainy Paris streets having smashed a shop window to steal perfume. Playing on the themes of the power of desire for objects and the irrationality of female shoppers, the advert's message is that criminality in pursuit of fashion is understandable, sexy and humorous.

During the Summer of 2011, riots swept across Britain. Sparked by the police killing of Mark Duggan in Tottenham, the rioters smashed town centres and torched buildings across the country. The causes of the riots – police violence, social exclusion, poverty – have been hotly debated ever since, but one recurrent feature was the looting of clothing and shoe shops. This has been attributed by many, including Camila Batmanghelidjh, founder and director of the charity Kids Company, as the result of social dysfunction, of a generation of young people 'continuously dispossessed in a society rich with possession'.[3] Amidst the chaos one particular image was seized on by the media – that of 22-year-old Shereka Leigh, filmed trying on shoes from a looted store before stealing them. She later received an eight-month prison sentence having been found with just several hundred pounds worth of goods.

The riots, and the harsh sentencing that followed, illustrate the tense disconnect between society's messages. People are taught: 'I shop therefore I am', that shopping equals success and that they should go to any length to consume. Our ability to shop, discard and replace has become the prime indicator of our social standing and personal success.[4] Even as adverts like those for *Covet* and *Addict* make light of criminality, they fail to mention that theft is acceptable only if the perpetrator is a beautiful, rich, white woman. Otherwise you can expect to serve 16 months for stealing ice cream or six months for the theft of £3.50 worth of water.[5]

The causes of the unrest have not been dealt with, in fact, they have intensified. People are brought to the boil through a combination of poverty on the one hand and the bombardment of images of things they will never have on the other. Expecting them not to boil over is foolish. As the eminent sociologist Zygmunt Bauman reasoned:

> Objects of desire, whose absence is most violently resented, are nowadays many and varied – and their numbers, as well as the temptation to have them, grow by the day. And so grows the wrath, humiliation, spite and grudge aroused by not having them – as well as the urge to destroy what you can't have. Looting shops and setting them on fire derive from the same impulsion and gratify the same longing.[6]

An Unequal Fashion

Attracting over 200 million visitors a year, Oxford Street in London's West End is Europe's busiest shopping street. Navigating through the crowds takes a shopper past several branches of H&M, with its turnover of up to 50 collections per year; Nike Town, where lines of fanatical shoe fans queue overnight; Primark, where fights break out during the sales and Uniqlo, the Japanese clothing company that boasts of making 613 different varieties of sock.

All of this is possible only because of the existence of a surplus in society. Whereas animals produce only what they need, humans go beyond their immediate physical needs to produce a surplus of food, shelter, clothing and other commodities. There is more than enough wealth in society to support everybody, but a walk down Oxford Street clearly shows that socially produced surplus wealth is not evenly distributed. Worldwide sales of luxury goods stand at

$150 billion,[7] while outside Bond Street underground station the homeless beg for spare change.

Despite these glaring inequalities, some still argue that fashion is now egalitarian. Charity shops and cheap chains like Primark have become fashion outlets; H&M and Target release collaborative 'designer' collections; Gok Wan presents 'cheap chic' TV shows; and magazines are filled with 'Scrimp or Splurge' columns. The widespread availability of relatively cheap clothing (of dubious quality) is not, however, the same as fashion democracy.

Fashion consumption is deeply unequal and generalisations about fashion consumers are misleading. The activist academic Juliet Schor says that instead of simply asking *Why do we consume so much?* it is important to clarify who is doing all the consuming.[8] A statistic such as the fact that in 2009 North Americans discarded 300 million pairs of shoes[9] seems straightforward, but it obscures the fact that some 50 million Americans live below the poverty line and another 100 million subsist on a low income.[10] Legitimate concerns about the impact of fashion on the world are not helped by blanket calls for everyone to 'shop less'. These calls are irrelevant to families forced to choose between a pair of shoes without holes and putting hot food on the table for their children.[11]

As well as inviting a false sense of equality, ignoring the link between fashion consumption and class ignores material circumstances in favour of theories of identity. The street fashion blog *The Sartorialist* published a photograph of a homeless man with the caption 'Not Giving Up Hope'. Scott Schuman and his fans expressed astonished delight that the homeless man had matched blue boots with blue glasses and gloves. This, they concluded, meant he was dignified and had 'Not Given Up'. Comments included: 'Powerful. He doesn't even look homeless. Blue is great on him', and 'I often look at homeless folks for inspiration on what to wear. There is a certain softness to the clothes after being worn day in, day out.'[12]

The academic fashion blog *Threadbared* argued that this approach summed up the problems inherent in reading clothes and style as expressions of identity. Whilst people express themselves through commodities such as clothes, this does not mean that making a judgement about someone's clothes and their identity should bleed into evaluating them as a person.[13] If style is taken for humanity, then the reverse can also be true. Presumably had the unnamed man been 'badly' dressed he would not have merited time or attention. This 'no style, no humanity' approach grades people's right to be treated as human beings based on their appearance, something that history, from the slave trade to Nazi ideology, has shown to be abhorrent. Ignoring class also implies that the wearing of 'bad' clothes is something people *consent* to because they have 'Given Up'. This approach neglects to mention the maelstrom of class, race, gender and economic crises that contributes to poverty and prevents people having control over their lives. As Engels pointed out in 1844, economic circumstance cannot be offset by a willingness to work, thrift, perseverance – or being well dressed.[14]

Without class there would be no fashion industry as we know it. Clothing is a key way for the rich to signal and reproduce their power.[15] Once the masses gain access to elite fashions (or close approximations of them) the rich move on in order to leave everyone else behind. Burberry's elite position suffered a temporary downfall when it became a working-class favourite. Corporate greed had led Burberry to sell hundreds of licences for its plaid print which led to mass production of a once exclusive product. At one point even Burberry print dog nappies were being manufactured. As one eighteenth-century commentator wryly noted: 'Nothing makes noble persons despise the gilded costume so much as to see it on the bodies of the lowliest men in the world.'[16]

King Consumer?

In the foreword to *Green is the New Black*, the model Lily Cole wrote that consumers need to take responsibility for their purchases because 'Capitalism is only as ruthless as its consumers. After all the consumer is king, right?'[17] Arguing that consumers are more powerful than corporations is indicative of a shift of responsibility, of blaming customers for the ills of the fashion industry. The previous chapters have shown fashion corporations to be more powerful than ever, yet, as Juliet Schor writes, growing corporate power has been accompanied by the dominance of an ideology that insists that the opposite is true and that the consumer is king.[18] One way to determine whether the corporation or the customer wears the crown is to examine why fashion is produced.

I am writing this on a day when most of the United Kingdom is blanketed in snow and I am wearing 18 pieces of clothing in an attempt to keep warm. Today it seems obvious that humans need clothes. Indeed, 40,000-year-old sewing needles have been found on Palaeolithic sites.[19] Yet I cannot argue that I need all the clothes that are hanging in my wardrobe. So why are they there? Because fashion is not about answering human need but about producing corporate profit. In *The Poverty of Philosophy*, Marx writes: 'World trade turns almost entirely around the needs, not of individual consumption, but of production.'[20] Corporations must produce fashion in order to make money. If everyone bought only the clothes they needed it would spell disaster for corporations, so instead 'false needs' are created to keep me and everyone else shopping. These needs are false because they are the manufacturers' needs not the consumers'.[21]

In 1690, the economist Nicholas Barbon called fashion 'the spirit and life of trade' because 'it occasions the expense of cloth before the old ones have worn out'. Barbon praised fashion's ability to 'dress a man as if he lived in a perpetual spring – he never sees the autumn of his cloth'.[22] 'Autumn cloth' – threadbare cloth that needs replacing – is never reached thanks to the cycle of fashion that replaces clothes long before it is necessary. Fashion is more than just clothes; it is a commodity cycle of newness that makes clothes go out-of-date and keeps retailers in business. This makes consumption the final stage in the production of fashion: 'A product becomes a real product only by being consumed,' wrote Marx. 'A garment becomes a real garment only in the act of being worn.'[23]

There is thus a symbiotic relationship between people and the fashion industry. Fashion should not be simplified as something that is merely imposed on people from on high. There is cross-pollination, with many trends originating at street level before being quickly co-opted, commodified and marketed. People are a vital component of fashion. If '*le mode*' is clothing and '*la mode*' is fashion, then as the fashion academic Ingrid Loschek explains: '*Le mode* becomes *la mode* when *le mode* reaches the streets.'[24] This was Gabrielle ('Coco')

Chanel's point when she remarked: 'A fashion that does not reach the streets is not a fashion.'

Fashion involves clothing being valued for something other than its use-value – the value of a commodity based on its ability to meet a human need. Instead of use-value, symbolic values, like love, wealth and power, are attributed to commodities.[25] It is possible to come home with the results of a good day's clothes shopping and immediately want more. If we were looking for things based only on their use-value we would be sated (and probably overwhelmed), but because we are looking for symbolism, we face a search based on empty belief which the ancient Greek philosopher Epicurus said 'plunges out to infinity'.[26]

Shopping is continually proffered as the way out of emotional pain. Yet shopping to repair the emotional pain of a broken heart, a lost job or boredom is like trying to fill a hole with air – the black hole of wanting does not go away no matter how many clothes you buy. The unfulfilled nature of modern society means that a lot of shopping gets done, and a lot of commodities fruitlessly consumed. Schor has called this 'the materiality paradox'. In modern society, the times when your need for non-material meaning is greatest are the times when you are mostly likely to maximise your consumption of material resources.[27]

Christmas on Oxford Street sees shoppers spend £1.5 million a minute.[28] New York's fashion market generates $15 billion in sales and $768 million in tax revenue a year.[29] Globally, fashion is a $1.5 trillion dollar industry.[30] Because stagnation would spell disaster for capitalism, governments and institutions sometimes intervene to ensure that what is produced is also consumed.[31] When the Adbusters Media Foundation tried to buy airtime for its *Buy Nothing Day* campaign in 1997, it was turned down by CBS on the grounds that it was contrary to the country's current economic policy.[32] In the days following the 2001 attacks on the World Trade Center, the US economy could not afford for people not to shop. President Bush announced that retail sales were strong: 'I encourage you all to go shopping more.' He reiterated the point in June 2004: 'If you own something, you have a vital stake in the future of our country. The more ownership there is in America, the more vitality there is in

America.' This is an example of the subordination of human needs to the imperative of corporations to accumulate wealth. Imaginary appetites and false needs are created without regard to whether they are real or dehumanising.[33]

Natalie Singh at WGSN described fashion as being 'all about making you feel that what you've currently got is not quite right already. It's ultimately about trying to make people feel insecure.'[34] Whilst fashion can provide an outlet for aesthetic creativity and enjoyment, this is subject to the demands of the markets that control fashion production. The human need for clothing and creativity has been commodified into the production of fashion for profit.

Shop to Live

The 'king consumer' ideology obscures fashion as a compelling economic need. Because it is constantly changing, fashion has become synonymous with being modern and competent. Keeping up with fashion can determine whether or not people find and keep employment, housing and their standing in society. The concept of aesthetic labour – of a person's job depending on their appearance – is generally applied to those working in the modelling, acting or music industries.[35] But maintaining a certain appearance is a prerequisite for people throughout the workforce. This makes fashion an economic necessity that people must consume to remain current. As *Vogue* described it: 'Just when you thought you had nailed your autumn/winter wardrobe – tunic (check), sheath dress (check), fuzzy knit (check), midi skirt (check), lace blouse (check – so many compliments) – a whole new set of options arrive in store.'[36]

One of the most enduring trends of the current economic crisis is that of work-wear. As unemployment and job insecurity rose, people were told to transform themselves with some well-tailored clothes. *The Times* reported that 'looking like someone who actually works for a living seem to be coming back into vogue'.[37] Jackie Newcombe emphasised this change to me, describing how: 'Work-wear is becoming more and more important to people as they think that it's more and more competitive in the workplace so they want to make sure that they look good.'[38] Another commentator summed up recession fashion by stating: 'It's OK to be redundant. It's not OK to look redundant.'[39] In this way fashion both promises and threatens – buying will keep you safe from harm, not buying courts disaster.[40] An extreme example was a magazine editorial that encouraged readers to buy an inordinately expensive necklace: 'Sure it's a recession but you're not dead yet!'[41]

Such is the importance of clothes for finding work that numerous charities exist to help people dress for interviews. Dress for Success 'solves the Catch-22 that confronts disadvantaged women trying to enter the workforce: Without a job, how can you afford a suit? But without a suit, how can you get a job?'[42] Similarly, in 2011 the New York office of charity Career Gear gave 1,192 impoverished and unemployed men a suit. Listed companies that participated in 'suit drives' include UBS, Citibank, J. P. Morgan Chase and PricewaterhouseCoopers – the very corporations that helped cause the financial crisis and put so many people out of work in the first place.

The need to maintain an appearance to secure work is not new. A factory worker's letter published in a newspaper in 1954 complained about the need to wear make-up: 'You can't go out hunting even a factory job looking as tired as you might feel. Cosmetics brighten up a weary face and give the illusion of the necessary vigour and youth.'[43] In the same series of letters another woman wrote: 'Personally, I would be greatly relieved if I could forgo the trouble and expense of make-up, but capitalism won't let me. I'm no sucker for beauty-aid ads, but economic pressure – I have to earn my living – forces me to buy and use the darned stuff.'[44] How many people today would happily give up make-up or fashion in its entirety if it were not for the need to earn a living?

The radical Evelyn Reed explained in 1954 that there is a difference between criticising people for enjoying buying and wearing fashion and criticising capitalism for compelling people constantly to buy new clothes. The freedom to wear and enjoy fashionable clothes must also be accompanied by the freedom not to do so. If we do not critique capitalist compulsions, then statements from make-up magnates like Helena Rubenstein ('There are no ugly women, just lazy ones') become truisms rather than merely grasping attempts to make billions by exploiting people's insecurities.

The feminist academic Sandra Lee Bartky wrote that while no one is marched off for electrolysis at rifle point, women are still compelled to conform to certain beauty ideals.[45] If make-up is a creative pursuit allowing women to express their individuality, why is the same picture painted day after day with little room for novelty or imagination? The woman who does not paint her face encounters sanctions that would never be applied to someone who 'chooses not to paint a watercolour'.[46]

Think of Me as Evil?

G. K. Chesterton declared: 'it is really not so repulsive to see the poor asking for money as to see the rich asking for more money. And advertisement is the rich asking for more money.'[47] Advertising is a bridge corporations use to reach consumers. Its purpose is to sell products to gain maximum profits. As such, the advertising industry is merely a symptom of the system that we live in and not the main problem itself. It represents massive waste, however, with $100 billion spent on advertising each year in the United States alone.

A hundred years ago, the pioneering consumption scholar Thorstein Veblen described production costs as being swamped by concealed sales costs. Today advertising alone (excluding other forms of marketing) accounts for up to 12 per cent of the price of everything from soap to jeans.[48] People see up to 3,000 adverts every day, neuro-marketing is on the rise and even babies are now turned into billboards. We are paying the price for adverts twice over, and 'if anything is following you around that doggedly, you're better off knowing what it's up to'.[49]

When accused of increasing pollution and poverty, advertising agencies argue that they merely redistribute existing desires rather than increase people's desire for 'stuff'. This premise is extremely important to cigarette advertisers, who argue that they do not cause more people to smoke, they just steal existing smokers from other brands. Similarly, fashion corporations claim that they are simply responding to human needs and use advertising to compete for existing markets – relieving them of responsibility for the millions of tonnes of textiles found in landfill. Yet the evidence suggests the opposite. The more people are exposed to advertisements, the more they consume. *Think of Me as Evil? Opening the Ethical Debates in Advertising*, a report produced for the World Wide Fund for Nature and the Public Interest Research Centre, stated that the implication that advertising increases aggregate material consumption means it can be pinpointed as an engine of the least sustainable aspects of an economy.[50]

For some liberal economists, seeing 3,000 adverts a day is a sign of healthy competition and choice. Competing companies, however, are already part of the monopoly of private property.[51] Working people have been dispossessed of any kind of ownership of productive property. Instead, corporations own everything from factories to farms to offices.[52] The fashion industry is particularly monopolised, with the majority of brands owned by a few multinational corporations, as discussed in Chapter 1.

Advertisements also act collectively to pump out the same message. The message is that we shop – we shop for clothes that will make us richer even though we've just spent all our money.[53] Real choice has been eroded and replaced by consumption choices.[54] Whilst a consumer cannot choose whether their taxes go towards cancer treatments or F16 fighter jets, or whether the firm they work for builds social housing or speculates on the cost of wheat causing famine in Africa, they *can* choose between 'tough girl' and 'flirty babe' trends for their Spring wardrobe.

Nor can we choose when we encounter adverts. The television can be switched off, adverts on billboards or public transport cannot. CBS, which controls most of the advertising space on the London Underground, claims that 64 per cent of commuters have bought or tried something as a direct result of seeing advertising on the Underground.[55] The authors of *Think of Me as Evil?* were so convinced by the impact of advertising that they recommended a disclaimer be placed on every billboard:

This advertisement may influence you in ways of which you are not consciously aware. Buying consumer goods is unlikely to improve your wellbeing and borrowing to buy consumer goods may be unwise; debt can enslave.

Deep in Debt

In 1966 a fashion commentator in the United States made the following prophetic statement: 'The credit card has become a badge of belonging. It began as a zephyr. It's a strong wind now. It may be the hurricane that blows up our economy.'[56] By 2012 credit card debt in the United States topped $1 trillion.[57] Debtors' prisons were abolished there in the nineteenth century, yet in 2011 *The Wall Street Journal* identified over 5,000 debt prisoners as wages dropped and homes fell into negative equity.[58] This is not a problem of irresponsible consumers: people are actively and officially encouraged to get into high levels of debt for systemic reasons. Interest rates are kept low to keep people shopping for goods that are becoming more expensive even as real wages drop. Debt offsets the drop in living standards that would otherwise occur.[59] Without debt the economy would shudder to a halt.[60]

Between 2000 and 2007, debt in the United Kingdom increased by 115 per cent[61] and by October 2007, individuals had been lent £1,200 billion for mortgages and £222 billion for unsecured consumer debt, a total of £1.4 trillion. With millions of people living below the minimum income standard and with the world sinking deeper into economic crisis, Step Change, the UK's leading debt advice organisation,[62] reported a 21 per cent increase in people asking for help between 2008 and 2010.

Fashion has become notoriously linked with debt. It has become commonplace for consumers, and in particular young women, to get into debt to keep up with fashion. This was characterised by an episode of the TV series *Sex and the City* where the lead character, Carrie Bradshaw, discovers that she has spent the equivalent of the down-payment on her apartment on shoes alone. Having spent $40,000 on shoes and facing homelessness she realises that she 'will literally be the old woman who lived in her shoes'.[63]

To keep consumers shopping with money they do not possess, debt has been rebranded as 'credit'. For shoppers, paying for a dress at the till is often accompanied by a sales pitch for a store card. In 2011, some 13 million people in Britain had store cards which had accrued a collective £1.83 billion in sales.[64] According to Step Change, single women are three times more likely to have store card debt than single men, with an average debt estimated to be £1,301. Step Change believes a large proportion of this debt comes from spur-of-the-moment fashion purchases.[65]

Store cards hide the reality of financialisation behind a façade of respectability or luxury. Customers make purchases in a familiar shop using a card stamped with a familiar logo. Operating the cards and lending the money, however, are third-party finance lenders like Santander, which owns the House of Fraser, Laura Ashley and Debenhams store cards. Santander even punishes card holders by fining them if they leave their card unused for too long.[66] Whereas credit cards generally offer an APR (yearly interest) of 15 to 18 per cent, store-card APR rates are often as high as 30 per cent. In a secret shopper sting, the consumer group Which? sent a heavily indebted graduate with no earnings to see how much debt he could accrue via store cards. Within two days he was in debt for £2,750.

Another serious source of fashion debt is catalogues. The Studio catalogue, for example, offers online and catalogue shopping and targets low-income families by offering the opportunity to spread payments out – buy now, pay monthly. At the end of their 21,000-word Terms and Conditions document, Studio state that shoppers can be charged an eye-watering 44 per cent APR. They also state that late payments will result in a £20 fine every time they send a customer a reminder. And they threaten: 'If you are late in making payments to us, we may pass your details to an external debt collection agency who may chase and collect any late payments on our behalf.' As the CEO of Macy's admitted 50 years ago: 'Customers who use a credit system pay for it.'[67]

Fetishes, Snake Oil and Alienation

An anonymous executive at Louis Vuitton has been quoted as describing the company's success as 'the biggest sleight of hand since snake oil. Can you imagine that this is all based on canvas toile with a plastic coating and a bit of leather trim?'[68] How is it possible for scraps of stitched canvas and leather to be given so much meaning?

Why do they sell for thousands of pounds? Marx termed this anomaly 'commodity fetishism'. The term was taken from early Portuguese anthropological writings in which amulets or charms were known as *feitiço*. The amulets were described as magically artful; possessing one was believed to give the owner special powers.[69] It is this same imbuing of objects with powers beyond their composition that still occurs today.

Each winter brings advertising copy implying that handbags can cure Seasonal Affected Disorder (SAD). Advertisements promise: 'Escape those January blues with Jeremy Scott's collaboration with accessories giant Longchamp. It's a ray of sunshine!' Or 'This highlighter yellow satchel is the perfect pick-me-up for right now.'[70] The only purchase that the NHS recommends as treatment for SAD is a light box. The fashion industry not ony ignores this, but hints it can also cure other ailments – Wonderbra: *Your Not So Secret Weapon*; Adidas: *Impossible Is Nothing*; Diesel: *For Successful Living*; and French Connection: *FCUK Advertising*.

Engels observed that under capitalism, competition and private property 'isolates everyone in their own crude solitariness'.[71] In a marketised society people are judged by their material worth. A designer handbag gives its owner status by signifying the amount spent. Under capitalism people are locked into a mindset where having is more important than being. We learn to value things only when we directly possess them rather than looking for happiness in ourselves, in labour, in society or in nature.[72]

Commodities acquire meaning because people are alienated. The Marxist John Berger described people balancing endless stretches of meaningless working hours with a dreamt future of exciting, enviable consumption: 'The more monotonous the present, the more the imagination must seize upon the future.'[73] Arthur Miller also noted how shopping is offered as a cure for emptiness in his 1968 play *The Price*: 'Years ago, a person, if he was unhappy, didn't know what to do with himself – he'd go to church, start a revolution – something. Today you're unhappy? Can't figure it out? What is the solution? Go shopping.'

Life as a 'servant of the wage'[74] is a familiar monotony for most people. The novelist Patrick Hamilton called London a 'crouching monster' that breathed commuters:

> Every morning [they] are sucked up through an infinitely complicated respiratory apparatus of trains and termini into mighty congested lungs, held there for a number of hours, and then in the evening, exhaled violently through the same channels.[75]

Under this system, people are forced to sell their labour without any control over what they produce or how they produce it. Few people ever have the chance even to imagine their full potential, let alone reach it, because they too are turned into commodities. Rather than being an end in themselves, people become a means for someone else's profit.

Take this description, by Dana Thomas in *Deluxe*, of expatriate Chinese workers in a Mauritian textile factory: during the break the workers 'slept on folded arms on their knitting machines. When the break was over, the Chinese girls snapped up and went right back to work. Their faces were blank, their eyes empty. No one spoke. All you could hear was the deafening sidth-sidth-sidth of the knitting machines.'[76] This is what Marx called the reduction of people to an abstract activity and a stomach.[77]

It is not only factory workers who experience alienation. Work in non-manufacturing industries is also carried out according to management edicts rather than personal creativity or judgement. This trend is predicted to intensify in the future, with only 10–15 per cent of people being granted 'permission to think' whilst at work.[78] The electronic revolution is expected to replicate the industrial revolution by chopping up, codifying and digitalising skills.[79] In Marx's words, alienation means a person only 'feels himself outside his work and in his work feels outside himself'.[80]

This devastating alienation means that people become alienated not just from themselves but from products. It is this distance that provides space for the idea that commodities can have special powers. Consumers are far removed from the production of goods like shoes, handbags or clothes. Items appear in shops without revealing a trace of the manufacturing process, seemingly independent of people. This gives the illusion that there is a source of wealth separate from human labour. We can admire a beaded evening gown or a solid pair of work boots without connecting them with the workers that produced them. This mystification of products means our society is arguably not materialistic enough.[81] Being materialistic does not here mean doing more shopping; rather it is a call for people to recognise that products such as shoes and handbags are dependent on nature and labour and have a physical, material reality independent of thought.[82] It calls for use-values to take precedence over endless symbolic values.

The fashion industry is adept at hiding human labour behind a glitzy façade. To create even a t-shirt requires a chain of designers, cotton pickers, sweatshop workers, dye technicians and freight drivers. Advertisements similarly conceal their means of production. Model agencies, photographers, stylists, make-up artists, cleaners and caterers, infighting, cellulite, boredom, starvation and Photoshop are all hidden because consumers are not allowed to look behind the scenes.[83]

This imperative comes from the need to generate surplus value. An inherent part of capitalism, surplus value arises from the difference between the value of labour-power and the value of the commodities that the labour-power produces. At one Disney subcontractor, workers each make 50 Disney shirts a day. These sell for $10.97 each or $548.50 for the batch. The eight hours of work earn the employee $2.22.[84] The difference between $2.22 and $548.50 is the surplus value that Disney creams off once the shirts have been sold.

Luxury goods also come with their true labour costs hidden from sight. Dana Thomas reiterates this point in her book: 'Yes, luxury handbags are made in China. Top brands.'[85] By hiding the real labour costs and the methods used to manufacture a 'luxury' handbag, corporations can charge more for it than if it was common knowledge that it was made in a Chinese factory. This mystifying process makes commodities appear independent of the labour that made them and thus capable of possessing independent powers. In an ideal world it would be the people who made the commodities who would be valued and respected rather than just the commodities.

Shopping is routinely proffered as a cure for everything from heartbreak to low self-esteem. Zygmunt Bauman describes how: 'From cradle to coffin we are trained and drilled to treat shops as pharmacies filled with drugs to cure or at least mitigate all illnesses and afflictions of our lives.'[86] In reality, a new dress cannot mend a broken heart, a new bag can only metaphorically and not literally satisfy hunger.[87] Because we live in a marketised society, it is little wonder that the 'visible divinities' of money and commodities are purported to cure heartache. Our real needs are ignored and what we experience instead are the artificial needs created by capitalist society.[88] In this way we lose out twice.

The artist Rob Montgomery 'space-jacked' a billboard with the message:

The spectacle of advertising creates images of false beauty so suave and so impossible to attain that you will hurt inside and never even know where the hurt came from . . .[89]

Far from being 'kings' who control the market, consumers of fashion are used to generate vast profits for corporations who create false needs. Our lives are inescapably linked to class and economic circumstances. There is no fashion democracy and no level playing field. Instead there is an ever-turning wheel on which we must all run.

CHAPTER FOUR

Stitching It

*In the Pearl River Delta, some 40,000 fingers
are severed each year in work-related accidents.*[1]

*The owners of the factories are ministers, ex-ministers, parliament
members, ex-parliament members, army generals, civil bureaucrats, even
university vice chancellors – this is the elite of society who have great
influence over state mechanisms.*
Amirul Haque Amir, President of the NGWF

On the morning of 24 April, 2013, a group of garment workers argued
with their managers outside Rana Plaza, a commercial building in
Dhaka, Bangladesh, which contained a number of clothing factories.
The garment workers said the structure was unsafe; that cracks in the
building's concrete had appeared and were growing in size; and that
they feared for their lives. They had fled the building the day before,
how could they now go back into such a death trap?

The managers replied that anyone refusing to enter the building
would have their wages docked, not just for that day but for the
entire month. In Bangladesh, losing a month's wages is tantamount
to starvation, so the garment workers were forced to climb the stairs
to their work stations, gingerly stepping around cracks in the floor.

An hour later, the eight-storey building collapsed on itself, its
illegally built top storeys shaken to bits by giant generators, placed
there to keep the factory running during frequent power cuts.
Thousands of workers dropped through floors and were crushed by
falling pillars and machinery.

Survivors were trapped in a living grave. One young woman,
Rogina Faidul, described lying buried in rubble for three days, her
arm trapped under a sewing machine. When rescuers located her
she had to amputate her own arm to escape. The official death toll
of Rana Plaza was 1,133, making it the deadliest garment factory
disaster in history. Another 2,500 people were injured, many
disabled permanently.

Retailers who have admitted to using the Rana Plaza factory
include Benetton, Bon Marché, Mango, Matalan, Primark and
Walmart, but hundreds more companies use low-cost Bangladeshi

factories, including upscale brands like Armani, Ralph Lauren, Michael Kors and Hugo Boss.

* * *

Apparel is one of the oldest, largest and most globally prevalent export industries, with most countries producing some kind of clothing product for the international market.[2] As an industry it is dependent on human labour. In a world where robots walk on Mars, the underwear you are wearing can only be produced by human hands. Because of this, fashion and human labour are inseparable. Everything we wear is the direct result of detailed, repetitive, human toil.

The profits accumulated by the fashion industry are huge – £759 million for Zara and £2.5 billion net for LVMH in 2011.[3] There is enough money in the industry for the entire workforce to be reasonably paid and fairly treated if only profits were reinvested and priorities realigned. The inescapable logic of the market means that wages, an elementary cost to cut, are driven as low as possible.[4] Fashion today is inseparable not only from human labour but from its extreme exploitation.

There are quite rightly countless books, films and campaigns highlighting the horrors of fashion's factories. Primark is notorious for making workers work an 80-hour week for 5 pence an hour, and for the death of over 100 workers in factories in a two-month period in 2006.[5] There is an inexhaustible list of brands caught using exploited labour. It extends well beyond the cheapest brands. It keeps growing to include H&M, Nike, Reebok, Adidas, Converse, Gap, DKNY, Levi's, Marks & Spencer, Karen Millen, Ralph Lauren, Burberry and hundreds of others. The key word here is 'caught', because no clothes exist that have been made without the exploitation of human labour.[6] With a supply chain that incorporates chronically underpaid agricultural, chemical, factory and shop work, such a thing is impossible. The Rana Plaza disaster was just one link in a chain of industrial tragedies that has long hung heavily around the neck of the world.

Sweatshops and Slavery

Sweatshops are often seen as a particularly abhorrent form of labour, somehow morally and politically separate from other lawful forms of low-paid work which appear acceptable by comparison.[7] I use the term 'sweatshop' to describe highly exploitative, and usually dangerous, workplaces where clothes are made. I am not imposing a size limit on a sweatshop so the term covers large factories as well as workshops. A Marxist understanding of the term 'exploitation' is that it occurs when people are not recompensed for the full value of their labour. Workers are not paid for the work that they do but for their 'labour power' – their ability to work.[8] Sweatshops are a particularly acute form of exploitation: Disney workers who earn $2.22 for producing $548.50 worth of merchandise are extremely exploited. Yet when the well-paid office worker produces more value than she is paid for, she is also exploited.

Recent decades have seen the rise of fast-fashion, a retail style that consists of the expedited production and distribution of short runs of trend-based fashion. Short runs mean seasonal sales are unlikely, which increases the pressure to buy quickly.[9] Fast-fashion necessarily involves aggressive pricing strategies in order to shift large quantities of stock at low prices rather than small quantities at high prices. Devised by discount clothing retailers like Walmart and Tesco, aggressive pricing has been adopted by traditional retailers threatened by discounters.[10] The result of short turnarounds and low costs is exploitation in the production chain. Yet there was exploitation before fast-fashion: the production systems might be abhorrent, but capitalism itself is the problem.

* * *

Factory production of materials like cotton emerged in Britain during the Industrial Revolution. Before the arrival of industrial machinery, cloth was made by families spinning and weaving raw materials in their homes. In 1764 James Hargreaves, a weaver in north Lancashire, invented the spinning jenny which vastly increased the amount of spun yarn that one person could produce by enabling eight threads to be spun at once. Later improvements increased this to 80 threads.[11] This reduced the price of yarn, which in turn increased demand. Wealthy members of the ruling class established factories containing multiple, water-powered spinning jennies. Automated machines required fewer workers, which in turn meant even cheaper yarn.

As advances in machinery accelerated, homeworkers were forced to replace outdated machinery more frequently in an attempt to keep up with production. It was an impossible race and one by one workers with the least money were forced to give up self-employment and seek factory work. When Dr Cartwright launched the power loom in 1804, the outpacing of workers by machines was complete. Home workshops could no longer produce yarn or cloth at the volume or price of factories. As Engels noted: 'the history of the proletariat in England begins . . . with the invention of the steam engine and of machinery for working cotton.'[12]

The wealthy family of Friedrich Engels owned a textile mill in Manchester where the 22-year-old German 'upstart' was sent to work in the hope that it would relieve him of his radical inclinations. Manchester had the opposite effect and led Engels to write his ground-breaking book *The Condition of the Working Class in England*. The move to Manchester also introduced Engels to the two loves of his life – the radical factory worker Mary Burns and, after her death, her sister Lizzie. It was these two women who guided Engels round Manchester and stopped him being robbed and beaten up in the slums as a wealthy foreign interloper.[13]

The scale of the Industrial Revolution can be seen in the enormous leap in cotton imports that Engels recorded. In 1775, 5 million pounds of raw cotton were imported into the UK; by 1844 this had increased to 600 million. This was cotton grown and picked by African slaves. The origins of the fashion industry and the slave trade share several disturbing intersections. By 1750 mills in Manchester were producing cloth modified to meet African tastes in prints and patterns.[14] As outlined in Karen Tranberg Hansen's book *Salaula*, it was clothes, both new and second-hand, which often filled the cargo holds of ships sailing to Africa from Britain. Once in Africa clothes were traded for slaves with African rulers like King Kazembe III of Luapula.[15] The West's Industrial Revolution abused Africa twice over, using the North Atlantic slave trade to gain slave labour and markets for clothes.

Engels reported that the Industrial Revolution led to 'a rapid fall in the price of all manufactured commodities, prosperity of commerce and manufacture, the conquest of nearly all the unprotected foreign markets'.[16] But the new 'national wealth' benefited only the rich. As workers were driven from the land and forced to seek employment in the newly industrialised towns, urban populations grew faster than the infrastructure could cope with. The 'slum-ification' of Britain began, and by the end of the nineteenth century over a quarter of Britain's population was estimated to be living at or below subsistence level. The 1833 Factory Act illustrates how bad things had become. It was considered highly controversial to ban children under the age of nine from working in textile factories and to restrict children aged between nine and 13 to working 12 hours a day. Those aged 13–18 could legally work a 69-hour week. As well as running sweatshops, industry owners also portioned out work to unregulated, starving homeworkers in order to undercut factory wages.[17]

As industry spread to the United States, so too did the modern sweatshops of the garment industry. The social worker Charles Bernheimer described conditions in Philadelphia:

> The room is likely to be ill-smelling and badly ventilated. Consequently, an abnormally bad air is breathed which is difficult for the ordinary person to stand for long. Thus result tubercular and other diseases which the immigrant acquires in his endeavour to work out his economic existence.[18]

As a result tuberculosis became known as 'the tailor's disease'.[19] Vast commercial laundries were set up, and it was these, with their sweltering, unsanitary conditions, that probably inspired the name 'sweatshop'.

Since its inception, the inhuman working conditions of fashion production have caused both industrial tragedies *and* industrial struggle on a truly momentous scale. It is no coincidence that out of these laundries, in Troy, New York, came the ground-breaking Collar Laundry Union, founded by Kate Mullaney.

Uprising

Garment workers have always fought for self-determined freedom from oppression. Media narratives of sweatshops often impose stereotypes of victimhood on garment workers, reinforcing stereotypes of passive Asian or immigrant women.[20] Yet what is clear is that groups of predominantly female garment workers (it remains a trade 90 per cent staffed by women)[21] engage in some of the bitterest and hardest fought battles of the international labour movement.

In the United States at the turn of the century these industrial battles were led by young immigrant women like Clara Lemlich. On 22 November 1909, Lemlich called for a general strike at a packed meeting of the Coopers Union in New York. The next day she took to the streets with 15,000 of her fellow garment workers. The strike, known as the Uprising of the Twenty Thousand, was a bitter, but ultimately successful, battle for better wages and working conditions. It lasted for over two months and set off a wave of women's strikes that spread from New York to Philadelphia, Cleveland, Chicago, Iowa and Michigan between 1909 and 1915.

Lemlich had arrived in the United States in 1903, fleeing with her family from the pogroms of Tsarist Russia. She described herself and fellow garment workers as reduced 'to the status of machines'. Unwilling to accept her fate, she joined the newly-formed International Ladies' Garment Workers' Union (ILGWU). Being an active member of the executive was a dangerous role. When she made her speech at the Coopers Union, Lemlich was still recovering from a severe beating by management thugs on a picket line.[22]

Yet the dangers of *not* struggling for change were far worse. On 25 March 1911, disaster struck at the Triangle Shirtwaist Factory in New York. A fire swept through the building killing 146 workers, mostly young Jewish and Italian women. The death toll was greatly increased by a lack of fire safety precautions and locked fire escapes. It was alleged that locking the doors meant that employees could be searched for stolen goods; it is more likely that they were locked to keep out union organisers as the factory had been a continual site of industrial action.[23]

One of the workers, Rosey Safran, who was interviewed in the days after the fire, explained that the union had been demanding adequate fire precautions: 'The bosses defeated us, so our friends are dead.'[24] Aided by a corrupt judge, the factory owners, Max Blanck and Isaac Harris, escaped responsibility. The tragedy galvanised the fight for workers' rights and in time led to the gradual implementation of fire codes for homes and workplaces.

Epilogue for a Fire

Over a hundred years later, as I write this book, the same avarice-fuelled fire that killed so many in New York has struck again – this time with a death toll twice as high. On 12 September 2012, approximately 289 garment workers perished in a fire at Ali Enterprises in Karachi, Pakistan. This industrial tragedy, the worst in Pakistan's history, reads like a grisly checklist of the Triangle Shirtwaist Factory fire: no fire exits, overcrowding, locked or blocked doors, and windows sealed by iron bars.

Pakistan's apparel industry accounts for 38 per cent of its workforce and more than half of the country's exports.[25] Its workers are paid some of the world's lowest wages – at Ali Enterprises workers reported earning an average wage of about $80 a month.[26] Pakistan's health and safety legislation has been swept aside at the behest of wealthy industrialists,[27] and as a result, factory fires are common. On the same day as the Ali Enterprises fire, 25 people died in a shoe factory fire in Lahore.

The New York Times reported that a prominent, New York-based factory monitoring group had recently inspected and certified Ali Enterprises as meeting internationally recognised standards. Two inspectors spent four days at the factory before issuing it with a prestigious SA8000 certificate.[28] The inspections were carried out on behalf of Social Accountability International (SAI), which describes its aim as being 'to advance the human rights of workers around the world'. As journalists investigated SAI, a shady world of corporate financing emerged, leading to accusations that certificates like SAI's are merely 'distractions meant to give corporate cover'.[29]

According to *Al Jazeera*, SAI receives between $10,000 and $65,000 a year from each of its 20 corporate 'programme members', including Gap, Gucci and Groupe Carrefour. SAI's board of directors includes a chairperson who previously worked for Toys 'R' Us for 20 years and a board member who simultaneously acts as Gap Inc.'s senior vice-president for social responsibility.[30] The 'watchtowers' that are supposed to protect workers' lives are nothing more than industry fronts.

The RINA Group, which was subcontracted to carry out inspections by SAI, has certified 540 factories, nearly 100 of these in Pakistan. With hundreds of workers dead, these certificates are shown to be worth less than the self-regulating paper they are printed on. 'Corporate-funded monitoring systems like SAI cannot and will not protect workers,' stated Scott Nova, executive director of the Worker Rights Consortium. 'The whole system is flawed.'[31]

Rana Plaza I, II, III, IV . . .

The garment industry represents approximately 80 per cent of Bangladesh's exports. After China, it is the second largest garment producer in the world, generating $19 billion worth of exports. Europe is Bangladesh's primary market, with 60 per cent of orders coming from European companies. Bangladesh is the United States second biggest clothing supplier.

To accompany this giant leap in production, there is a long roll-call of Bangladeshi garment factory tragedies: Rana, Spectrum, Tazreen, Smart and many, many more. The sheer scale of Rana Plaza made it a horrific watershed, however, as consumers grasped the grim realities behind the 'Made In Bangladesh' labels in their clothes.

Sick of their warnings going unheeded, after Rana Plaza global trade unions, Uni Global Union (20 million members of 900 unions across 150 countries) and IndustriALL capitalised on the outpouring of anger by serving retailers with an ultimatum. Working with NGOs and the National Garment Workers Federation in Bangladesh (NGWF), Uni Global and IndustriALL drafted the *Accord on Fire and*

Building Safety in Bangladesh and told retailers: this time, you sign our deal. Due to union and public pressure, by the end of September 2013, 90 global brands including H&M, Zara and even Primark had signed the Accord.

The Accord has powerful opponents. Walmart and Gap have formed yet another voluntary, corporate-led initiative that has, of course, shunned union involvement. This model of voluntary self-inspection that excludes unions, is fundamentally flawed. War on Want point out that Rana Plaza had twice been audited by Western brands, which, shockingly, did not identify any risks with the eight storey building. As a result 1,133 people were crushed to death.[32]

According to Philip Jennings, General Secretary of Uni Global, 'The Accord is different – it is legally binding in the case of dispute, it covers 1,500 factories, and workers are involved locally, regionally, and globally.'[33] Consider that under the Accord, garment workers can rightfully refuse to work in unsafe factories. What's more, workers must continue to be paid until dangerous working conditions are resolved. Imagine what a difference this agreement would have made to the Rana Plaza workers who begged their managers for clemency on that fateful April morning.

Building Unions in Bangladesh

Even with the Accord there is an extremely long way to go until the country's labour laws become consistent with international standards. Regardless of what they sign whilst under pressure, corporations are not to be trusted. They are in Bangladesh to benefit from a severely exploitative factory system. Export Processing Zones (EPZs) were established in Bangladesh in the 1980s; it was these, coupled with a ban on labour organisations, that attracted the multinationals.[34]

Amirul Haque Amir is the president of the NGWF, he described to me the struggle against 'termination clauses' – enshrined in legislation to allow factory owners to fire anyone engaging in union activity. By law 30 per cent of workers have to be signed up to a union before it becomes official. 'Imagine this,' he said, 'in a factory employing 10,000 workers.'[35]

'From the government side they never protect the workers.' Amirul Haque Amir continued, 'Inside the government there is a significant number of people directly involved with the textile business. They are totally against trade union organisations because there are inhumane conditions in the factories which they fear a trade union would highlight.' High levels of unemployment also mean people are sometimes scared to organise – factories can easily fire 500 people and recruit another 500 from Bangladesh's reserve army of labour.

This said, it is still trade unions who are leading the ongoing struggle for human rights. After mass strikes and protests in 2010, the government (caught between workers and the Bangladesh Garment Manufacturers and Exporters Association), raised the minimum wage to 21 cents an hour. By 2012, inflation had eroded this to 14.7 cents in real terms. In protest half a million garment workers went on strike for a 6.3 cent rise, to bring the minimum wage to 27.3 cents an hour, or back to 21 cents in real terms. In the aftermath of Rana Plaza there have been more demonstrations by garment workers demanding justice for the fallen and injured, and for better pay and conditions. Strikes numbering 200,000 workers took to the streets in September 2013.

The striking workers are accused of treason, of bringing Bangladesh into international disrepute and of threatening the country's ability to attract foreign contracts. Those trying to organise for workers' rights face a hostile state apparatus that routinely uses rubber bullets, tear gas and beatings to disperse protesters. Labour movement figureheads face kidnapping, torture and murder. Aminul Islam, the chief organiser of the Bangladesh Centre for Worker Solidarity, an initiative backed by US unions, was found tortured and murdered in 2012.[36]

According to the Workers Rights Consortium, the cost of implementing decent standards in Bangladesh's 4,500 factories would be $3 billion spent over five years. Consider that the five siblings of the Walton family, which controls Walmart, each have personal fortunes of $18 billion. Just 3.5 per cent of their wealth would ensure that the people who slave for them do not die horribly in the process.

Bra Wars

By the 1920s growing trade union strength in Manhattan and other industry hubs had improved pay and working conditions. But wary of shrinking profits, suppliers looked for ways to get round the unions. The solution they found was to subcontract work away from union strongholds to smaller contractors.[37] Old-style competition among contractors returned and standards dropped through the floor.[38]

If this sounds familiar it is because this is the pattern that has characterised the garment industry ever since. The apparel industry is the site of a perpetual struggle between labour and capital. Subcontracting complicates this conflict because, unlike in other industries, fashion retailers do not own the factories that produce their stock. Retailers hire manufacturers, who hire contractors, who hire subcontractors, who hire garment workers. This chain allows retailers to claim that they are not responsible for garment workers. In fact, retailers exercise almost total control over the pay and conditions of garment workers by forcing factories to accept rock-bottom prices.

By the 1970s the 'outside production' of subcontracting had come to mean outside the United States.[39] It was a new system, impervious to domestic campaigns or legislation. The term 'global scanning' has since been coined to describe the way corporations systematically seek out the most profitable sites for production.[40] Typically, they have a very cheap urban workforce; no pension, health care or insurance requirements; no trade unions, protests or strikes; little or no democracy; and a state apparatus ready and willing to crack down on dissent.[41] As a result, Latin America, Asia, South East Asia, North Africa, Sub-Saharan Africa, Turkey and Eastern Europe have all become sites for cheap apparel production.

Whilst cheap imports benefit retailers, they are often ruinous for domestic manufacturers in countries like the United States and United Kingdom. Cheap imports of Chinese wire coat-hangers, used by dry cleaners, put huge pressure on American firms. In 2004 there were eight significant American manufacturers. Three years later there was just one.[42] Competition between different sections of the industry shows the ruling class to be a 'band of warring brothers'[43] rather than a homogeneous bloc.

Subcontracting led to the establishment of a new world manufacturing map. In the first decade of the twenty-first century there were two other major upheavals in apparel manufacture. The first was the expiry of the Multi Fibre Arrangement (MFA) in 2005. The MFA was established in the 1970s to set quotas and preferential tariffs on apparel and textile imports to the United States, Canada and Europe. Whilst most trade was being increasingly liberalised, apparel and textiles were not. The MFA had a variety of effects in the developing world. Some small countries were given guaranteed import quotas. Because the MFA covered the volume not the value of imports, others, like South Korea, got round the MFA by diversifying and increasing the quality of its exports. South Korea also started subcontracting to countries without quotas, then moving on once quotas were imposed.

For a country like Bangladesh, too poor and unskilled to diversify, the MFA was devastating.[44] It is estimated that the MFA took millions of jobs and billions of dollars of exports away from developing countries, with the global welfare cost of the MFA reaching $7.3 billion a year in the mid-1980s.[45]

When the MFA came to an end in 2005, the loss of 30 years of restricted access caused a tremendous flux in the global geography of fashion.[46] Saipan is one of 14 Northern Mariana Islands located in the northern Pacific Ocean. As part of the United States Commonwealth, anything 'Made in Saipan' can be certified as 'Made in USA' and is both duty- and quota-free. While the MFA was in force, Saipan became a giant compound housing tens of thousands of workers – predominantly young, female and Chinese.[47]

With the lifting of quotas, factories left Saipan and returned to South East Asia where labour costs were even lower. An apparel factory is easy to move, being merely rooms full of sewing machines. In 2005 Saipan had 34 garment factories producing $1 billion worth of goods a year. By 2013 none were in operation. Abandoned factories with walls crumbling in the humidity, dusty floors, and bin bags full of labels that would have once been sewn into clothes bear mute testimony to a vanished industry. Young women workers without the means to return home now work in Saipan's sex tourism industry.[48]

After the MFA, textiles and apparel fell under the jurisdiction of the World Trade Organisation. The predictable showdown between China and the European Union quickly ensued, with 48 million pullovers, 18 million pairs of trousers, 8 million t-shirts and over 11 million bras being seized and held in warehouses at EU ports during the summer of 2005.[49] A truce in the 'Bra Wars' was eventually negotiated, with new tariffs imposed on China.

Shortly after the MFA expired, the economic crisis erupted in 2008. The effect of the economic crisis on apparel production should not be underestimated. By 2009 imports into the United States had dropped by 15.7 per cent and every major garment supplier in the world was reporting a decline.[50] In China, 10 million Chinese textiles and apparel workers, a third of the country's total of 30 million, lost their jobs as production slowed.[51] One million (1 in 35) Indian apparel workers also lost their jobs, as did approximately 20 per cent of the Cambodian apparel workforce (75,000 out of 352,000).[52]

World Bank economists have declared that, despite factory closures and some social unrest, China is 'the clear winner in the global apparel export race of the past fifteen years'.[53] China's exports in 2009 were valued at $122.4 billion.[54] To put this into perspective, the next six exporters combined (Turkey, Bangladesh, India, Vietnam, Indonesia, and Mexico) export just half of China's total output.[55] This is despite China no longer being an extremely cheap place to produce commodities, with wages and benefits for blue-collar workers in Guangdong rising by approximately 12 per cent a year.[56]

Rising wages have far from signalled the end of manufacturing in China. In part, the country has moved up the value chain to produce more high-tech commodities. Whilst some apparel production has moved to cheaper places like Bangladesh, or places closer to Europe like Turkey or North Africa, much has stayed in China because it provides a guarantee of quality. China also benefits from a growing domestic market, a government highly supportive of industry, established supply chains and a truly huge workforce. Whilst Chinese wages are rising fast, so too is Chinese productivity. Chinese workers are being paid more to produce more.[57]

A Stitch in Time

Economists have neatly divided the production of fashion into different processes.[58] The first is known as CMT which stands for 'Cut Make Trim'. This is the most basic form of apparel assembly and involves no design work. It generally takes place in EPZs and involves very poor countries importing consignments of fabric to be cut, sewn, trimmed, then exported. Typically, each worker focuses on one aspect of garment production, for example sewing on back pockets or button loops, or snipping off loose threads for 16 hours a day. Prices are kept low because there are thousands of factories competing with each other.

Places that have limited capabilities other than CMT are Cambodia where 85 per cent of exports are from the apparel sector,[59] and also Sub-Saharan Africa and Vietnam. CMT is an extremely cheap production system which relies on millions of exploited workers. However, CMT's complex logistical processes mean it may soon become obsolete.[60]

Beginning in the 1970s, some East Asian suppliers upgraded from CMT to OEM – Original Equipment Manufacture. OEM (a method adopted from technology manufacture) focuses on manufacture rather than design, but a supplier will source and finance piece goods and provide the finishing, packaging and delivery to retail outlets according to designs and fabrics chosen by the client.[61] The shift from CMT to OEM is often associated with the development of a domestic textile industry.[62]

The biggest manufacturing profits are found upstream from OEM and CMT in areas of industry that require large amounts of capital and so are more difficult for poor countries to access. Consequently, poor countries that cannot afford to overcome the barriers to entry specialise in labour-intensive sectors like CMT, whereas richer countries specialise in capital-intensive sectors like synthetic fibre production (China) and machine manufacture (Japan).[63]

The most profitable areas of apparel production are the intangible ones – design, branding and marketing. This marks a recent shift of value from tangible to intangible aspects of production. Original

Design Manufacture (ODM) is a business model that adds design capabilities to OEM. Places able to deliver this full package service are the European Union, Turkey, India and China. Original Brand Manufacture (OBM) involves a focus on branding rather than design or manufacture. OBM can also mark the beginning of branded products aimed at a domestic or local market. An example is the Chinese menswear brand Bosideng which competes in China with multinational brands. With the economic crisis slowing imports to the United States and European Union, domestic markets are predicted to become more of a focus for countries like China and India.[64]

Once OBM status has been reached, suppliers can attempt to become lead firms – retailers, brands, marketers and brand manufacturers whose sheer size and sales mean vast market power. Walmart, Target and Tesco are examples of 'mass merchant retailers' with private labels that they stock alongside other labels. H&M, Gap and Benetton are 'speciality apparel retailers' whose label matches the name of the shop. Nike, Hugo Boss and Gucci, on the other hand, have their own brand but it is sold through multiple retail outlets; they are 'manufacturers without the factories'. Fruit of the Loom and Inditex (Zara) are 'brand manufacturers' – they typically own the brand and the manufacturing.[65]

Once a lead firm has a shop full of cheaply produced clothes, they still have several systemic imperatives to overcome. Clothes must be turned into money otherwise they are useless: 'Goods are produced to be sold. They are "commodities" that have to be exchanged for money before the producers get any benefit from their effort.'[66] Retailers must try to outsell their competitors. This 'intra-sectoral' competition means that companies face constant pressure. There is also the threat from 'inter-sectoral' competition,[67] whereby clothing companies must convince consumers to spend money on clothes rather than on other commodities such as cars, holidays or computers.

The Path to Development?

A common, 'well-meaning' pro-sweatshop argument is that factory jobs are better than hod-carrying, prostitution or sewer cleaning, and that this is 'proved' by how sought-after they are. It is indisputable that people in developing countries want jobs in factories, since they are indeed better than some other forms of subsistence. But what pro-sweatshop arguments tend to ignore is that the poverty that drives people into sweatshops is a recent phenomenon caused by colonial and neoliberal strategies.[68]

Poverty wages were used by colonial powers to create mass destitution that forced people to take any work that was going at whatever cost to themselves. Neoliberalism has followed this pattern, with the IMF and World Bank pushing structural adjustment programmes that have destroyed local industries such as fishing and small-scale farming. This has created the hordes of people forced to migrate to cities in search of work. Couple this need for work with the loss of protective trade tariffs and labour laws and it becomes clear why companies like Nike or Primark rush to exploit the situation in the third world.[69]

Under capitalism there is a mass of unemployed, semi-employed, casually or precariously employed people. Marx called them the 'reserve army of labour'. Anyone who has read John Steinbeck's *Grapes of Wrath* will recall this mass as the means by which capitalist landowners are able to pit starving workers against each other to drive wages down and down. Since the Great Depression of the 1930s, the reserve army of labour has become a global phenomenon. This army is purposefully maintained to allow capitalists to play a global game of 'race to the bottom'.[70]

Thus sweatshop jobs have systemic causes. These jobs might be in demand, but this does not mean they do not shackle people into poverty and abuse or that they are not the result of a destructive system. There are very few women over the age of 40 to be found in China's export factories – 'spent and discarded the women move on'.[71]

Another supposedly well-meaning argument in favour of sweatshops was infamously summed up in an article for *The New York Times* entitled 'Two Cheers for Sweatshops'. The article begins with a description of Thai workers eating beetles – the premise being that sweatshops are acceptable in South East Asia because people there have 'a different perspective from ours, not only when it came to food but also what constitutes desirable work'. The article continues:

'Nothing captures the difference in mind-set between East and West more than attitudes towards sweatshops.'[72]

An entire book could be written detailing everything that is wrong with this 'clash of civilisations' argument. First, if sweatshops are suited to this fictitious 'Asian mind-set', why are there countless examples of industrial struggle in Asia in recent decades? Nike workers were repeatedly on strike during the 1990s: 10,000 Indonesian workers protesting against low and unpaid wages, 1,300 Vietnamese Nike workers fighting for a raise of 1 cent an hour, and 3,000 Chinese Nike workers striking against dangerous working conditions and low wages. More recently, in 2012, there were 500,000 workers on the streets of Bangladesh and 5,000 Cambodian workers from a single company striking for better pay.

Wherever there is oppression there is resistance, and wherever there are sweatshops there are struggles to improve them – not only by the NGO campaigners that the article was attacking, but by the very people working in conditions the article describes as 'tantalizing to a Thai labourer getting by on beetles'. The article also misses the fundamental point of why people eat beetles in the first place: because they are poor. Beetles do not constitute the diets of wealthy Thais. The difference is not one of 'mind-set' but of poverty versus life-threatening destitution. Superficial differences like diets or skin colour should not be used to justify exploitation.

Far from being an Asian phenomenon, sweatshops are as 'American as apple pie'.[73] As we have seen, industrial sweatshops are an Anglo-American concept that continue to exist in both Britain and the United States today. Whilst these are typically staffed by new immigrant workers, this is not because immigrants are predisposed to being 'insect-eating drones', but because they represent the most impoverished section of the workforce. They have the fewest opportunities due to their ethnicity, class, gender and language barriers[74] – hardly something that should prompt cheering. It is a slippery slope to cheer something just because it is marginally better than the alternative: 'Slavery is better than death.' Two cheers for slavery?[75]

A third pro-sweatshop argument is that sweatshops lift countries out of poverty. This has the bizarre effect of portraying multinational corporations and exploitative factory-owners as benefactors. The reality is that these factories are often a step backwards in terms of workers' rights. Many companies, Nike being a prime example, have histories of persuading governments in developing countries to let them flout the minimum wage or circumvent laws by paying workers 'apprentice wages', as Nike did in Indonesia. In Haiti, factories making clothes for companies including Dockers, Nautica, Hanes and Levi's actively prevented Haitian legislators from raising the minimum wage above 0.31 cents an hour. The Haitian Parliament passed a law in 2009 raising the minimum wage to 0.62 cents an hour but this was blocked by factory owners with the help of the US Agency for International Development.[76] A 2008 Worker Rights Consortium study found that a Haitian family of one adult and two children needs a minimum of $12.50 a day to survive, yet Haitian garment workers are paid $3.70 a day.[77]

China is often cited as a sweatshop success story, with commentators arguing that sweatshops have lifted tens of millions of Chinese out of poverty. But as one economist explained:

> A move from abject poverty to poverty is not enough. Whilst China has seen an increase in productivity, the benefits of this increase have not gone to the people doing the work, but straight to the top of society. As a result China is one of the most unequal societies in existence.[78]

The environmental costs of China's factories are also catastrophic.

Development, if it happens at all, takes place despite multinationals not because of them. Corporations deliberately seek out countries without minimum wages, labour laws or trade unions, and help keep them that way. There are numerous links between foreign industry and tyranny that have kept dictators in place. A long list of fashion brands, including Karen Millen, L. K. Bennett and Reiss, have been named and shamed for refusing to deny that they manufactured in Burma under the military dictatorship. According to one report: 'Burma appeals to manufacturers because of its very cheap labour, ban on trade unions and lack of health and safety laws. Factory wages are as low as 5p an hour.'[79]

Nor does economic growth alone lead to development. Legislation and trade unions are vital components for worker protection but these are vehemently opposed by dictators propped up by corporations. The inescapable march of neoliberalism, of competition and the creation of a global reserve army of labour combine to make sweatshops an inescapable fact of capitalism.

Pro-sweatshop arguments also ignore the fact that the wealth created by the factories is extracted by corporations, leaving little behind in the host country. The Haitian earthquake of 2010, which killed 300,000 people and decimated the desperately poor country, allowed what Naomi Klein calls a 'shock doctrine' to commence. Previous US plans to turn Haiti into a Caribbean sweatshop had met with resistance from (amongst others) President Aristide and the Haitian labour movement. After the earthquake, work began on vast factory complexes, termed Integration Economic Zones (IEZs). One such industrial park has been described as an oasis in northern Haiti because it has the paved roads and functioning health services that the rest of the country lacks.[80] The Caracol Industrial Park was built using funding from Washington, yet it is Sae-A, a South Korean textile company and supplier to Gap, Target and Walmart, who will be employing 20,000 Haitian workers on slave wages whilst enjoying an alleged first four years rent-free package. Essentially, the US taxpayer is building industrial parks in Haiti for the benefit of South Korean companies.[81]

Haiti is in the process of being turned into a tax-free zone for foreign investors at the expense of Haitian agriculture. No tax or customs duties are paid to central government on imported materials. Despite millions of dollars of investment, in 2011 Haiti raised less tax than the per capita rate of Sub-Saharan Africa.[82] All the 'aid' has gone to benefit corporations, and with wages precipitously low, precious little goes in taxes to Haiti's national treasury at a time when Haitian-run infrastructure and social welfare are desperately needed.

A Living Wage

The final 'well-meaning' argument from those in favour of sweatshops is that wage increases would cause manufacturers to flee from developing countries. The logic here is that a wage increase would cause clothing prices to rise, which would alienate customers, forcing corporations to take flight. Initiatives like the Asia Floor Wage Alliance seek regional wage rises to circumnavigate the threat of factory closures. Rolling out the recommendations of the Asia Floor Wage Alliance on a global scale would ease the poverty faced by garment workers.

Yet the argument that corporations might take flight obscures one vital fact – that the wages of garment workers could be *doubled* without there being a noticeable impact on the price of clothing. The wages of garment workers account for 1–3 per cent of the cost of clothing – 1.8 per cent in a 2002 study by the economist Robert Pollin.[83] According to some experts: 'for a typical sportswear garment, doubling labour costs (by doubling wages) would result in retail price increases of roughly 1–3 per cent; tripling wages would result in price increases of 2–6 per cent.'[84]

A flesh-tone dress, worn by Catherine Middleton to the White House, was discovered to have been made in a Romanian sweatshop by women workers paid just £168 a month (99p an hour).[85] The dress, from the serial sweatshop offender Reiss, retailed at £175. Had wages been doubled, the dress would have cost just £178.15 – an inconsequential price rise for a customer.

It is worth noting here that the vast majority of consumers do not buy things based on price alone.[86] Rather than just buying the cheapest possible clothes, consumers pay a premium for other considerations, the prime example being the Nike tick on a shoe. Other examples are the Louis Vuitton stamp on a bag, the words Ralph Lauren or Manchester United on a shirt, soft cashmere or leather, certain colours, guarantees of longevity, favourite brands, clothes that act as badges of identity, or whatever is currently in fashion. It is not the case that sweatshops are driven by a demand for the cheapest possible clothes.

If the price of clothes is not the fault of consumers, and if doubling wages would have such a meagre impact on the price of clothes, why don't corporations 'just do it' and alleviate the suffering of millions? Suffering is not, and will never be, alleviated under capitalism because the top link in the chain, Nike, Tesco or, in this case, Reiss, has a vested interest in keeping wages as low as possible. Doubling the wages of Romanian garment workers to £1.98 an hour would after all detract from the £125 million fortune accumulated by CEO David Reiss.[87] Under capitalism corporations must compete with each other to maximise profits, and satisfy shareholders and investors. Costs are therefore compressed as far as possible.

Corporations under capitalism flat-out refuse to alleviate poverty for billions of people. The transformation of society is tantalisingly close – the difference of £3.15 more for a Reiss dress. But under capitalism this will never happen. Even when small wage increases are won they are under constant threat because history is not a linear march towards social progress. In the 1930s, Frances Perkins, US Secretary for Labor, warned: 'The red silk bargain dress in the shop window is a danger signal. It is a warning of the return of the sweatshop, a challenge to us all to reinforce the gains we have made.'[88] Every morsel of progress has had to be fought for against those who seek to keep exploiting people. In *Reform or Revolution* Rosa Luxemburg gives the example of the struggle for reforms being like the myth of Sisyphus, who was condemned to keep rolling a boulder up a steep hill only to have it come crashing back down once his back is turned.

Working for reform of the industry remains vital; every struggle for a wage rise or better conditions must be supported internationally. Those seeking change should support trade unions, pickets, boycotts, solidarity movements and strikes on a global scale. Yet this should never distract from the fact that the issue of labour rights in the fashion supply chain is insoluble without a fundamental change in the structure of society. Real, lasting change in the fashion labour system will not happen without an international struggle that creates a world based on the principles of equality, justice and people and planet, rather than capitalism's competition and profit.

CHAPTER FIVE

A Bitter Harvest

*Have we fallen into a mesmerized state that makes us accept as
inevitable that which is inferior or detrimental, as though having
lost the will or the vision to demand that which is good?*

Rachel Carson, *Silent Spring*

Picture a desert, a diseased salt-rock desert plagued by winds that
blow carcinogenic dust into villages causing throat cancers and
tuberculosis, a pesticide-infused desert that acts as a graveyard for
abandoned boats. The fishermen have gone, their children suffering
from malnutrition and high infant mortality rates. The summers are
hotter and the winters colder. Teaming schools of fish have been
replaced by camels grazing on scrubland and a few cows seeking
shelter in the shade of a rusting hull. This desert was once the Aral
Sea, the world's fourth largest lake, home to 24 species of fish and
thriving fishing communities and surrounded by lush wetlands
teaming with wildlife and rare forests. This has all gone. Now there is
just 15 per cent of the sea left, an inhospitable stretch of water whose
saline levels have risen by 600 per cent. 25,000 miles of sea bed lie
exposed – the equivalent of six million football pitches.[1]

Two thousand miles to the east, picture a multitude of waste pipes
pumping 2.5 billion tonnes of toxic waste water a year into the rivers
and lakes of just one country.[2] Picture 300 million people without
access to clean drinking water because 70 per cent of their rivers,
lakes and reservoirs are polluted.[3] Imagine 75 per cent of all disease
and 100,000 deaths a year resulting from polluted water. Picture
China's 'cancer villages' and the 12 million tonnes of grain polluted
by heavy metals each year. Imagine the dead fish, the dead birds, the
colourful sludge clogging the rivers as women struggle to find the
least dirty bit of water to cook and clean with. All this taking place in
the shadow of giant factories whose owners wilfully commit violation
after violation without fear of censure.[4]

Next, picture a hot, dusty farm in the outback of Australia, the
sun beating down on a series of large concrete tanks filled with a
writhing mass of crocodiles. The tanks stretch on and on, housing
70,000 factory-farmed reptiles,[5] which will get a bullet in the head
once they have grown enough scales to satisfy European handbag
manufacturers. Picture crocodiles that have lived in the wild for over

200 million years now in overcrowded tanks. Picture their wounds from fighting and their deformities from being unable to walk or swim. Picture filthy, overcrowded water with a distorted bacterial balance that leads to infected wounds.[6] In the wild, crocodiles can live to be 70 years old; on factory farms, they are shot at the age of three.

Finally, imagine a chemical so toxic that just one teaspoon can kill an adult human if it touches their skin. Picture gallons of this chemical being sprayed onto the cotton fields of the United States. Picture the chemical run-off from these fields draining into food sources and poisoning 2,000 people. Picture leaks at production plants in the United States that hospitalise hundreds of people living nearby. Then picture the scene when 40 tonnes of this chemical exploded into the atmosphere of Bhopal, India, cloaking the city in poison and killing at least 15,000 people:

> The poison cloud was so dense and searing that people were reduced to near blindness. As they gasped for breath its effects grew ever more suffocating. The gases burned the tissues of their eyes and lungs and attacked their nervous systems. People lost control of their bodies. Urine and faeces ran down their legs. Women lost their unborn children as they ran, their wombs spontaneously opening in bloody abortion.[7]

* * *

There is nothing 'natural' about a single one of these environmental catastrophes. They are all the result of the workings of the fashion industry under capitalism. Earth, air, animals, water and human health, all are subject to fashion's bitter harvest.[8] The draining of the Aral Sea is due to its waters having been appropriated to irrigate Uzbekistan's 1.47 million hectares of cotton. This practice began under Soviet rule and has continued under the current dictatorship. Cotton is hugely water-intensive: a single cotton bud uses 3.4 litres of water, and a single cotton t-shirt consumes 2,000 litres. Uzbekistan is now the world's fourth largest exporter of cotton, with most of its 800,000 tonnes being exported annually to Europe. Every Autumn, schools are closed and students and teachers forced to harvest cotton. Head teachers are given cotton-picking quotas and students face punishment and even expulsion for non-compliance.[9]

Whilst Uzbek cotton farmers are paid only a third of the value of their cotton, the crop provides Uzbekistan's brutal dictator, Islam Karimov, with the vast majority of his export earnings.[10] There are no civil liberties in Uzbekistan and Karimov has carried out brutal mass killings of journalists and protesters, including 800 people in Andijan in 2005. His daughter Gulnara is a self-styled socialite who was described in a US diplomatic cable leaked to Wikileaks as 'the single most hated person in the country'.[11] In 2011 she attempted to stage a fashion show at New York Fashion Week. Having been barred due to protests by human rights campaigners, she moved her show to Cipriani's, a private venue. Britain and the United States continue to have a close and uncritical relationship with Karimov.

China produced $197 billion worth of garments in the first three months of 2012.[12] The Chinese textile industry ranks as the third worst water polluter out of the country's 39 industries.[13] Water scarcity catches people between the pincers of drought on the one hand and pollution on the other. Much of the pollution is due to the hugely inefficient textile industry, which uses more water than almost any other industry and pollutes all the water it uses. Eighty per cent is used in dyeing and finishing, 12 per cent in fibre processing and 8 per cent in other areas of the supply chain.[14] The Institute of Public and Environmental Affairs (IPE) is a registered non-profit organisation based in Beijing. It studies the impact of corporate polluters on China's water and air. Its report *Cleaning up the Fashion Industry* exposed large international brands as contracting to factories committing serious environmental violations. The Panyu Kamking Bleaching and Dyeing Company, rated 'red' due to its environmental violations, supplies Gap, Diesel, YSL, Levi's and DKNY, amongst many other brands.

Nike, Reebok, Tommy Hilfiger and Abercrombie & Fitch are clients of Fountain Set (Holdings) Ltd, a major company that installed secret waste-water pipes to discharge untreated dark red waste-water into rivers with chroma levels 19.5 times higher than the acceptable standard.[15] Having been exposed as discharging 20,000 tonnes of toxic water and fabricating water usage data, the company simply moved to a different province of China where there is even more serious water scarcity.[16]

The IPE followed up its research by writing to 48 brands, confronting them with 'suspicions of pollution in their supply chains'. At factories used by Zara, major pollution violations had taken place, and at one suspected Zara supplier, workers died as a result of cleaning out waste-water treatment pools. The response from Zara? 'We regret that we cannot respond to individual requests for information from schools, universities and professionals regarding our work.'[17]

Crocodiles are kept in squalid captivity and then shot or bludgeoned to death to meet demand from fashion houses like Hermès. The economic crisis has made the poor poorer but the rich richer. Consequently, Hermès announced in 2009 that it would be entering into exclusive partnerships with crocodile farms in Australia to meet demand for its inordinately expensive leather bags.

A crocodile typically has a brain the size of a finger encased in bone 2 cm thick. It is impossible to stun them for a humane killing. In Australia farmed crocodiles are supposed to be shot through the head, but killing methods in the United States include severing the spinal cord with a chisel, which can take five to eight blows with a mallet and merely paralyses the animal. Other methods include beheading crocodiles with machetes and trying to smash their skulls with baseball bats or mallets. Speaking on the cruel methods he has witnessed as a farm inspector, reptile biologist Dr Clifford Warwick stated: 'Few people would realise that an alligator or crocodile with his head cut off will be alive for an hour before it loses consciousness.'[18]

The longer a crocodile is kept alive, the less money the farm makes, so as soon as it has grown the required centimetre belly width it is killed.[19] Once a crocodile has been killed, its belly, throat and leg skin is removed and blasted with water jets to remove excess flesh. The skin is then dipped in chemicals, drained, salted and shipped in chilled freezers to tanneries in South East Asia. Hermès uses a tannery in Vietnam to stretch, oil, polish and dye its skins.[20] The 'luxury' company uses between three and four crocodiles to make one handbag. These bags can have $200,000 price tags and waiting lists are years long. This difference between the actual cost of a factory-farmed but so-called 'luxury' material, and the marked-up price of the handbag allowed Hermès to post record net profits of £495 million in 2011.[21]

Aldicarb (known commercially as Temik) is one of the most toxic pesticides ever registered in the United States.[22] It was banned in the European Union in 2003. Aldicarb is made of methyl isocyanate (MIC) mixed with aldicarb oxime and methylene chloride. Until 1987, Union Carbide (now Dow Chemicals) was the sole manufacturer of aldicarb.

The company built a huge plant in Bhopal, believing India represented an enormous untapped market. But Union Carbide underestimated the poverty of Indian farmers who were too poor to buy their pesticides. The Bhopal plant ceased production in the early 1980s and, still containing vast quantities of poisonous chemicals, was left to rot. Falling into disrepair, safety systems that should have prevented a leak were left unmaintained. Thus in December 1984 an explosion released 40 tonnes of methyl isocyanate into the atmosphere of Bhopal. Between 3,800 and 15,000 people died instantly, up to 200,000 people have since experienced increased morbidity or mortality – premature death, or partial or total disability.[23] There has been no justice for Bhopal from Union Carbide or Dow Chemicals.[24] In the 28 years since the disaster, survivors have been plagued with an epidemic of cancers, menstrual disorders and what one doctor described as 'monstrous births.'[25]

The pesticide industry is a product of the Second World War, when insects were used to test chemicals as agents of death for people.[26] It should come as no surprise then that such brutal carnage followed the explosion. Linking the horror of aldicarb and Bhopal to fashion is its primary use as a pesticide for cotton (along with beans and peanuts). In the United States, cotton has in the past accounted for 83 per cent of aldicarb use.[27] In 1984, when only an American company was producing aldicarb, the United States was the world's second largest cotton producer[28] – a deadly harvest to be turned into disposable clothes and goods.

Just one year after the Bhopal disaster, aldicarb caused the United States' largest case of food poisoning. Two thousand people in

California fell ill after eating toxic watermelons, with one source of poisoning thought to have been run-off from cotton fields.[29] Six deaths and two stillbirths were reported in sufferers, though coroners' reports did not record the pesticide as the cause of death.[30] That same summer, 135 people were hospitalised when a Union Carbide plant in Western Virginia leaked a mixture of aldicarb oxime and methylene chloride.[31] Attempting to shed some of its more controversial assets, Union Carbide sold the West Virginia Plant to Rhône-Poulenc, which sold it to its present owner, Bayer CropScience, in 2002.

In 2008, about 75,000 pounds of aldicarb were applied to California crops – almost entirely cotton.[32] That year tragedy struck again when an explosion at Bayer CropScience killed two workers at the plant and narrowly avoided causing a disaster that congressional investigators stated 'could have eclipsed the 1984 disaster in India'.[33] A tank just 80 feet from the explosion contained more than 13,000 pounds of MIC – the same chemical that exploded over Bhopal 24 years before.

In 2011, after concerted campaigning by local residents, Bayer CropScience was banned from restarting production of aldicarb at its West Virginia plant. Undeterred, the company laid off 163 workers and moved production of the deadly chemical to China. Under an agreement with the Environmental Protection Agency, Bayer CropScience – still the United States' sole manufacturer – is set to end worldwide production of aldicarb by 2015 and to end distribution by 2017. Commenting on the ban, Pesticide Action Network North America stated: 'It never should have been registered in the first place back in 1970, and by the mid-1980s there was sufficient data to suggest it should have been taken off the market. The system is designed to leave things like this on the market as long as possible.'[34]

Environmental Crisis

Drastic change is urgently needed. As communities dependent on the Mao Zhou river in China understand, nothing comes for free, there will always be someone or something that pays. There are only so many rivers, so much clean air, so much topsoil. So why does the fashion industry persist in inflicting such serious environmental devastation on the planet? The short answer is: because it has to.

Corporations need to maximise profits. To do this they must acquire the component parts of their products as cheaply as possible. Other than under slavery, labour has to be paid for, whereas nature is seemingly available for free. Dilys Williams, director of the Center for Sustainable Fashion, describes the current system as 'based on the fact that resources have been very cheap to get hold of, oil has been very cheap and there have been limitless supplies of water etc., so it's been an easy economic model'. Whilst it has been 'easy' and 'prolific', Williams points out that this economic model is 'very short term-ist. Not just from a resources perspective but also from a human fulfilment perspective.'[35]

The environmental crisis is not the result of bad corporations or bad executives but of a bad system. Capitalism's mantra is, in Marx's words: 'accumulate or die'.[36] Fountain Set Holding Ltd spews out toxic waste because it is bound by the logic of competition, of finding the cheapest way to produce a higher rate of profit than its competitors.[37] This is why costs are cut, safety measures ignored and pollutants discharged into rivers. We are not faced merely with the challenge of persuading those at the top of society to change their ways. We are faced with crunch time.

As resources shrink, flashpoints grow. There are increasing numbers of ecological issues around the world, crises in weather conditions and crop failures. If the fashion industry, or capitalism in general, was forced to internalise all of the social and environmental costs for water, air, soil and animals it generates, it would go out of business.[38] Capitalism should therefore be regarded as an economy of unpaid costs.[39] Humanity's ecological debt to nature is now huge, and if nothing changes, this may ultimately be repaid at a terrifying price.

Whilst the fashion industry functions according to the unavoidable imperatives of capitalism, it does seem to be particularly predisposed to high levels of pollution and waste, with the Chinese textile industry ranked as the third worst water polluter out of the country's 39 industries. In 1977, 31 million tonnes of textiles were produced worldwide; by 2007 this had risen to 80 million tonnes; the vast majority of this going into the fashion industry.[40] Turning this amount of textiles into clothing requires 1,074 billion kilowatt hours of electricity, 132 million tonnes of coal and up to 9 trillion litres of water. Having added up these resources plus all the pesticides, acid dyes, animal products, labels, strings, zippers and metal buttons, Lucy Siegle, author of *To Die For*, concluded that fashion's footprint resembles a scorched earth strategy.[41]

What is it about fashion in particular that makes it so wasteful? In Chapter 3 we discussed the important link between use-value, symbolic value and rampant consumerism. Fashion is a deregulated, subcontracted, trend-based industry that relies on selling billions of short-life units every season at a maximum profit. Brands sell clothes not of the highest quality, ensuring that they can make them cheaply, that they will wear out and that you will be forced to buy new ones.

The throw-away culture of the fashion industry is hugely encouraged by the domination of exchange value over use-value.[42] Capital's sole aim is to expand by selling goods and accumulating surplus wealth.[43] It does not matter whether an item fulfils a need or will last a long time. All that matters is how much it can be sold for. This spells disaster for the environment and led Marx to describe capital as having a vampiric relationship with nature, 'a living death maintained by sucking the blood from the world'.[44] Fashion is not just based on exchange value, it is an active champion of forgetting about use-value altogether.

Flight from Nature

The concept of alienation is particularly pertinent for understanding fashion's impact on nature. People are far removed from the production of the clothes that they wear. The average high street shopper will never experience 20 years of picking cotton in sweltering heat or work in a polyester factory in Zhejiang. This gives the impression that clothes exist independently both of people and of nature. The fashion industry is adept at hiding the human labour behind its wealth and power; it is even better at hiding the materials that go into producing our clothes.

Take the use of living creatures in fashion production. As well as crocodile – mink, dog, fox and snake all sell for exorbitant prices. Whilst still alive, a python has a hose pipe inserted into its mouth. The water makes the snake swell and stretches its skin. Once swollen, the snake is impaled on a meat hook and skinned alive.[45] Foxes, minks and dogs are mass-farmed across the world, mostly in China but also in places like Finland and the United States. Fur production has been banned in the United Kingdom due to its cruelty, whereas China has no animal rights legislation at all (except that which covers endangered species).

Eighty-five per cent of fur is factory-farmed, a trade whose despicable cruelty is well documented. Animals are crammed into tiny, filthy cages and when it is their turn to die they are often electrocuted, hung or bled to death – any method that protects their fur and increases factory profits. The idea that fur is ethical or sustainable is a lie. The production of a farmed fur coat uses 20 times the amount of energy used to make a *faux* fur coat. Fur dressing, the application of chemicals to stop fur and skin from rotting in your wardrobe, is rated as one of the world's five worst industries for toxic metal pollution.[46] Fur is a prime example of profit taking precedence over well-being. Its current resurgence is largely the result of fur manufacturers plying impoverished student and graduate designers with fur for use as a free material.[47] The ability to degrade nature and commodify animals, all the while labelling it 'luxury', is an example of capitalism's sleight of hand, used to generate huge profits for corporations.

Under capitalism we relate more to commodities than we do to nature itself. We no longer see ourselves as a *part* of nature; rather, nature is something to be gloriously conquered for profit.[48] Everything becomes property: land becomes real estate, animals become fur, the Lake District becomes a nuclear waste dump and oceans become sources of fish. Everything must have a profit squeezed out of it.[49]

Rather than exist in harmony with each other and with the planet, humans are taught to measure themselves by their distance from the rest of the population and from nature itself.[50] Bertell Ollman described alienation as the 'splintering of human nature into a number of misbegotten parts'.[51] Ecologists now argue that losing sight of the fact that humans are part of nature means all exploitation becomes easier. Vociferously exploiting nature is one and the same as exploiting people. Environmental degradation is the degradation of human relationships.[52]

The exploitation of the planet is produced by the same imperatives that result in the exploitation of people in sweatshops. They both result from alienation from nature. If we were not alienated, we would not even be able to *conceive* of abusing the planet. Losing sight of the fact that humans and the planet are utterly intertwined is the starting point for our destruction.

Marx is sometimes accused of Prometheanism, of being in favour of industrialisation at any cost. In fact, he believed deeply in the oneness of humanity and nature, saying that it was their separation, not their unity, that required explanation.[53] The flight from nature encourages the idea of the duality of humans and nature (including animals) rather than their oneness. It is no coincidence that the things we are taught to aspire to are ruling-class symbols of cruelty and power over nature – furs and skins. What is a skin handbag other than a sign that you are rich and powerful enough to command and destroy nature? That you can have living things die for your decoration and pleasure?

Buy Less, Spend More?

We live in an era of unprecedented consumption. The United Kingdom deposits 1.4 million tonnes of textiles in landfill every year.[54] Are consumers to blame for the state of the fashion industry? Is it primarily people's shopping habits that must change for fashion to be sustainable? According to the green fashion book *Eco Chic*, 'the issue is clear: buying fewer, but longer-lasting items is the way forward.' It concludes: 'Buying fewer, but better-made clothes may be more expensive but will serve you better in the long term.' A similar line is taken in *Green is the New Black*: 'It could be argued that haute couture is the most ethical fashion of all.'[55] It recommends that shoppers become 'ethical' by having bespoke suits made and joining the waiting list for a Balenciaga bag because they will still want it next month.

The logic of 'buy less, spend more' easily unravels. Not only is it true that planning ahead is a measure of class,[56] but spending thousands of pounds on *haute couture*, whilst people go hungry does not fit within most people's definition of ethical. *Haute couture* is currently affordable for a just few thousand people in the world. It stems from a deeply unequal social environment, which could be rectified only by the large-scale redistribution of wealth. Nor does a large price tag guarantee clothes are ethically made. Designer labels are often made in Chinese factories in the same polluting conditions as cheaper products. To reiterate Dana Thomas: 'Yes, luxury handbags are made in China. Top brands.'[57]

It is also worth remembering what happened when the economic crisis caused millions of people inadvertently to buy fewer clothes as they ran out of disposable income. The result, as imports to the United States dropped by 15.7 per cent, was that ten million Chinese workers lost their jobs, along with 1 million Indian workers and approximately 20 per cent of the Cambodian apparel workforce (75,000 out of 352,000).[58] This is the reality of a sudden drop in consumption – it is catastrophic for local workforces. Factory jobs are so desperately needed due to neoliberalism's decimation of traditional local industries like farming and fishing. What is needed is an overhaul of the entire system to stop big businesses and the IMF destroying the ability of communities to survive.

The premise of 'buy less, spend more' is that people who buy expensive clothes buy fewer than other people. In fact, the wardrobes and carbon footprints of those who can afford *haute couture* vastly exceed those of everyone else. The world's population currently stands at approximately 7 billion. Just 8 per cent of the population (500 million people) emit 50 per cent of the greenhouse gases.[59] In Canada, the top 10 per cent of the population has an ecological footprint nine times that of the bottom 10 per cent.[60] The super-rich of the United States have an ecological footprint up to 1,000 times that of those at the bottom of society: more a 'death-style' than a lifestyle.[61] The poor might be easier to harangue but it was not a teenage Primark customer that reportedly owns 4,000 pairs of shoes (Anna dello Russo) or who allegedly owns £1 million worth of Birkin bags (Victoria Beckham).

In the midst of an economic crisis, and with many people living from pay cheque to pay cheque, there needs to be a more realistic analysis of the highly pressurised role that fashion plays in people's lives. With debt and fashion so closely tied, it seems unethical to recommend people get deeper into debt by buying expensive clothes. 'The consumer is no freer than the producer,' wrote Marx. 'His judgement depends on his means and his needs . . . Both of these are determined by his social position, which itself depends on the whole social organisation. World trade turns almost entirely round the needs, not of individual consumption, but of production.'[62]

Fashion environmentalists are often accused of being elitist and of using fast-fashion to blame the poorest members of society for climate change. Should fast-fashion be left alone because it makes working-class life better in the same manner as cheap flights? The short answer is no. Fast-fashion is a false emancipation that is disastrous for the global working class. It is the working class that are held captive in sweatshops, have their unions smashed by Walmart and their homes flooded or turned to dust by climate change. It is the working class that end up wearing poor-quality clothes that easily wear out and are quickly scorned as unfashionable. It's the working classes that are forced by low wages and the homogenisation of high streets into shopping or working at cheap shops like Primark.

It is also the working class that are driven to anxiety and a sense of inadequacy for not being able to keep up with fashion. The feminist academic Sandra Lee Bartky has written of the double shame borne by impoverished women: the socially created and imposed 'shame of poverty', as well as shame from the inability to keep up with appearance requirements. These are not merely psychological burdens, since the ability to conform to accepted standards of dress and appearance are critical for social mobility.[63]

The ability to buy something should not be confused with freedom.[64] This cheapens freedom by narrowing it to the right to choose between different styles in the shops. Imagining that the right to buy limitless clothes at whatever cost to the planet equals freedom is to lose sight of what freedom actually means. Fast-fashion is not pro-working class; it must be critiqued as a product of corporations' drive for profit, not as the fault of the poor.

This is not to say that we can continue as we are. Environmentalists cannot make it much clearer: 'All that human societies have to do to destroy the planet's climate and biota and leave a ruined world to future generations is to keep doing exactly what is being done today.'[65] Arguing that fast-fashion is not the fault of the working class should not be taken for an assurance that life can carry on as normal. If things continue as they are, the working class will just sink together beneath rising sea levels.

To stop environmental devastation, everybody's consumption habits will have to change. Some people, like the very poor, need to consume more. Many others need to consume far less or differently. This is not to be feared. The idea that something will be lost through environmental protection is an inversion of what is real.[66] The term 'inversion of what is real' was coined in response to environmentalists who are ironically concerned more in preserving capitalism than in saving the planet and humanity.[67]

It is no coincidence that for many people it is easier to imagine the end of the world than the end of the fashion industry or of capitalism.[68] Those benefiting from the capitalist system work hard to maintain the idea that capitalism is a natural state of affairs without alternatives. Because an alternative seems unthinkable, capitalism can sometimes seem more real than the planet we live on. Yet maintaining the fashion industry or capitalism is meaningless when compared with maintaining the planet. Only the loss of one would signal the end of humanity. We need to end capitalism; being afraid to say this is to advocate environmental destruction.

Corporate Change?

Corporate Social Responsibility (CSR) has been described as CEOs taking credit for what they should be doing anyway.[69] As illustrated in Chapter 4, terrible working conditions for millions of people create giant profits for multinational fashion corporations. There is currently a concerted effort by corporations to shift attention away from sweatshops and onto 'green issues' – an area where, unlike sweatshops, they can at least pretend to be making progress.

One CSR initiative came from Gucci when, in 2009, the company pledged to go green and eliminate paper made from Indonesian rainforests and from controversial suppliers such as Asia Pulp and Paper. Its press release declared:

> Shoes will be packed in one flannel instead of two. Gift boxes will only be given out when requested. Gucci is going to replace all of its mannequins with a new eco-friendly version, designed by Frida Giannini, made with shockproof polystyrene – a long-lasting and 100 per cent recyclable raw material – fully made in Italy and finished with water-based paints.

Other energy-saving promises included the reduction of approximately 10,000 tonnes of carbon dioxide emissions and 4 million litres of gas oil consumption.[70]

But for whose benefits are such energy- and cost-saving exercises carried out? The environmental scholar Wes Jackson has pointed out that 'When the Walmarts of the world say they're going to put in different light bulbs and get their trucks to get by on half the fuel, what are they going to do with that saving? They're going to open up another box store somewhere. It's just nuts.'[71] Being primarily a leather goods company, Gucci products have a high environmental impact. Cattle farming is highly carbon-intensive and creates a great deal of methane. Methane is a key contributor to climate change and is 25 times more potent per kg than CO_2. Processing and dyeing leather also uses highly toxic compounds.[72]

H&M has been widely criticised by Greenpeace for using Chinese factories that discharge untreated chemicals into rivers, and for selling clothes, including children's clothes, impregnated with chemicals such as the known hormone disruptors nonylphenol ethoxylates (NPEs). NPEs break down into the toxic nonylphenol (NP) which is hazardous even at a very low concentration.[73]

Having earned a reputation as a major polluter and having had its shops stickered by activists, H&M launched its green drive, which includes pledging to tackle the use of dangerous chemicals, launching a range of 'sustainable red carpet dresses' and ensuring that 'all cash desk receipt rolls are made of FSC [Forest Stewardship

Council] certified paper'.[74] H&M's 2013 Conscious collection came with the inevitable and unimaginative 'jungle and birds' print, as if sticking a picture of a toucan on a t-shirt will give people climate-amnesia, or as if churning out millions of bags dyed green makes a company environmentally green.

Such environmental pledges cannot contend with what has been called the fashionably dressed elephant in the room: ethical fashion is an oxymoron.[75] How can an industry claim to be ethical when it churns out billions of items of clothing, sending new stock to shops up to 50 times a year? Environmental initiatives are the result of genuine and widespread public concern over climate change and environmental degradation. Yet much of the 'greenwashing' that takes place is just that – a crude attempt to take advantage of these concerns. The risk of being hoodwinked by sympathetic corporate greenwash is greater today than ever.[76]

Techno-change?

Science and technology are often proffered as the cure for climate change. Albert Einstein, however, pointed out that science 'cannot create ends and, even less, instil them in human beings; science, at most, can supply the means by which to attain certain ends.'[77] Only if you control technology can you determine how it is used – for the good of humanity or for profit. Why, for example, are some scientists mapping crocodile DNA to produce more belly scales rather than working on a cure for HIV/AIDS? Why is technology being applied to the efficient production of even more aldicarb rather than the long overdue clean-up operation in Bhopal?

This misuse occurs because technology is not neutral; rather it reflects the power structures of capitalism.[78] For the Marxist scholar István Mészáros, believing that science and technology will solve all our problems in the long run is far worse than believing in witchcraft because it ignores the question of who has control of science and technology. The key question is not which technologies might help solve the planet's problems, but how to change the direction of technology away from its current narrow focus on profit maximisation.[79]

Technological innovations such as recycling are vital, but they can become an excuse for governments and corporations not to change. Sceptical of the idea of a circular fashion economy, Dilys Williams is uncertain that it would ever be possible to close the energy loop and recycle old clothes to make something new without using up new resources (even if using renewable energy). Her concern is that recycling can perpetuate a model of throw-away culture: 'Being sold the idea that whatever we do is OK because we can just recycle products when we are done is actually quite dangerous.'[80] Our ability to recycle some clothes should not become an excuse for inactivity or for corporations to keep producing at the same unsupportable rate.

Every so often, science produces a 'miracle' fabric that is launched amid claims that it is the answer to the fashion industry's sustainability and green issues. In 2003 a product known as Ingeo™ fiber was launched by Cargill Dow. Cargill Dow was a 50:50 joint venture formed in 1997 by the Dow Chemical Company (responsible for the Bhopal disaster) and Cargill, Inc. Its purpose was to create new markets for the products of its parent companies.[81] Cargill is the world's biggest corn merchant, so it should come as no surprise that Ingeo™ fiber is made from corn. In 2005 Cargill bought out Dow Chemicals from Cargill Dow and renamed the company NatureWorks LLC.

The two big green claims for Ingeo were that PLA (polylactic acid) is made from the sugar in corn rather than from oil and that it is biodegradable. Both of these claims were quickly discredited. To launch their product, Cargill Dow worked with the outdoor clothing company Patagonia. The project imploded when Patagonia learned that Cargill Dow was using genetically modified (GM) corn to produce Ingeo. Patagonia has campaigned widely against GM crops, which have the potential to be the greatest environmental disaster in history.[82] It has been alleged that Cargill hopes to create such expansive markets for non-food 'green' GM products that GM crops become a *fait accompli* – an underhand tactic that fashion environmentalists must remain aware of. Patagonia publicly dropped Ingeo saying: 'It seemed almost too good to be true. Unfortunately, it was.'[83]

Whilst its production creates less pollution than plastics, the claim that PLA is biodegradable is also misleading. PLA will not compost in a compost bin; what it needs is a specialised industrial facility at a controlled temperature, of the sort few people have access to. Large amounts of PLA can interfere with composting as it reverts to lactic acid. In landfill, PLA will last as long as a plastic PET bottle – up to 1,000 years. Corn also uses more nitrogen fertiliser, more herbicides and more insecticides than any other crop grown in the United States. These practices contribute to soil erosion and water pollution as nitrogen runs off the fields into streams and rivers.[84] Lastly, is it ethical to turn food into clothing and packaging when malnutrition causes a third of all child deaths?

The production of fashion fabrics by industrial chemical companies is nothing new. After the Second World War a number of companies, including DuPont, Imperial Chemicals Industries (ICI), Courtaulds and Dow Chemicals, began producing fabrics like nylon, rayon and polyester. *Eco Chic* describes how 'Advertising in magazines like *Vogue* was a rebranding exercise – from makers of arms and ammunitions to easy-care blouses and dresses.'[85] Rebranding is still taking place today. Dow Chemicals is responsible for Bhopal, the largest industrial disaster in human history which it is refusing to clean up. Cargill is a major buyer of Uzbek cotton and is charged with using child slaves on its African cocoa plantations. Both companies are accused of so many dreadful human and environmental violations that I do not have the space to list them all. They are not environmentally friendly in any sense of the word.

Being 'green' can also mean being naïve.[86] We must not let corporations dupe us into thinking they have our best interests at heart.

* * *

Einstein's definition of insanity is: *doing the same thing over and over again and expecting different results*. The fashion industry is taking a devastating toll on our world. It inflicts serious harm on people and the biosphere. For every kilogram of textiles that is produced, an average of 10 kg of chemicals are used.[87] In 2002, even when still restrained by the Multi Fibre Arrangement (MFA), China produced over 20 billion pieces of clothing – about four for every person in the world.[88] This is the scale of the problem we face. Yet proffered solutions currently include getting people to buy fewer clothes, recycling, trusting corporations to do the right thing and the invention of wonder fabrics – all solutions that appear more concerned with keeping capitalism intact than with saving the planet. After 20 years of these 'solutions' how can it not be insanity to think that capitalism – the cause of the disasters we face – is the key to saving the planet?

Those wanting the overthrow of capitalism are often accused of being dreamers. Yet, there is no greater illusion than that of utopian reformism which believes you can fundamentally change a system without touching its power relations.[89] The scale of change needed to halt our current trajectory towards disaster is not going to be possible under the current system of competition and profit. What we need is a system fundamentally built on respect for the planet and each other, so that the biosphere, including people and animals, turns from a plundered resource into a revered community.

CHAPTER SIX

Fashion and Size

Unreachable beauty is a reminder to make an effort.
Karl Lagerfeld, creative director, Chanel

There were six of us in a two-bedroom apartment and a few of the girls were starving themselves. One of them ended up in hospital because her stomach was eating itself. They would feed themselves on nuts and a lot of the time spit out the nut after chewing it.
Dunja Knezevic, president of the Models' Union

Fashion is an innately visual industry that sells itself as a creator of choice, change and creativity. Yet fashion is a world devoid of variety, where anyone who does not fit within its slim visual confines is rendered all but invisible. The most indicative instance of this is the industry's approach to the size and shape of the female body. As catwalk imagery has proliferated and the fashion model has become an accepted beauty role-model, fashion's influence has spread far beyond just governing what people should wear.

This chapter echoes the fashion industry by primarily focusing on *women*'s bodies. Male body dissatisfaction is certainly increasing, and male cosmetics, eating disorders and overly thin male models have become more common. Pressure on men to conform to a certain image is, however, incomparable with the pressure borne by women.

Some women baulk at the idea of fashion being able to affect their self-image, seeing it as an insult to their intelligence.[1] Some women experience shame and guilt at not meeting size and beauty standards, then shame and guilt when they try, because they 'should know better'.[2] This cycle of shame and guilt, and not wanting to admit to feeling inadequate, obscures the normalisation of compulsory thinness. To begin to break away from this, we must confront the reality of life under capitalism.

It is, therefore, no insult to say that a $1.5 trillion industry, whose images blanket the planet, has an effect. Nor is it insulting to discuss the overwhelming evidence that fashion has a destructive impact on women employed by the industry as models.

Bodies

The history of human beings is one of body alteration and marking. Bodies have always been used to express the sexual, religious and cultural practices, and the geography, of specific periods.[3] Yet never have attempts at alteration been so widespread, nor the 'ideal' so out of reach. The social desirability of an impossible version of beauty serves to torment all those who cannot attain it and as a constant source of pressure for those who supposedly do. This results in normalising body dissatisfaction, which carries serious consequences. Young women do not perform actively at school when they are not feeling confident about their appearance.[4] Eating disorders such as bulimia and anorexia nervosa are thought to be on the rise, affecting 1–2 per cent of Britain's population.[5] At the same time obesity – believed to be caused partly by body dissatisfaction and dieting – is rising sharply.

Homogenised beauty is linked to an international rise in body dissatisfaction. In her book *Bodies*, psychologist Susie Orbach outlines how desire for an idealised, slim, Westernised body has spread with globalisation. Eating disorders followed the introduction of television to Fiji, Chinese women undergo leg-breaking surgery to make them taller, and some of Tehran's 3,000 plastic surgeons carry out five rhinoplasties ('nose jobs') a day. Size is intimately linked with race – a Western ideal is promoted at the expense of 'indigenous bodies'. For Orbach this is a new frontier of colonialism,[6] with brand iconography replacing religious iconography to determine aesthetic norms.[7]

Digital Beauty

We live in a world soaked in visuals. People see between 2,000 and 5,000 images of bodies every week.[8] These images display something unobtainable while simultaneously assuring us of a beauty democracy. Their message is that everyone can and should work towards looking 'great'. Beauty missionaries push the myth that our bodies are in constant need of attention and taming. Life is turned into one long round of 'improvements': plucking, waxing, dyeing, dieting, exfoliating, filing, painting and squeezing yourself into a particular shape in the vain attempt to resemble an advertisement. The 'advert look' focuses on two key criteria – thinness and symmetry of features.

The fashion industry collapses the space between aspiration and fantasy.[9] Its rhetoric of 'choice' and 'empowerment', coupled with our ability to consume clothes, means that people are given the impression that they can become what they see. But this beauty democracy does not exist. It is a mirage hiding insurmountable obstacles – obstacles hidden by their very obviousness.

Models employed by the fashion industry have a body type shared by just 5 per cent of women in the United States.[10] If you are not born with it then there is nothing that you can do to achieve it. Many women exist without the time or resources to attain a healthy lifestyle, including a nutritious diet, let alone attain a top model lifestyle.[11] One stylist said of models' hair: 'a lot of people don't realise, in editorial, how much is fake'.[12] Plus the images we see are not just of augmented supermodels, but of digitally enhanced augmented supermodels.

Walking past H&M, shoppers could be forgiven for thinking they were seeing double or even triple. Despite having different faces and ethnicities, H&M swimwear models all look suspiciously similar, with identical stomachs, thighs and arching arms. In 2011, a Norwegian website exposed H&M as using computer-generated bodies to market its lingerie and swimwear. The digital bodies are pigmented to match the head of the models that are stuck on top. H&M defended its use of fake bodies by saying that it is merely following industry standards.[13]

This forgery is replicated in high fashion. In 2008, the *New Yorker* profiled Pascal Dangin, fashion's most sought-after 'photo-shopper'. He had just retouched 144 images in the March 2008 edition of US *Vogue* – 107 adverts, 36 fashion pictures and the Drew Barrymore cover image. Dangin's presence in the fashion industry is described as necessarily 'shadowy' and he is not credited by magazines. He admits that 'this world is not reality – it's about drawing people towards an ideal vision'.[14] For one image he described altering a woman's feet, knees and collarbones as well as having 'minimized the actress's temples, which bulged a little, tightened the skin around her chin and excised a fleshy bump from her forehead'.[15] Society is in the process of making reality unpalatable.

The Dangin profile was highly controversial because he described retouching Dove's 'Real Women' campaign – adverts featuring 'real women' of different shapes, sizes, ages and nationalities. Dangin stated: 'It was great to do, a challenge, to keep everyone's skin and faces showing the mileage but not looking unattractive.' Unilever, however, which owns both Dove and the overtly sexist brand Lynx, officially denied that the retouching occurred, stating that Dangin had worked only on colour correction and dust removal.

The Body Beautiful?

Fashion models appear to hold a deified status as women who have won the 'gene pool lottery'. But what is the impact of the fashion industry on the lives and physicality of these women? The debate over the industry's responsibility for eating disorders continues. Anorexia nervosa is a serious psychological illness that can be provoked by a wide range of causes and I would not wish to crudely generalise the disease or those it afflicts. The negative body image that contributes to disordered eating and eating disorders is unlikely to be solved until sexism is expunged and women are no longer taught that their appearance is paramount.

Families and female role-models also hugely influence body confidence. Ending 'fat talk' and raising self-esteem are not the sole responsibility of the fashion industry, and yet this does not absolve the industry of culpability. There is no doubt that the fashion industry seriously harms its employees by requiring them to conform to a certain aesthetic.

In August 2006, a 22-year-old Uruguayan model, Luisel Ramos, died having just stepped off a catwalk. The cause of death was heart failure caused by anorexia nervosa. Tragedy repeated itself a few months later when Luisel's younger sister, 18-year-old model Eliana, also died from a heart attack caused by malnutrition. A Brazilian model, Ana Carolina Reston, died in hospital also in 2006. Having been told at a casting call that she was 'too fat', the 22-year-old starved herself until at 5 ft 9 in tall she weighed just 6 stone.

In the early twenty-first century, the fashion industry equates beauty with thinness and requires models to be thin. Catwalk models today are on average just 15 years old and 80 per cent of all the models at the 2007 London Fashion Week were foreign workers.[16] Young, far from home and under extreme pressure, models face serious exploitation.

What chance do unknown models have when even top fashion models have painful stories about body scrutiny and being told to lose weight. Amy Lemons, who sits on the Advisory Board of the Models Alliance, started modelling women's clothing at the age of 12 and did a *Vogue Italia* cover when she was 14. As puberty matured her body, her agent told her to eat one rice cake a day and if necessary to drop to half a rice cake: 'They were telling me to be anorexic – flat out.'[17] The model Crystal Renn was told that she would make it as a supermodel if she lost 40 per cent of her body weight. She did and as a result battled with anorexia nervosa for years.[18] Another top model, Coco Rocha, was told when she was 15: 'The look this year is anorexic. We don't want you to be anorexic, just look it.'[19]

In 2013 a Swedish eating disorder centre was forced to change its policy of letting patients go for a walk unaccompanied in the neighbourhood because model scouts were attempting to recruit girls with eating disorders. One scout even approached a young woman who had become wheelchair-bound by her illness.[20]

A Shrinking Industry

The designer Elsa Schiaparelli is credited with first using tall thin models in catwalk shows. Other designers like Charles Worth and Paul Poiret used a wide range of women as models. A fitter for Cristóbal Balenciaga famously reassured clients that 'Monsieur Balenciaga *likes* a little stomach'. Balenciaga's clothes, created to suit women of many sizes, were often modelled by 'short, stocky' women.[21]

The 1960s saw the introduction of very thin 'waif' models and during the 1990s the fashion industry was criticised for 'heroin chic' which replaced the more athletic aesthetic of the 1980s. In 1996 Jo Fonseca, director of the Models 1 agency, stated: 'I can think of nothing worse than being fat. The only reason that thin girls look so unusual at the moment is because there are so many fat people.'[22] Then came 'size zero'. In 2013 catwalk models were thinner than ever with waist measurements comparable to that of a seven year old.[23] Size zero is the US equivalent of a UK size 4. It is as slight as it sounds, particularly in the context of over half of North American women wearing a US size 14 or larger.[24]

It is a highly enforced thinness. Dunja Knezevic, president of the Models Union, explains: 'There is such a tiny percentage of girls who are naturally that way and that is mostly because they are young. If you are 20 your hips can't be a certain size when you are six foot tall unless you are starving yourself. Your hips have developed, so it's just impossible.'[25] According to one booker in New York: 'The thin thing now is beyond anything I have ever seen. This is the thinnest time in modelling. It's ridiculous.'[26] Crystal Renn puts it more bluntly: 'Any thinner means dead.'[27]

> Models are told to lose weight or get liposuction. The mentality is that you can never be too skinny. I have seen girls come in through agencies who are 15 and haven't developed hips, and they are told 'lose some weight' – just because *everybody* should lose some weight. It's not even 'eat healthy to be skinny'; it's just 'don't eat'. A lot of agencies recommend living off water. Water, coffee and cigarettes are a recommended diet still. There are agencies who provide a nutritionist, but mostly, and especially when Fashion Week comes round, it's just 'starve yourself'. (Dunja Knezevic)[28]

Women had to die before the dangers of size zero were taken seriously. After Luisel Ramos died, Madrid and Milan Fashion Weeks banned size zero models and agreed a minimum body mass index (BMI) of 18.[29] Paris and London refused to act. British *Vogue* editor Alexandra Shulman wrote an article in the *Daily Mail* entitled 'Size zero hysteria at London Fashion Week'. She dismissed calls for a ban: 'If I started to photograph all our shoots on size 14 women . . . would everyone want to look like them? I think not.'[30]

In the face of continuing pressure, in 2012 Condé Nast announced the *Vogue* Health Initiative. The pact commits *Vogue* editors to hire models 'who, in our view, are healthy and help to promote a healthy body image'. Yet there was little discernible change in the international June 2012 covers of *Vogue*, which was when the initiative launched.

The pact also banned the use of models under the age of 16. *Vogue* has become notorious for devising fashion shoots that, if conducted outside the industry, would certainly have led to arrests for child pornography. One particularly disturbing shoot by *Vogue* Paris featured a heavily made up ten-year-old in sexually provocative poses. Dunja Knezevic agrees that there is a lot that goes on in the fashion industry that elsewhere would lead to arrests: 'like the sexual harassment, like the child labour . . . People don't realise that these girls in the campaigns are 15. The industry just goes "she doesn't look it so who cares if her tits are out."'[31] In a revealing interview, legendary model Kate Moss described how doing provocative shoots as a young girl gave her a nervous breakdown. Of one of her most lauded images, a topless photo shot by Corinne Day, Moss said: 'They were like, "If you don't do it, then we're not going to book you again." So I'd lock myself in the toilet and cry and then come out and do it.'[32]

There have been some notable moments of change with regard to size. The designers Giles Deacon and Mark Fast have employed a greater variety of models on their catwalks. Organisations like *All Walks beyond the Catwalk* and *AnyBody* have campaigned to increase diversity. The June 2011 publication of *Vogue Italia* was a 'plus size' edition. The cover featured three 'plus size' models in underwear sitting at a café table bearing plates of spaghetti. This token change has, however, been criticised as amounting to little more than a symbolic stand-in for diversity which may hinder real change.[33]

What has definitely not helped the debate is journalists attacking thin models, describing them as 'Skeletor's bastard offspring' with 'cold dead eyes and antelope legs'.[34] Shaming is the worst possible way to confront someone with a weight disorder, no matter what the intention of the remark. Topshop model Codie Young, whose body was criticised in the *Daily Mail*, spoke out: 'Just because I'm a model doesn't mean you can just attack without any sort of hesitation.'[35] Models experience public criticism for being 'fat' or 'thin' and then more criticism if they lose or gain weight. Calling for people to stop watching women's bodies as if it were a sport, the website *Fashionista* was right to question: 'Can models – or regular women – ever win when it comes to weight?'[36]

Why Size Zero?

Excuses periodically emerge from within the industry about the 'need' for size zero because it lets clothes hang better and allows buyers to better envisage how clothes will look in the shops. This 'woman as living coat-hanger' argument should not be entertained. Humans model clothes to bring them to life and make them look beautiful; otherwise clothes could just be displayed on rotating racks. What claim can the fashion industry have to creativity if its buyers cannot visualise clothes without extremely thin models or indeed if designers cannot design clothes for a variety of sizes, as Cristóbal Balenciaga did?

Ashley Mears describes in *Pricing Beauty* how 'editorial producers are looking to shock in a high-stakes game of distinction'.[37] Designers value sexual unavailability – the body stripped of sex – as part of creating a high-end look. She quotes one designer: 'You're displaying your clothes on this ageless unattainable beauty.'[38] Mears also describes the attempt by brands to portray an 'ideal' world in which fat women (and women of colour) do not exist.[39]

Much is made of models needing to be ultra-thin in order to fit into sample sizes. Some argue that small samples are due to economies of scale since small sizes require less material. But a conglomerate that makes millions in profit can scarcely argue that a few extra inches of cloth will bankrupt them. Sample sizes could be produced at US size 6 or in a variety of sizes, something that would reduce pressure on models and benefit the health of society as a whole. Dunja Knezevic describes the refusal of anyone to take responsibility: 'The agencies blame the designers – "How can we stock models who are a size 8 when they only want a size 6?" But the designers say: "They only give us small models".'[40] With no sector of the industry willing to start a process of change, industry regulation seems the most effective route for moving away from size zero.

These excuses do not justify or explain why young (poor) people are required to starve themselves to death for the visual entertainment of the rich. So what is really behind size zero?

A Modern Condition

The economic theories of Karl Marx were his attempt to mirror the relations he observed in the real world.[41] Marx describes the physical condition of the working classes of Victorian Britain – their stunted height, bent backs, gnarled fingers, missing limbs and deathly pale complexions. This, he said, was the result of labour being external to workers, of their having no choice about what work they do, how it is done or what is produced.

In working, the worker 'does not affirm himself but denies himself, does not feel content but unhappy, does not develop freely his physical and mental energy, but mortifies his body and ruins his mind'.[42] This sheds light on twenty-first-century capitalism's focus on the body and on extreme thinness because it is startlingly similar to the predicament of the vast majority of women workers in the fashion industry. They have been reduced to 'living appendages of the machine'.[43]

The ultimate poverty or loss of being has been described as being left with nothing to work with except your body, like an animal. This was the original definition of the proletariat.[44] It is the situation for the vast majority of women working as fashion models.

Take Dunja Knezevic's description of modelling: 'You are essentially this object that things are done to. They make you into a product, then they shoot you as this product that they sell.'[45] The way models are treated shows them to be commodified labour like other workers. The production of fashion is the production of commodities by commodities.[46] These young women are shown no respect.

An agency got a call one afternoon with a request for a model to go finish off a photo shoot that had started that morning and which was using very strong flashlights. The model sent by the agency ended up having the first layer of her corneas burnt off by the flashlights. She was rushed to hospital – the same hospital where the original model from the morning was being treated! They burnt the corneas of the model in the morning but didn't change the lights or change anything they were doing – just called up and got another model. (Dunja Knezevic)[47]

Maintaining extreme thinness turns every hour of a woman's day into work. There is no physical or mental rest from dieting. It is an obsession, as this traditional saying describes it: *A person with bread has many problems, a person without has only one.* For young models, this work is physically and mentally draining:

Sometimes I don't know how these girls function. They're not eating anything at all, all their bones are sticking out, they are really struggling. You walk into a casting and there's these girls just slouched over half asleep and you try and talk to them and they're just dazed. (Dunja Knezevic)[48]

Models' work is not restricted to catwalk and photo shoots. Behind the scenes, their work is to starve themselves to maintain an illusion that makes money for the fashion and beauty industries. Models are not coughing up soot, but their damaged bodies are a sign of the system at work, a system that has control of them.

Sometimes their work brings death. This is partly because models are subject to the massive pressure and insecurity of a giant reserve army of labour. If they do not 'measure up', thousands are waiting in the wings to take their job for worse conditions, less money and less food. This reality is hidden behind statements like this from one top model: 'We don't wake up for less than $10,000 a day'.[49]

Enforced thinness – starvation to the point of death – is emblematic of the industry's treatment of people and the planet, of the pressure the industry exerts on all its workers. But there is also something more sinister at work. Making unnaturally obtained or sustained extreme thinness a condition of employment is a reactionary but effective means for the industry to maintain control of employees, for taking away their agency.

Dunja Knezevic explains:

The industry is literally weakening people. A lot of people with anorexia or bulimia say that eating is the one thing they can control. For models especially this is the only thing they can control as their agencies are controlling their life. For clients or agencies – if you can control models in the sense that you can get them into this mentality, then you've got them. You can tell them what to do and push them around and manipulate them. Eating disorders are really a great way to do that. If you think about it, it really takes over the mind. It is a weakening of the mind.[50]

Strength is replaced by obsessing over extreme thinness. If taught that they are weak, women are less likely to fight back against poor treatment.[51] They are also less able literally to fight back against physical attack.[52] Attacks on women, including rape and sexual assault, are widespread across society but take place with disturbing regularity within the fashion industry. Several top industry figures, including the photographer Terry Richardson and American Apparel CEO Dov Charney, have stood accused of the alleged routine sexual abuse of young women.

More than a Trend

The cult of thinness has spread throughout society beyond just those who have it as a condition of employment. So why do people strive to be thin?

For Susie Orbach, thinness has become fashionable because the West has accumulated vast riches and now has 'some need to exhibit, amongst this abundance, its opposite: to be free of need, to be highly selective, to be able to control the food that we require, to do away with the materiality of the body'.[53] Orbach argues that if extreme thinness were not in fashion, it would be something else. In the 1950s, companies sold Wate-On and scolded women for being too thin for 'fun'.[54] Today the fashion industry, along with its 'handmaidens',[55] the diet, food and pharmaceutical industries, make billions from body insecurity. Described as 'merchants of body hatred,'[56] they 'depend on the breeding of body insecurity [to] create beauty terror in so many people'.[57] Women are too profitable a market to be allowed to relax into their physicality. Instead they are given an impossible quest for self-perfection which keeps them spending money.

The Lagerfeld quote that opens this chapter reads in full: 'Unreachable beauty is a reminder to make an effort. But if you see something and you can reach what you see, then you do not have to make an effort anymore.'[58] Effort entails buying clothes, accessories, cosmetics and perfumes – preferably from Chanel. As part of the wider capitalist system, fashion fuels 'consumer demand by creating a craving that can't be satisfied'.[59]

Whilst it might be problematic to argue that there is a natural state of being, women's bodies today are augmented with silicon injections into breasts and buttocks, botox injections, skin bleach, hair dye, enamel teeth, hair extensions, fake nails, vajazzles (crystals applied to the genitals), surgically modified noses and chins, and leg bone grafts. They are also starved. The results are then photo-shopped to within an inch of their life – this is the epitome of the flight from nature.

Alienation leads people to be alienated from the planet, from each other and from their own bodies, as discussed in Chapter 5. These three things become something to be conquered. Human nature 'splinters'[60] into fractured parts and the body becomes something to be starved and hated, rather than a part of nature, perfect as it is. This conquering of the body comes partly from the way humans are taught to measure themselves by their distance from the rest of the population and 'from nature itself'.[61]

Promoting a fake body ideal is also deeply disempowering. It leaves women feeling so inadequate that they spend large amounts of their time trying to alter their appearance. The promotion of a particular fetishised body shape – in this case airbrushed thinness – forms part of the process of exclusion carried out by the fashion industry. Chapter 7 further explores the idea that the fashion industry defines beauty through a process of exclusion – this time of race – benefiting those that do the excluding and having nothing to do with the actualities of those being excluded.[62]

Yet thinness is more than just a trend in the continuing cycles of fashion. Why are starvation and life-threatening extreme thinness currently propagated as beauty? In *The Beauty Myth*, Naomi Woolf argues that extreme thinness through dieting did not exist until women's emancipation entered law. When women received the vote in the 1920s, dieting and thinness became a preoccupation for women. This change is blamed on the social expediency of making 'women's bodies into the prisons that their homes no longer were' since women were now entering 'male spheres', including the workplace.[63]

Wolf writes that fashionable dieting and extreme thinness has occurred simultaneously with every advance in women's rights. Examples include the popularisation of the Twiggy 'waif' silhouette during the women's liberation movement of the 1960s and 1970s to cancel the contraceptive pill's most radical implications.[64] 'Heroin chic' ('the look of sickness, the look of poverty, and the look of nervous exhaustion')[65] was, Wolf argues, brought into fashion in the 1990s as a way of curbing women's hopes for advancement and gratification.[66]

A particularly pernicious aspect of dieting – of doing it to yourself – has been illuminated by Sandra Lee Bartky in *Femininity and Domination*. She outlines the key concept of prisons as being the maintenance of a state of conscious and permanent visibility for all prisoners.[67] Society, she argues, keeps women prisoner by keeping them on display. She describes how women check the mirror half a dozen times a day to see if their make-up has smudged; worry that the wind or rain will ruin their hair; and, being scared of getting fat, monitor what they eat. Women therefore self-enforce their prisoner status: because they know they are being watched, 'inmates' police themselves.[68]

There has been an important change since *Femininity and Domination* was published in 1990. The rise of the internet means that never before have ordinary people been so on display. If life was a visual prison before the internet, now it is a concentration camp. From sonograms of babies in the womb to photos of funerals, Facebook in particular means that every aspect of our lives is captured and posted online for inspection. Being constantly on display means 'Facebook facelift' is now a term recognised by the *Cambridge Dictionary*: 'facial cosmetic surgery as a result of vanity brought on by seeing too many photos of oneself on social networking websites'.[69] The forced urge to diet, and the ability to be judged for not dieting, is thus more prevalent than ever.

An illuminating article by the blog *Threadbared* applied academic Rob Nixon's definition of 'slow violence' (violence that occurs gradually and out of sight; an attritional violence that is typically not viewed as violence at all, and which has a delayed effect)[70] to body dysmorphia and eating disorders. For *Threadbared*, adult women tacitly told to strive for a pre-pubertal body is a goal that spawns a myriad of linked acts of slow violence: low self-esteem, anxiety, depression and for some, drug and alcohol abuse, self-harming and disordered eating behaviour. In this way, eating disorders can illuminate the society we live in. Rather than being 'a white girl's problem', race and racial violence play a strong role in the development of body dysmorphia.[71] This normalisation of distress adds to women's inequality in society.

Global society is weighed down by war, extreme poverty, financial upheaval, tyranny, imperialism, shrinking resources, nuclear disasters, terrorism and neoliberalism. If we include the slow violence of climate change – and, I would argue, the alienation of modern life – early-twenty-first century capitalism presents us with perhaps the greatest crisis in human history. It is a time of extremes.

Today's society is also different in that markets have spread to every area of the globe; what is left to conquer is the minutiae of the human body. Current Western capitalist society also differs from other societies because, since the 1980s, the sale of products has become increasingly dependent on myth and fantasy.[72] Especially in fashion, use-value has been overtaken by the brand fantasies needed for exchange value to work. The idea that women can not-eat and stay healthy and that adult women can attain pre-pubescent bodies is the height of fantasy.

Emaciation or Emancipation?

Outside of the 'plus-size' industry, fashion – both high-end and high street – has all but refused to give women attainable beauty ideals. This may be doing them out of profits. Research has found that (contrary to what Alexandra Shulman argued) women are more motivated to shop when models in adverts reflect their body size and shape. Purchase intentions are said to rise by up to 300 per cent when models reflect the weight, age or ethnicity of customers.[73] Sales of Dove products in the United States increased by 600 per cent after their 'Real Women' advertising campaign.[74] As the economy shrinks, corporations may begin to diversify their advertising campaigns in a cynical attempt to attract more customers. The point of diversity is not, however, to increase profits for corporations.

One positive step is the increasing use of collectivity by models to stand up for their basic rights. The idea of a trade union of models originated with Victoria Keon-Cohen and Dunja Knezevic, who founded the Model Union in London in 2009 as a branch of the British trade union Equity. 'The industry has been so unregulated for so long that people just behave however they want whenever they want,'[75] stated Keon-Cohen, pointing out that models cannot turn to their agencies if they run into trouble because they rely on them for work and visas. The Model Union has produced a Code of Conduct which is supported by the British Fashion Council and the Association of Model Agencies. It aims to regularise minimum wages, work breaks and nudity requirements and to facilitate the provision of healthy food and drink at shows. Members also get facial disfigurement insurance, legal support and access to counsellors and nutritionists.

The industry is slowly getting used to the idea and the union has not encountered discrimination against its members for joining: 'After a few years of us explaining, people are becoming supportive: "OK, you don't want to die at a shoot – fair enough".'[76] One problem it has encountered is low expectations from the models themselves: 'They are mostly from Eastern Europe, some are from Africa, there are a lot from South America – girls for whom not having food available for eight hours is acceptable because their mother works in a factory and doesn't have any food for 12 hours a day.'[77]

Sara Ziff, a fashion model whose film *Picture Me* exposed the sleaze and exploitation endured by teenaged models, has since founded the Model Alliance in the United States. 'There's nothing funny about a workforce that is overwhelmingly young, female and impoverished, working for some of fashion's wealthiest, most powerful brands,' stated its co-founder Jenna Sauers.[78] The Model Alliance has successfully campaigned for legislation to protect child models in New York State. It takes courage to unionise and protest against ill-treatment in any industry, but particularly in such a competitive and deregulated industry as modelling.

Fatshion

Another site of body-image subversion is the internet. Out of the blogosphere has come the self-styled fatosphere. I have used the term 'fat' in this chapter because that is what is what bloggers use: 'By calling myself "fat", I'm saying this is who I am. This is the body I have. This is the right body for me because it's the one I'm living with. "Fat" is not a bad word. Rather than saying "overweight," which implies there is a correct weight, I use "fat" purely as a descriptive word.'[79]

Fatshion sites have provided a platform for women rendered invisible by the fashion industry and is helping to change fashion's visual culture from the bottom up. A cursory search for 'Fatshion' on Tumblr will reveal how the fatosphere provides a great deal of pleasure for the women it represents. The internet has become a lifeline for women who have been told both implicitly and explicitly that they are ugly:

> Your confidence has inspired me to be comfortable with who I am. For more than a decade I had been battling with bulimia and now that I am in recovery I have gained weight and my natural shape and curves have returned. Not knowing how to go about dressing myself and completely at a loss as to how to carry myself now, your website has been a source of inspiration. Thank you!'[80]

When American Apparel held an online 'plus-size' modelling contest, the fatosphere found the perfect opportunity for an online protest. Notorious for producing sexist and exploitative ads, American Apparel is also known to discriminate against fat people: 'That's not our demographic.'[81] The company sought to salvage its image by running *The Next BIG Thing* modelling contest. Women

– known as 'things' by American Apparel – were asked to submit photos of themselves and describe why they were 'bigger, better and more booty-ful than the rest'. Members of the public then rated each woman on a scale of 1 to 5 to choose the winners.

The contest badly backfired thanks largely to the work of Nancy Upton, a Dallas-based blogger. Upton entered the competition with a series of satirical photographs under the caption: *I'm a size 12. I just can't stop eating.* Her submission featured her eating a roast chicken in a swimming pool, bathing in ranch sauce and posing provocatively with pies. Her message was that the women entering the competition were not beautiful because of or despite their size. Upton was voted the winner but was quickly disqualified by American Apparel: 'We have decided to award the prizes to other contestants that we feel truly exemplify the idea of beauty inside and out, and whom we will be proud to have representing our company.'[82]

The downside to the internet, as well as constant visual exposure for people, is bullying, trolling and the fact that the fatosphere remains marginal. Whilst pockets of resistance are important, few 'fat activists' would be happy settling for this. The internet is also utilised by people caught in the throes of severe eating disorders. 'Thinspo' (thinspiration) and pro-ana (pro-anorexia) sites post 'motivational' quotes, pictures and tips to encourage readers to lose weight. Facebook, Tumblr and Pinterest have worked with groups like the National Eating Disorders Association to close down pages that explicitly encourage self-harm and to redirect viewers to advice on eating disorders.

Other campaigns for change call for companies like Weight Watchers to be sued for false advertising. Campaigners point to 95 per cent failure rates and the high levels of repeat customers: 'The only thing that gets thinner is people's wallets.'[83] There have been similar moves to tackle airbrushing, with adverts being withdrawn in the United Kingdom after trading standards battles. Some commentators describe the task of regulating advertisers as 'Sisyphean in a digital age'.[84] Yet a public health message such as *Warning! This perfection is an illusion* on every airbrushed advert could challenge the onslaught of fake images.[85]

Body Image

Media literacy classes are also becoming more commonplace in schools as a means of teaching young people how media images have been altered. Media literacy is not a solution to poor body image. First, it leaves the media untouched and instead shifts responsibility onto young women. It requires them to become savvy media dissectors, and if they *still* lack body confidence after the classes, then it is they who are to blame, not the media. As the academic Rosalind Gill explains, media literacy classes are yet another way in which young women must strive to perfect themselves. They imply that what needs to change is how people engage with the media rather than the media itself. A good comparison would be telling the black community to deal with racism by taking a media literacy class.[86]

It is possible to intellectualise and criticise the portrayal of women in the fashion industry and still be caught up in feelings of inadequacy and low self-esteem. Unless people are also taught and encouraged to fight for change, they may end up feeling more 'trapped'[87] and powerless than they did to begin with. The SPARK (Sexualisation Protest Action Resistance Knowledge)-led *Body Peace Treaty* is one example of young women campaigning against the fashion media to bring about change. Teen activist Julia Bluhm organised petitions and protests against the airbrushing of female celebrities, which led to a change of policy by *Seventeen* magazine. The UK high street chain Debenhams have also pledged not to airbrush their adverts.

Studies have shown that restricting photographs of underweight models and prohibiting size zero models would be justified as a method of easing pressure on young women.[88] Yet much of the industry remains vehemently against regulation, arguing instead for self-regulation to protect fashion as 'art'.

As well as starvation, models report being painted with car paint instead of body paint, having their eyes burned with cosmetics and having their hair fall out after it has been bleached three times on a shoot.[89] These are real people not canvases. This 'art' has consequences.

Cries to reject protective regulation exist against a backdrop of some of the most fastidious industry regulations in existence. The *Chambre Syndicale de la Haute Couture* in Paris, for example, governs *haute couture* with legal definitions covering issues such as the number of fittings for each dress and the number of employees a company must have. There is no excuse for rejecting health and safety regulations in the fashion industry.

Self-regulation has resulted in countless sick or dead fashion models and has allowed the cult of thinness to spread insecurity throughout society. Regulatory bodies, campaigners and governments should demand more from an industry whose products, philosophies and influence leave society so marked. For many women it is too late to undo the damage; for millions of others, proper regulation could bring relief.

*   *   *

The pushing of a single beauty ideal follows the pattern of an industry that caters for profits not needs. Beauty ideals about symmetry and size zero do not exist to benefit society, in fact they do great damage. They exist to keep women spending their time and money on altering their appearance, to create a climate of self-doubt and to control a large section of the fashion industry's workforce. To counteract this, the very idea that there is just one version of beauty must be discarded, along with the system that propagates it.

Beauty must be recognised as an intrinsically individual trait, rather than a measure of how well someone is able to conform to the same old accepted aesthetic.[90] Women must be released from the idea that their appearance is what matters most and employees of the fashion industry must not be faced with starvation as an employment requirement. Real freedom of expression for the individual will bring comfort, freedom and the possibility of real creativity and choice. It will free up all the hours and resources now spent despairingly striving to alter the way we look. There is nowhere to go with size zero and the current aesthetic. To reiterate Crystal Renn's point: 'Any thinner means dead'.

CHAPTER SEVEN

Is Fashion Racist?

Some of those other countries are, um, Muslim countries and for a
fashion magazine like Vogue that poses issues. I'm not sure the culture,
the political culture or the fashion culture, is compatible with the values
of Vogue. I'm not saying we'd never go to those countries, but we'd have
to carefully consider. On an economic level some of them aren't ready. I
certainly don't think Bangladesh, Nigeria or Pakistan are ready for Vogue.[1]
Jonathan Newhouse, Chair of Condé Nast International

The production of fashion is a highly lucrative business. Because of
this, it has historically been guarded as a domain reserved for one
demographic: rich, thin and white. This has resulted in the myth
that those outside this demographic do not 'do fashion'. They are
relegated to 'the people without history' or, in this case, 'the people
without fashion'.[2] This essentially racist premise – that what Paris,
Milan, London and New York produce is fashion and what everyone
else produces is just clothing – is the setting for this chapter. It is a
premise that allows for the dehumanisation, and thus the guiltless
exploitation, of the so-called third world. It is a perception that faces
serious challenges from shifting economic power.

Exclusion Zone

In February 1959, photographs of China Machado (born Noelie
Dasouza Machado) appeared in *Harper's Bazaar*. It was the first time a
model of colour[3] had featured in a fashion magazine, something that
Machado's photographer and colleague, Richard Avedon, fought to
accomplish. In 2012, China Machado, aged 82, once again began
working as a model. Of her childhood in Shanghai she remarked:
'We [non-whites] had no images. We had nothing that told us we were
nice-looking. Nothing. So I didn't think of myself as good-looking at
all. It never occurred to me.'[4]

Not until 1966 did *Vogue* magazine put a model of colour on one
of its covers. British *Vogue* went first, featuring Donyale Luna. In the
photograph Luna's hand covers part of her face – an attempt, it is
thought, to mask her ethnicity. It took another eight years before
Beverly Johnson was featured on the front cover of the US edition

in 1974. *Vogue Paris* stayed resolutely white until as late as 1988 when Yves Saint Laurent threatened to sever ties with the magazine unless 18-year-old Naomi Campbell was put on its cover.

Several decades on and all-white catwalks, all-white advertising campaigns and all-white fashion shoots are still the norm. In fact, the fashion industry has drawn so much 'whitewash' attention to itself that the July 2008 edition of US *Vogue* led with the story 'Is Fashion Racist?' The edition conceded that catwalks present an eerily homogeneous spectacle: 'the same procession of anonymous, blandly pretty, very young, very skinny, washed-out blondes with their hair scraped back'.[5]

Catwalk statistics show a disturbing lack of diversity. New York Fashion Week 2009 consisted of 116 different labels presenting shows with 3,697 modelling opportunities. Of these 668 (18 per cent) went to models of colour. This is even less inclusive than it sounds because repeat appearances from three top models made up half the spots. In the multicultural city of New York in 2009, 82 per cent of all Fashion Week appearances were by white models. A breakdown of these statistics reveals that out of 35 spots Calvin Klein used only one model of colour, while Donna Karan used three out of 45.[6]

These statistics marked a 50 per cent increase after campaigners fought to diversify American catwalks. New York Fashion Week 2007 was quite literally a whitewash with 101 shows (a third) having no models of colour whatsoever. The increase between 2008 and 2009 has also been credited in part to the election of President Barack Obama and the appearance of the first black First Lady. The heavy scrutiny of Michelle Obama's wardrobe means that she is capable of providing much-needed publicity for designers, leading some to try to appear more racially inclusive.

By industry standards there is only mild segregation in New York. The 2008 Paris Fashion Week, with shows by 40 designers, did not include a single model of colour. Industry insiders talk of endemic racism in Europe: 'In Paris and Milan, if you offer a black girl, they drop the book like it's hot.'[7] Clients tell casting directors: 'We want a black girl, but don't let her be too black'.[8] The model Renee Thompson, who featured in the documentary *The Colour of*

Beauty, described her experiences in the industry: 'Sometimes it's so blatantly racist, it's disgusting.'[9] Prada did not have a single black model on its catwalks between Naomi Campbell in 1997 and Jourdan Dunn in 2008. London is said to be marginally better than the rest of Europe but booking agents still receive casting briefs which say 'no ethnics'.[10] This accepted level of racism is unimaginable in almost any other industry.

Deviants, Animals, Slaves and Backdrops

Magazines are also discriminatory. Take, for example, the substantial September 2011 edition of British *Vogue*. The magazine carries a cover story on the 'Turbulent Life of John Galliano'. With fashion designer Galliano's conviction for anti-Semitism, the edition makes an interesting context for the exploration of race representation. Flicking through the pages, a reader will see 402 images of white people but only 22 of people of colour. Among these 22 images, five people were in one small picture illustrating a white actor's visit to Haiti; three images were of servants, two of which accompanied an article on 'tactile glamour', where Edouard Manet's painting *Olympia* (complete with black slave) had been used to depict the 'splendour' of days gone by.

The advertisements followed a similar pattern: 373 adverts depicted white models, only 24 featured models of colour. Seven of the latter were tiny, newspaper-style adverts in the back pages. On the main pages the majority of models of colour appeared in group portraits like the Tommy Hilfiger advert. There were just three adverts where a model of colour was given a page to herself.

As well as routine exclusion, models of colour face being caricatured. The fashion media routinely casts black female bodies as illicit, hypersexualised, primitive or obscene.[11] Commonplace stereotyping of models of colour occurs whenever the industry wants to invoke 'tribal' imagery. Anyone who reads fashion magazines will also be aware of fashion's continuing predilection for portraying women of colour as akin to animals. Jean-Paul Goude's 'Wild Things' shoot for *Harper's Bazaar* in 2009 featured Naomi Campbell running with a cheetah, skipping with monkeys and riding on an elephant and a crocodile. Other famous examples are Peter Beard's photographs of Iman naked with a cheetah and Maureen Gallagher feeding a giraffe – also while naked.

Fashion shoots also typically utilise everyone from Mongolian herders to Balinese children as mere exotic landscapes. The 'exotic people' are there to provide a contrast to white models and expensive clothes. It is an unoriginal and tedious theme rich with the history of colonialism and exploitation.

In August 2008 *Vogue India* ran a 'Slum Dwellers' shoot, juxtaposing impoverished people who survive on $1.25 a day with $100 Fendi baby bibs, $200 Burberry umbrellas and a $10,000 Hermès bag. Kanika Gahlaut, a journalist at *Mail Today* in India, stated: 'There's nothing "fun or funny" about putting a poor person in a mud hut in clothing designed by Alexander McQueen. There are farmer suicides here for God's sake.' *Vogue* did not list the slumdwellers' names, they are just 'lady' or 'man', unlike the clothes which are fully identified. *Vogue India* retorted: 'Lighten up. Fashion is no longer a rich man's privilege. Anyone can carry it off and make it look beautiful.'[12]

Displacing Whiteness, edited by Ruth Frankenburg, describes how women of colour are fetishised as being 'on a slippery slope from exotic beauty to unfemininity and ugliness'.[13] Because of this it is also common for models of colour to be chosen for shoots portraying deviance. One magazine editor stated: 'Black girls have a harder-edge kind of look. Like, if I'm shooting something really edgy, I'll use a black girl.'[14] An example of this stereotyping is a 2011 *Stylist* 'S&M shoot' of Sudanese model Alek Wek in handcuffs, masks and a horse's tail. Alek Wek has spoken about how she has been portrayed in the past. She compared a Lavazza campaign where she was pictured as the 'coffee' in a giant cup to previous images of black people used by the advertising industry: 'There was the big-lipped jungle-dweller on the blackamoor ceramic mugs sold in the forties; the golliwog badges given away with jam; Little Black Sambo, who decorated the walls of an American restaurant chain in the 1960s; and Uncle Ben, whose apparently benign image still sells rice.'[15]

In 2011, the shoe company Christian Louboutin issued a series of advertisements that were indicative of the second-class position of women of colour in the fashion industry. Billed as a celebration of 'the power of femininity', the adverts showed re-enactments of iconic paintings including Georges de La Tour's *The Magdalen with the Smoking Flame*, François Clouet's *Elisabeth of Austria* and Jean-Marc Nattier's *Marquise d'Antin*, amongst others. All of the women portrayed were aristocratic, wealthy or saints, except for the final picture – a reproduction of Marie Benoist's *Portrait d'une négresse*. This painting's subject is a former slave, made a servant during the brief outlawing of slavery in France. The unnamed woman, who belonged to Benoist's family, did not have a choice about whether she was painted or about how her body was portrayed, a dilemma akin to that faced by models of colour in the twenty-first century.

Whilst it has been argued that Benoist may have had sympathetic, feminist and emancipatory intentions, the image is one of white privileged power enforcing black servitude.[16] Unlike the fine robes of the other pictures, the woman in *Portrait d'une négresse* wears a headwrap and has one breast exposed. The slave trade meant that the headwrap came to symbolise servitude and poverty for black women in the European colonies and in the United States.[17] Art historians argue that the exposure of the woman's right breast is a visual reference to the slave auction block where black bodies were stripped, beaten and violated in public to prove white power.[18] This is in sharp contrast to the other paintings in the Louboutin set. According to one art historian, the facial expression and body language of the woman in the picture portray the psychological damage resulting from her vulnerable situation.[19]

Models of colour are far more likely to be portrayed in a nude or semi-nude state than their white counterparts and are routinely depicted in a way that suggests they are inferior. It is impossible, for example, to imagine the reversal of this scenario – six photos of black aristocrats and the seventh of a half-naked white woman who has been born and raised in servitude.

Why the Negative Stereotypes?

It would be easy to reduce all fashion race-related stories to the question of whether the wrongdoer is a racist or not. But this approach is generally unhelpful since intention, whether a person intended to offend or not, is only part of the story.[20] It does not matter whether Prada excludes black models *intentionally* or whether Louboutin set out to be offensive; what matters more is the result. For the majority of people in the fashion industry – and in society as a whole – racism is perpetuated unconsciously and unintentionally, but it is still racism. 'No matter the intention, the result is racism,' wrote Naomi Campbell, Iman and campaigner Bethann Hardison in an open letter to designers in September 2013. 'Not accepting another based on the colour of their skin is clearly beyond aesthetic.'[21]

The notions of racial difference that constitute racism are human creations, not predetermined categories. Because of this they are subject to change.[22] But while race, like sexuality or gender, is a social construct, it still has tangible effects on the world and a very real impact on the lives of individuals.[23]

Racism, in the form of derogatory stereotypes that are constantly re-articulated in culture, supported slavery, lynching and colonialism. In *A Quiet Revolution*, the Harvard academic Leila Ahmed describes nineteenth-century European ideas about the hierarchy of races and the racial and civilisational superiority of Europeans. This racist narrative aided European colonialism by casting Europeans, not as bloodthirsty, murderous exploiters, but as virtuous men bringing civilisation to backward people.[24]

Today, war is still justified by racism. Support for the wars on Iraq and Afghanistan was sought through the idea that the invaders were a civilising force. Women and women's dress have become key issues for neo-imperialists trying to justify war. Gayatri Spivak labelled this form of rhetoric: 'white men saving brown women from brown men'.[25] Step one in any war is to dehumanise your opponent so that your actions appear justified. On a local level, negative stereotypes, like those found in the fashion industry, serve to encourage everything from discriminatory police stop-and-searches to subordinate housing, job and education opportunities.[26]

Frederick Douglass, an escaped slave and leader of the abolition movement, argued that racism exists to benefit the small minority who are in control of society: 'They divided both to conquer each.' Racism divides people so that they do not unite in action to win higher wages or stage a revolution. By this measure, racism comes from its beneficiaries – those who extract huge profits from a divided and distracted society.

In eighteenth- and nineteenth-century cotton-weaving towns like Manchester, while a tiny minority of white people lived lavishly off the backs of black slaves in plantations, the majority of white people lived and died in filthy slums, suffering under a system that thrived on inequality and oppression. This is not to say that working people cannot be racist as well. Competition for jobs and resources leads to surface divisions in society being exploited. Because of this, racism must be fought against in order to unite people to fight for real change.

'Ain't I a Beauty Queen?'

As president of the Council of Fashion Designers of America, Diane Von Fustenburg encouraged the organisation's members to create multicultural fashion shows.[27] But will diversifying catwalks end industry racism or is integration into an exploitative system counterproductive?

In 1968, there were not one but two important protests at the now infamous Miss America beauty pageant. The first was a feminist protest outside the pageant which rejected the idea of Miss America on the grounds that it was sexist and objectified women. At the same time, in the nearby Ritz Carlton Hotel, the NAACP (National Association for the Advancement of Colored People) held a Miss Black America pageant in protest against Miss America being racially segregated.[28] Segregation was formalised by rule 7 of the Miss America rule book: 'Contestants must be of good health and of the white race.'

Many feminists in 1968 could not understand why the black community wanted to be integrated into the exploitation of beauty pageants. They did not appreciate the desire to overcome the dominance of Eurocentric beauty that Miss America perpetuated. In *Ain't I A Beauty Queen?* Maxine Leeds Craig explains that being excluded from the dominant beauty ideal does not mean you escape objectification.[29] Instead, you get a double dose of shame – that of being excluded and that of having an 'unacceptable' body.[30] Whilst the protests unfortunately did not unite to find common ground, both carried important messages about discrimination. The first black contestant to feature in Miss America was Cheryl Browne in 1970, but there was no black contest winner until Vanessa Williams in 1983. In 2013, Nina Davuluri, the first winner of Indian heritage, was subjected to a flood of racist criticism on social media.

Beauty is a site for political resistance, though a problematic one. In *Venus in the Dark*, Janell Hobson questions whether power can ever be achieved from beauty recognition. Do women of colour who have been recognised as 'beautiful' have the power to elevate the status of all women of colour? Are they agents for change or just sex objects?[31] Taking an unequivocal position against the goal of integration, the Black Power activists Stokely Carmichael and Charles Hamilton stated that any black people 'absorbed into a white mass are of no value to the remaining black masses. They become meaningless show-pieces for a conscience-soothed white society.'[32]

The token use of models of colour has certainly been used by the fashion industry to excuse racism. In addition to US *Vogue*'s 'Is Fashion Racist?' edition, *Vogue Italia* has attempted to deflect accusations of racism by producing 'all-black' issues – a tactic that commentators describe as a backward step which reproduces and secures white as 'normal'.[33] *Vogue Italia* is certainly guilty of producing racist shoots, for example, its 2012 *Haute Mess* fashion spread – an offensive parody of stereotyped black and Latina 'ghetto' fashion; or the 'Slave Earrings' scandal in which it advertised gold hoop earrings as bringing to mind 'the decorative traditions of the women of colour who were brought to the southern United States during the slave trade'. After an outcry, the article was changed to an advertisement for 'Ethnic Earrings'. 'Ethnic' as used in the fashion industry is a catch-all phrase designed to group together anyone and anything that is 'not white'.

The fashion media also routinely and wilfully disregard the progress made in combating racism by the rest of society by shooting white models engaging in 'blackfacing', 'redfacing' and 'yellowfacing' (including taping back their eyes). Too many current examples of this racist practice exist to list here. This (mis)representation of African, Native American and Japanese culture gives the impression of having stepped back in time.[34] The pathetic excuse is often given that these shoots are 'just art', as if the fashion industry was not merely enacting and compounding age-old patterns of oppression. When the former *Vogue Paris* editor Carine Roitfeld was accused of racism for blacking up Lara Stone in 2009, she defended herself by saying: 'I once did an entire issue on a black model.'[35]

Despite the complexities, campaigns for fashion diversity are an important anti-racist struggle. Catwalk shows and magazines define beauty by a process of exclusion. This exclusion extends to questions of size, age, class, disability and the minutiae of personal appearance, with race as a fundamental category. Whilst the *Black is Beautiful* campaigns of the 1960s did not bring change to black people's economic life, they were a significant cultural victory which ended one form of discrimination.[36]

Ending catwalk and magazine racism will, however, take more than the inclusion of models of colour. The entire industry also needs diversity. Currently, the role of editors, journalists, casting agents, designers and photographers suffers from 'white opportunity hoarding'.[37] The fact that so many racist fashion shoots are produced points to a serious lack of diversity in the industry. Student selection committees at art schools have also been found rejecting black applicants for citing hip hop as an influence whilst waving through white students who they acknowledge are less talented.[38]

Ending racism in fashion cannot be achieved in isolation. It requires ending racism in society. This requires a systemic change to remove a tiny minority's ability to exclude everyone else; it requires an end to the system that needs racism: capitalism.

Inspiration or Appropriation?

While the people of the world may be rejected, their cultures are commodified and vociferously consumed.[39] In 2012 Urban Outfitters produced a 'Navajo' range of clothes and accessories. The range had no links to Navajo designers or artisans, items merely displayed a faux tribal print. The marketing of inauthentic products using Native American tribal names is outlawed under the Indian Arts And Crafts Act. Amid popular protest, the Navajo Nation served Urban

Outfitters with a cease and desist letter, highlighting their particular objection to the 'Navajo Hip Flask' and the 'Navajo Hipster Panty' which contravened their spiritual beliefs about modesty, and the reservation-wide ban on the consumption of alcohol. Refusing to apologise, Urban Outfitters were sued by the Navajo Nation. Court-ordered mediation failed and a court case is scheduled for 2015 in which Urban Outfitters have submitted a shocking counter claim to cancel the tribe's federal trademark registrations. The fashion industry is notorious for profiting from the co-option and reproduction of cultural dress from across the globe. Fashion has rightly been compared to Godzilla for devouring everything in its path.[40] Designers frequently acknowledge a wide variety of inspirations for their collections. To defend himself against charges of anti-Semitism, John Galliano stated in court: 'I travel the world, not just as a tourist but to understand cultures. I've lived with a Masai tribe.'[41]

This merging of cultures could be taken as a sign of progress, of an inspiring, globalised world in which different cultures are celebrated.[42] Artists after all do not live in isolation and it is impossible not to be influenced by our multi-layered world of international foods, music, clothes, religions, ideas and art. Yet this approach ignores the historical and political context of the spread of culture. While the fusing of cultures can, in part, be celebrated as exchange, for the most part it is the outcome of domination.[43] The cultures of the world have not spread and merged through an organic process of cross-cultural harmony; instead, colonialism and neo-colonialism have resulted in the supplanting and harnessing of those cultures they have encountered.[44] In 2009 Dior provided a disturbing example of this with its 'Fertility Goddess' shoe from Galliano's 'tribal chic' collection. The heel of the strappy shoe was a miniature replica of an African fertility goddess statue. Each step caused the wearer to tread on the goddess, replicating the colonial relationship between Europe and Africa.

The use of Native American designs by giant multinational corporations reflects this deeply unequal relationship whose history is one of subjugation and terror. They represent the theft of cultural identity and lost homelands.[45] In imitation goods, history and meaning are lost: 'Native American people are reduced to one dimensional outdated stereotypes, or worse, as an extinct exotic race that once roamed the land, but who no longer live and breathe and resist today.'[46] This inequality dictates who is allowed to do the appropriating. The sociologist Erving Goffman noted that: 'Immigrants can impersonate Native Americans in dress and in patterns of decorum but it is still a doubtful matter to Americanise one's name or one's nose.'[47]

Cultural appropriation remains a sensitive issue. Many consumers remain resistant to the idea that their $5 feathered earrings are an offensive by-product of oppression and colonialism. A writer from the Cree people explains the need for sensitivity by asking: 'What does the Victoria Cross, the Order of Canada, a framed Bachelor's degree, the Giller Prize, and an eagle feather all have in common?' The answer is that each is a visual recognition of a certain kind of achievement, imbued with important symbolism. Each of these symbols has rules governing its use and imitation will cause offence.[48] Picture, if you will, the effect on a decorated war veteran of seeing fake Victoria Cross earrings being worn to a rave and then tossed in a bin.

Vast profits from fake cultural products rarely translate to jobs or benefits for indigenous communities whose artists are left struggling to make a living from authentic products.[49] In 2012, the designer label Rodarte brought out a collection based on Australian Aboriginal art. An Aboriginal member of the United Nations Permanent Forum on Indigenous Issues described the collection as 'completely insensitive to Aboriginal art, spirituality and land'. Attracting criticism for copying 60,000-year-old rock art, the Rodarte sisters finally stated that whilst they had not been to Australia themselves, they had bought the designs from an Aboriginal artist, the late Benny Tjangala.[50]

Fashion's penchant for imitating culture reinforces the idea that cultural dress is fabulous and exotic when worn by some, but backward when worn by minorities.[51] Chanel can show a *faux*-Indian Paris–Bombay collection at Paris's Grand Palais, Hermès can sell saris costing from $1,800 to $100,000, but the same styles when sold or worn by Indians are considered 'backward'. Similarly a white US citizen, for example, can wear fashions from the subcontinent of

India without taking any of the 'heat' of oppression that goes with these clothes when worn by Indians in the United States.[52]

Calling for cultural traditions to be afforded respect does not mean that people should dress only according to their national identity and eschew all contact with other cultures. As one Native American commentator says: 'It's OK to love our stuff.'[53] To reform the fashion industry there needs to be more diversity – indigenous artists being afforded the same opportunities as corporations to determine what their culture looks like and how it is represented in the global fashion arena.[54] But ending cultural appropriation means overturning the power structures that it mirrors. Ending the racism that appropriation stems from, and the imperialism that it reflects, means ending capitalism and replacing it with a global equality that does not value people based on the colour of their skin.

Fashion's Global Shift

> One hundred or more years ago, our prejudice was that 'mysterious Orientals' were jolly good at arty stuff, at imagery and making fabulous carpets and so forth, not to mention spell-binding poetry and jewellery fabrication. We Westerners on the other hand, and the British in particular, were the hard-headed types who could run factories, build steam locomotives and battleships and generally run an economy. We were practical; they at best were 'charming' in a childlike and rather untrustworthy way. Now, they are the drones who can not only turn out factory-made goods but lend us their savings in order that we may buy these goods. Not to worry, however, because we have the artists, the designers and the creative brains. We have also those personable if somewhat slippery characters in advertising, public relations, marketing and the City.
>
> Who are the charming, feckless, childlike Orientals now?[55]

The waning power of Europe after the Second World War was marked by New York becoming an important fashion centre. Since the start of the economic crisis in 2008 the centre of economic power is shifting again. Whilst in a state of financial disarray, Europe and the United States have witnessed the rise of the BRIC nations – Brazil, Russia, India and China. In 2013 the United States was still the world's largest economy with by far the greatest military arsenal, but China was recognised as the world's factory and for the first time Asia had more billionaires than the United States.[56] It is more than possible that the next generation of powerful corporations will not be American or British and, even if they are, will not be employing American or British workers.[57]

This has major implications for the fashion industry. The fashion supremacy of Europe and the United States has lain all but unchallenged for decades. Partly this is because fashion hubs tend to be located in powerful centres of industrial capital. The industry needs cities full of skilled workers, customers with plenty of money for shopping, and media industries for promotional purposes. Fashion houses need the political and economic clout of a powerful country that can negotiate advantageous terms for its products and establish cultural hegemony for its ideas. As an industrial fashion centre, Paris benefited from industrialists, financiers and the historical encouragement of the French government, which passed laws to prevent copyright infringement. Likewise, Italian industrialists worked closely with their government after the Second World War to create an export-led fashion industry that could rejuvenate the economy.[58]

In 2013 there exist new centres of fashion to challenge the old guard. It was once inconceivable that fashion could be created outside of Paris; now the importance of Fashion Weeks in places like Beijing, Lagos and Rio is growing. As with fatshion, the internet is providing a means for more people to gain a platform in fashion. As a result, designers in a wider range of countries are gaining attention. The question for the established industry will be how to expand its market whilst keeping the club doors closed.

Designer China

What China needs is recognition that it produces designers, not just products. Despite a proliferating industry, China has yet to be accepted as a legitimate fashion power. Unsurprisingly, finding a Chinese fashion star has become something of a preoccupation for Chinese entrepreneurs and journalists. The media mogul Hung Huang (the 'Oprah of China') is a tireless promoter of Chinese fashion. As owner of the Brand New China boutique (BNC), she aims to create a China 'where modern women reject increasingly ubiquitous foreign luxury goods, and their counterfeit reproductions, in favour of raiment designed by local Chinese fashion talent'.[59] Her words must strike fear into the hearts of luxury brands that have come to rely on China as a key market.

The desire for domestic designers is mirrored by China's youth market. Natalie Singh, Head of Youth and Street at WGSN, explains: 'You now have all the Chinese kids out there who want to wear Chinese branded clothing. They want "Made in China" by and for Chinese people. They don't want second best, they want brands that are servicing them.'[60] The longer the effects of the economic crisis are felt, and the longer consumers in Europe become accustomed to living with less, the more domestic markets in places like China will become the focus for brands.[61]

Well aware that there has been a geographical shift of sources of money and power, the industry is responding in two ways. First, existing fashion houses are scrambling to strengthen their appeal to Chinese consumers. Modelling agencies based in the United States hold recruiting competitions in China, and Chinese supermodels are hired for campaigns. Collections like the Louis Vuitton Spring/Summer 2011 collection are so targeted that in a *New York Times* article headlined 'Camping it up in Old Shanghai', the fashion critic Suzy Menkes remarked: 'You didn't need a Master's in Mandarin to get the message that China is hot retail property.' This unsubtle targeting is not always well received. Susanna Lau (Stylebubble) described the look as sometimes replicating 'those weird connotations that traditional Asian dress signifies in Western cultures (docility, demureness, opium-den slutiness, etc.)'.[62]

The second response from the fashion industry is a strengthening of its racist practices to exclude the competition. Edward Said wrote in *Culture and Imperialism*: 'The power to narrate, or block other narratives from forming and emerging, is very important to culture and imperialism.'[63] By seeing the fashion industry as a source of power for multinational corporations and states we see why its racial identity is so closely guarded. Fashion in France directly generates €35 billion in sales each year and employs 150,000 people. France is the world leader in perfumes, cosmetics, *haute couture*, and *haute joaillerie* (exclusive jewellery);[64] it does not want to share this with potentially monolithic Chinese corporations. Becoming inclusive would mean losing the power to exclude.

Exclusion in fashion is characterised by the simultaneous commodification of culture and rejection or racist portrayal of people. *The Economist* describes fashion insiders dismissing Mumbai Fashion Week:

> Foreign buyers complained that although the fabrics were gorgeous, the cuts were often poor, and it was difficult to spot a single trend amid the riot of styles, even within one show. Many Indian designers also lack the organisational skills and infrastructure needed to handle large orders. Veronique Poles, a fashion consultant from Paris, said producing half a dozen of the same frocks could be a stretch for some Indian designers, '*and then getting it delivered on time – pah!*'[65]

'*Anti-Semitic, Homophobic and Ridiculously Snobbish*'

In February 2011 John Galliano was arrested following complaints that he had hurled racist and anti-Semitic abuse in a Paris café. The incident had been filmed and the video went viral. As more reports of racist outbursts surfaced and Natalie Portman, Hollywood star and face of Miss Dior perfume, publicly severed ties with Galliano, he was sacked by both Dior and his namesake label. He was subsequently found guilty of anti-Semitism by a French court. Avoiding jail, he was fined a mere €6,000.

Galliano's role as chief designer at Dior renewed speculation over the behaviour of Christian Dior himself during the Nazi occupation of Paris. Having spent much of the war employed by the couture house of Lucien Lelong, Dior's clients were the wives of Nazi officers and French collaborators.[66]

Whilst she despised Dior's New Look, Coco Chanel also became deeply embedded with the Nazis in Paris. She is described as 'a wretched human being. Anti-Semitic, homophobic, social climbing, opportunistic, ridiculously snobbish, and [she] actively collaborated with the Germans during the Nazi occupation of Paris.'[67] Closing down her fashion house, Chanel spent the occupation of France in the Paris Ritz with Hans Gunther von Dincklage, a spy sent to Paris as part of an advance party preparing for the Nazi invasion. Chanel used laws banning Jewish people from owning businesses to try to rob her partners, the Wertheimers, of the perfume business they had co-founded. Chanel moved in the highest Nazi circles in Paris and even played a part in the failed 'Operation Modelhut' plot, which involved her being an intermediary to Winston Churchill.

Disgraced and arrested in post-war France, Chanel was inexplicably released. Fearing attacks and being forcibly shaved as a *collaboratrice horizontale,* she fled to Switzerland with von Dincklage and lived there in exile for 15 years. Her comeback in the 1950s was coolly received in France. Only the American market saved her from disappearing into obscurity.

Despite this history, Chanel is usually portrayed as a woman who struggled through hardship to liberate women from restrictive clothing and create the 'little black dress'. The film biopic of Chanel starring Audrey Tatou crudely ended before the Second World War. At the time, Tatou was the face of Chanel and the film effectively an hour-and-a-half long advertisement for the brand, – which had an estimated net worth of $18.5 billion in 2013.[68]

Louis Vuitton is another fashion house that aligned itself closely with the Nazi occupiers in Paris. Under the stewardship of Gaston Vuitton, grandson of the founder Louis Vuitton, the company benefited from a close relationship with the occupying forces. The company went so far as to produce busts of the Vichy regime leader Philippe Pétain in their factory. Gaston's son Henry Vuitton was commemorated for his services to Nazi Germany. This history was purposefully suppressed until being exposed in Stephanie Bonvicini's book *Louis Vuitton: A French Saga.* The book was met by silence from the French press – for LVMH (owners of Louis Vuitton) are amongst France's biggest advertisers. A spokesperson for LVMH denied being involved in the lack of coverage of the book: 'We haven't put any pressure on anyone. If the journalists want to censor themselves, then that suits us fine.'[69]

The German designer Hugo Boss owned a small textile company in Metzingen, Germany. One of his early contracts was to manufacture brown shirts for the emerging Nazi Party. By 1938 the firm had become a key supplier of Nazi uniforms, including for the Army, Hitler Youth and the paramilitary SS. As the war progressed, Hugo Boss's factories were staffed by forced labourers from France and Poland, most of whom were women.

These details came to light in 2011 with the publication of the economic historian Roman Koester's *Hugo Boss 1924–1945*. The book was commissioned by the Hugo Boss corporation but Koester denies that this influenced his findings. More than just a business relationship, Hugo Boss was ideologically aligned with the Nazis, having joined the party as early as 1931. He was prosecuted and fined for his involvement after the war.

The Spanish designer Cristóbal Balenciaga designed numerous dresses for Carmen Polo, wife of the fascist dictator General Franco. Fleeing the Spanish Civil War in 1937, Balenciaga moved to Paris, where he also became a designer for the Nazi elite, though he did turn down the opportunity, when asked by Hitler, to help make Berlin a centre for couture. Having closed his fashion house in 1968, Balenciaga came out of retirement in 1972 for just one commission: a wedding dress for General Franco's granddaughter, María del Carmen Martínez-Bordiú.[70]

Should artists be judged by their political beliefs? If so, should we judge their art by the same standards? Whilst disappointing, it should come as no surprise that so many lauded designers collaborated with fascist dictatorships. The Russian Revolutionary leader Leon Trotsky described artists as living 'in a bourgeois milieu, breathing the air of bourgeois salons, they receive and are receiving hypodermic inspirations from their class'.[71] Many top designers would have been sympathetic to Nazism because it was what surrounded them. By 1939, fascist and authoritarian ideology had become the dominant force of the political Right across Europe.[72]

Bourgeois business interests would have also been paramount for these designers: if it is your job to create anything from yachts to furniture to fashion for the very rich, then you are destined to bow to their wants and opinions. In this way, life determines consciousness.[73] It is of course these same fashion houses that continue to clothe dictators today.

Yet making dictators look powerful, and siding with a reactionary authority, involves a criminal loss of principle. Nor is it automatic. Dior's sister Catherine became a noted member of the French Resistance and Elsa Schiaparelli repeatedly turned down invitations to work with Benito Mussolini's fascists in Italy. Who knows how many other creative minds were lost through resisting fascism. So if we reject people's opinions, should we reject their art?

Sometimes an artist's political sympathies are expressed in the content of their work. Dior's collusion with the Nazis arguably echoes in his designs. The Nazis believed women should look virtuous and feminine, and restrict themselves to *Kinder*, Küche, *Kirche* (children, kitchen, church). It was an ideal that Paris fashion houses catered for during the occupation. Dior's restrictive, hyper-feminine form was arguably 'more than merely reactionary, nostalgic and backward looking; it became the persistence in the late 1940s of the romantic styles that had flowered under Nazism'.[74] Portraying this Nazi ideal of womanhood also intersected with the aims of Dior's capitalist cotton-baron backer.

When art and such politics merge, we must reject the art. Beauty should not take precedence over political meaning, as Elizabeth Wilson explains in *Adorned in Dreams*. It would be wrong to view patterns made by people being blown up by shells as 'beautiful' as the Futurists did; or to view Leni Reifenstal's film of Hitler's Nuremberg Rally simply as a great work of light and shade. To do so would be to ignore the meaning of events and allow the pursuit of style to justify cruelty and death.[75]

Yet someone like the resolutely anti-Semitic Coco Chanel could produce an aesthetic that challenged sexist assumptions about women. Sometimes abhorrent people produce art worthy of consideration. This is not to say that wearing Chanel is a progressive act. Chanel products are stamped with the name Chanel and her symbol of linked 'C's. Ironically, people wear them as symbols of liberty and élan as well as luxury and expense. But Chanel was anything but a symbol of freedom: she was a homophobic, anti-Semitic bully who sought to crush liberty.

To edit out the industry's role in bolstering such regimes is a betrayal of those that suffered at the hands of fascists. Edward Said wrote that we are better off exploring history rather than repressing or denying it.[76] Accepting that the fashion industry has a racist past and continues to perpetuate racism today is a step towards preventing a racist future. This involves recognising the realities of the fashion industry – that it is premised on the ability to exclude groups and individuals. This exclusion benefits those that do the excluding and has nothing to do with the actualities of the excluded.[77]

CHAPTER EIGHT

Resisting Fashion

The charge sheet against the fashion industry could read as follows: fashion reinforces racism, sexism, gender stereotypes, class and unequal power relations. Fashion seriously exploits its impoverished workers and its customers. It pushes the values of wealth and greed, and promotes body insecurity and dissatisfaction. Fashion is a monopolised industry with large corporations controlling both the luxury and the mass markets. Corporations control the factories and the shops, the fashion magazines and the cotton fields. Fashion's endless quest for profit means scant regard is ever shown for people, animals or the environment. In an industry that sells itself as a promoter of individuality, the reality is one of conformity with billions of pieces of trend-based clothing churned out each year and sent to identikit stores from Birmingham to Bangkok, with magazines on different continents promoting the same styles.

And yet fashion is for many people an immense source of joy and a means for creative expression. This and the next two chapters examine attempts to change the fashion system so we can keep the good and exorcise the grim. This chapter looks at resisting the fashion industry – what happens when people use their clothing and appearance to defy fashion; Chapter 9 examines attempts to reform the industry; and Chapter 10 explores the possible impact of revolution on fashion.

Attention Seekers, Lost Boys, Sceptics and Protesters

Throughout Western history clothing has defined people's roles, status and gender. In recent history, clothing has also been used as a means for protesting against these definitions and against society. Examples of dramatic, norm-defying dress include Punks with their tampon earrings, Harajuku Kids in Tokyo, Thai Rastas and Goths in Moscow. Immediately, a question arises: Are these not merely expressions of personal style rather than significant attempts to change society?

There is no single reason why people use their clothes for rebellion.[1] Some people dress differently merely to shock and gain attention, some do it to lampoon something in society they detest, some are relieving boredom and sometimes fashion is alienation masquerading as individuality.[2] A jaded photographer summed up the Harajuku scene in Tokyo: 'The rest of their lives are going to be crap, so they might as well enjoy themselves while they can.'[3] Others avoid fashion as 'conservative sceptics'; they are opposed to the latest bizarre trend the industry is attempting to foist on them rather than against fashion *per se*.[4] But there are people for whom style is protest, a way of making a deliberate political point about their plight or the plight of others.

Some commentators argue that a wide variety of styles shows fashion to be a system of expression in which people express chosen meanings through their clothes.[5] Yet whilst clothes are a form of non-verbal communication, they are not simply a phenomenon of communication or culture. Clothes are not just signs.[6]

Ideology

> The ideas of the ruling class are in every epoch the ruling ideas, i.e. the class which is the ruling material force of society, is at the same time its ruling intellectual force. The class which has the means of material production at its disposal, has control at the same time over the means of mental production.
>
> The ruling ideas are nothing more than the ideal expression of the dominant material relationships, the dominant material relationships grasped as ideas.[7]
>
> Karl Marx

Fashion is ideology. The statement 'thin is beautiful' is an example of the ideology pushed by the industry. 'Black models are not aspirational' is another example; 'Fashion means European' is another, and on goes the list.

These ideas necessarily benefit the status quo. They reinforce class relations and allow the ruling class to establish, sustain and reproduce their position of power.[8] Under sumptuary laws certain colours and materials were illegal for all but the nobility. One demand of the Peasants' Revolt in Germany in the sixteenth century was the right to wear red.[9] Today, the pricing of brands enacts the same hierarchy. If you are rich you can dress in Dior, Prada and Lanvin; if you are poor you must dress more or less in Primark, F&F at Tesco and New Look. This makes fashion a signifier of difference that lets class appear natural and legitimate. Malcolm Bernard, in *Fashion as Communication*, describes how dressing expensively is used by the upper classes who are eagerly, if not frantically, trying to naturalise their higher status through fashion and clothing.[10]

So what of those who reject ruling-class beauty ideals, who shout with both their voices and their dress that the Emperor is naked and relying on society's silent obedience to his ideologies? Punk is one such form of dress that challenges beauty ideals. Its confrontational assault on the aesthetic values of the dominant classes arguably makes Punk ideologically opposed to capitalism itself.[11]

Challenging ruling-class ideology is a dangerous path to take. To prevent disobedience, society metes out punishments to those who disobey fashion etiquette. Dress can influence the ability to gain employment, rent a flat, avoid assault or arrest, be found 'not guilty', get a visa, appear in the media, win elections, get on planes, make friends or marry the person you love.

Rebel with a Cause

Despite these risks, and the role of fashion in enforcing ideology in society, does dressing differently really count as rebellion against the fashion system? After all, donning the anarchist uniform of vegan trainers and all black clothes is hardly guerrilla warfare. What would a serious challenge to society's material relations look like? When trying to bring about change, does it matter how we dress? Is how we dress really anything more than an individual act? Does it count as resistance?

In his autobiography, Malcolm X rejects attempts to use style to defy the system despite having been a rebellious 'zoot-suiter' in his youth. The 'zoot suit riots' took place primarily in Los Angeles in the early 1940s. White servicemen and the authorities clashed with disaffected Latino and Black youth who wore the zoot suit to reject a society that rejected them. Zoot suits were flashy. With long jackets and wide legs, they used far more material than was considered patriotic whilst rationing was in place. Zoot suit 'girl gangs', like the Slick Chicks and Black Widows, wore feminised versions of the zoot suit.[12]

For Malcolm X (later influenced by the conservative mindset of the Nation of Islam) dressing outlandishly became a distraction from 'real' resistance. Today, some argue that fashion acts as a pressure-valve enabling disgruntled elements in society to let off steam that would otherwise build up.[13] There is no reason, however, why dressing differently should necessarily be a substitute for politics or engagement with serious issues.

The correct way to define resistance is widely debated in James C. Scott's *Weapons of the Weak*. Conventional political wisdom states that 'real' resistance needs to be 'a) organised, systematic and cooperative; b) principled or selfless; c) have revolutionary consequences; and/or d) embody ideas or intentions that negate the basis of discrimination itself'. Dressing as a Goth is arguably none of these things, even if done *en masse*. It could be dismissed as token, incidental and not aiming to change the structures of society because it is 'a) unorganised, unsystematic and individual; b) opportunistic and self-indulgent; c) has no revolutionary consequences; and/or d) implies in its intention/meaning an accommodation with the system of domination'.[14]

Scott makes the compelling argument that it was scattered and isolated (though numerous) desertions from the Tsarist army in 1917 that made the Russian Revolution possible.[15] According to Scott, whilst acts are rare and isolated, they are of little consequence, but when a consistent pattern appears it is resistance.[16] He argues that to dismiss individual acts of resistance is fundamentally to misconstrue daily life for those living under oppression, because most people are simply trying to survive day by day.

A similar argument has been made with regard to rebellious dressing by African-American women in the 1960s. The popularity of the Afro hairstyle grew in support of the political prisoner Angela Davis. As Davis herself states, this led to the largely forgotten arrest and harassment of hundreds of black women who were persecuted as Davis look-a-likes.[17] Whilst for some, clothes, accessories and hairstyles might be their only means of political engagement, what links desertions from the Tsarist army with Afro hairstyles is the fact that there were significant movements behind them both. In Russia there was a large Bolshevik-led revolutionary movement agitating wholeheartedly for dissent, and in the United States there was a growing Black Power movement.

Whilst the Punks of 1970s Britain endured a certain level of oppression, there are far more extreme examples of people using clothing to resist. Under the system of slavery in Jamaica, slave-owners instigated practices designed to strip slaves of 'their pride, their dignity and, most of all, their African identity'.[18] Steeve O. Buckridge describes in *The Language of Dress* how slaves were given clothes made of osnaburg linen by their owners, a uniform meant to humiliate and rob them of their cultural dress practices. Yet these fabrics were fashioned and accessorised to reflect African modes and aesthetics. This was one way for the slaves to prevent cultural alienation and hence psychic annihilation. Clothes became the means to rebel, signifying absolute resistance to the theft of self-definition, history and culture.[19]

Clothing has frequently been used as one, but not the only, method for women to resist oppression, particularly whilst under colonial rule. Yoruba women resisted the British occupation of Nigeria by wearing only their traditional clothes and speaking to the authorities only in Yoruba – their medium for expressing far-reaching dissent.[20] For women in Palestine during the First Intifada, the traditional *shawal* was frequently modified into a Palestinian 'flag dress', worn to signify resistance to the Israeli occupation.[21]

Dress *can* be an act of resistance and a powerful force in resistance movements, particularly amongst women. Its significance, however, depends on whether there is a movement behind it. Fashion and clothing should be seen as simmering dissent not as a decisive and final revolutionary act.[22]

Refusal

In *Fashion as Communication* Malcolm Bernard identifies 'refusal' and 'reversal' as two key forms of resistance in dress, refusal being the attempt to separate yourself from offensive power structures and reversal being the attempt to reverse the power and privilege around which the power structures revolve.[23]

Punk

She lounges against a lamppost, a safety pin through one ear and another through her nose, her hair has been shaved except for two bleached cat ears on the top of her head. Her leather jacket is ripped and the scowl on her face completes a wholesale rejection of all things pretty or acceptable. She is Punk, a classic instance of 'refusal'. In Britain, Punk was most prominent in the late 1970s and early 1980s, decades when disaffected working-class youth faced rising unemployment and limited opportunities. A severe form of refusal, Punk was an anti-authority reaction to a system that left many people disenfranchised: 'Beneath the clownish make-up there lurked the unaccepted and disfigured face of capitalism.'[24]

The Women's Liberation Movement

The radical women of the Women's Liberation Movement also refused fashion. They rejected the outlandish make-up of the 1980s, as well as the decade's high heels, tight clothes, short skirts and anything else considered sexualised and repressive.[25] The movement resented society's fixation with youth, beauty, thinness and a narrow sense of the erotic. They believed that women had been indoctrinated into spending far too much time on their appearance, and that clothing designated for women actually (not just symbolically) subjugated them.[26]

Fictitious bra-burning stories gained notoriety because they fitted so well with the belief that feminists wanted to destroy anything they felt oppressed them. A 'Women's Libber' was stereotypically portrayed wearing a boilersuit and Doc Martens, with a make-up free face and severely cropped hair.

The hijab

Some 50 years ago experts predicted the *hijab* would soon disappear; at the start of the twenty-first century, it is firmly in the ascent.[27] *Hijab* fashion is widespread and diverse; there are literally hundreds of ways to wear the headscarf. When she first began researching *A Quiet Revolution: The Veil's Resurgence from the Middle East to America*,

Leila Ahmed was alarmed by its resurgence. Yet what she found fundamentally challenged, even reversed, her initial expectations.

After the 2001 bombings of the World Trade Center and the start of the so-called War on Terror, the wearing of the *hijab*, *niqab* and *burqa* suddenly emerged as a matter of state for Western nations. Anti-feminist, pro-war hawks in both the United States and the United Kingdom repeatedly used Muslim women to justify imperial war and domination. This was the same hypocritical tactic used by the colonialist Lord Cromer in Egypt in the late 1800s.[28]

Historically, when faced with such a climate, movements like Black is Beautiful have reacted to painful prejudice by proudly reasserting their scorned identity.[29] This is what happened with the *hijab*. Faced with attack and a polarising society, many women chose to take up the *hijab* as 'an affirmation of identity and community, of pride in heritage, of rejection or resistance to, or even protest against, mainstream society'.[30]

Further polarisation took place as *hijab* bans came into force around the world. This was typified by France where in 2004 the *hijab* was banned in schools. In 2011 another French law banned face coverings in public – a law aimed primarily at the *niqab* and *burqa*. For the French philosopher Alain Badiou, the *hijab* ban was the result of two things: fear and capitalism. Badiou described the ban as a capitalist law that removed a woman's right to undress only when she wants to: 'Whoever covers up what she puts on the market is not a loyal merchant.'[31]

Primarily, attacks on Muslim women's dress have been part of an imperialist agenda seeking support for war. If Muslim societies can be framed as needing to catch up with 'civilised' societies, then war looks justified as a civilising and liberating force. Certainly, there is a feeling amongst many Muslim women that they are exhausted by the debate over their dress and that they want to be judged by what's in their head not what's on their head.

* * *

Refusal styles encounter one insurmountable problem – there is no escape from planet fashion. You can refuse to participate in the system but unless you overthrow it, it will still be there when you open your eyes. Regardless of how you dress, you are still living in a capitalist system. Even the most covered-up woman will still encounter thousands of fashion messages telling her she is too fat, too dark or too ugly. Committing to wearing a boilersuit for the rest of your life does nothing to help the oppressed women in China who made that boilersuit. Home-made or second-hand clothes are still produced using materials made under capitalism. It is impossible to refuse to participate.

Reversal

Reversal is an act of resistance that attempts to reverse positions of power and privilege. It has most frequently been used as a tactic by women or women's advocacy groups in an attempt to change the position of women in society, particularly with regard to the right to wear controversial, bifurcated articles of clothing – in other words, trousers.

Trouser-wearing women

It is important to note that whilst trousers for women were controversial in Europe and the United States in the nineteenth century, they were worn by women in many other parts of the world. Albanian Muslim women wore trousers in the nineteenth century as did Mughal Indian women in the early seventeenth century and Mongolian, Inuit and Japanese women throughout the ages.[32] Debates about trousers for women often ignore these cultures as people without fashion.

The dress reformers of nineteenth-century North America chose fashion as their site to challenge long-standing beliefs about women. In *Pantaloons and Power* Gayle Fischer describes how reformers wanted to show that rather than just being a covering for the body, clothing was a powerful cultural symbol, emblematic of women's place in society.[33] In nineteenth-century North America, trousers for women were completely socially unacceptable. Women were expected to be ornaments, devoted to and dependent on pleasing men.[34] Fashion consisted of debilitating corsets, layers of petticoats and floor-length dresses that restricted movement. Dress reformers advocated knee-length dresses worn over pantaloons. Amelia Bloomer, after whom the bloomer outfit is named, wrote: 'The costume of women should conduce at once to her health, comfort, and usefulness; and, while it should not fail also to conduce to her personal adornment, it should make that end of secondary importance.'

As a campaign, dress reform emphasised individual change rather than changing state or national laws; having failed to gain momentum, it fizzled out by 1879.[35] Over the next century trousers for women slowly gained acceptance in Europe. In 1911 the daring 'harem skirt' was presented as part of a collection in Paris.[36] During the two world wars women agricultural and munitions workers wore trousers to work. The 1920s saw women gain the right to bare arms and a bit of leg as leisurewear became more daring, and cycling and swimming became acceptable for females. In the 1930s Hollywood stars like Marlene Dietrich and Katharine Hepburn eroticised and glamorised trousers for women. But it was not until the 1960s that trousers became a widespread female fashion after André Courrèges showed trouser-suits for Spring 1964. By the late 1960s women in the West wearing jeans had become widespread.[37]

Trousers threaten conservative elements because they represent male power, independence, ease of movement, physical work and sexual independence – the alarming spectacle of both promiscuity and non-participation. In 2009, the Sudanese journalist Lubna Ahmed al-Hussein was put on trial for wearing trousers – an act considered indecent under Sudan's strict morality laws. Rather than use the immunity granted to her by her job as a UN worker, Hussein resigned from her post and insisted on a public trial to which she wore the trousers that had resulted in her arrest. Facing imprisonment and 40 public lashes Hussein told journalists: 'When I was in court I felt like a revolutionary standing before the judges. I felt as if I was representing all the women of Sudan.'[38] The court found Hussein guilty and, whilst sparing her the lash, fined her the equivalent of $200.

Far from being an isolated case, in 2008 alone 43,000 women were arrested in Khartoum state for clothing offences, with the chief of police unable to say how many of these women were flogged. Lubna

Ahmed al-Hussein continues to fight for women's rights: 'Islam does not say whether a woman can wear trousers or not. The clothes I was wearing when the police caught me – I pray to my God in them. Let them show me what the Qur'an or Prophet Muhammad said on that issue. There is nothing.'[39]

For all its liberal talk, the fashion industry remains rigidly divided into 'menswear' and 'womenswear'.[40] Yet it has recently taken to its heart a number of models who model both male and female clothing. Andrej Pejić is a male model with long blonde hair best known for womenswear catwalk appearances and lingerie campaigns. Saskia de Brauw and Erika Linder ('I have too much imagination to be just one gender') are female models who also model menswear. Another line was crossed in December 2012 when Casey Legler, a woman, was signed to Ford exclusively as a male model.

Sycophantic Surrender?

Reversal styles can challenge ideas about gender and women's role in society. But they become problematic when they tacitly subscribe to the idea that male is superior. Simple reversal implies that the world according to (ruling-class) men is the only viable one. If the purpose of reversal dress is to be radical, why sycophantically surrender to the dress code of men?[41] Why does 'gender-neutral' clothing always look like men's clothing when shirts, ties, smart shoes and suit jackets are hated work uniforms for many men and symbols of exclusion and oppression for most working-class men and women? Why does the 'gender-neutral' body have to resemble that of an emaciated young boy?

Nor is reversal automatically a challenge to the underlying structures of society. The assumption of reversal is that it is enough to reverse roles and attributes rather than challenge the underlying structure that has created such inequality.[42] Some female hip hop emcees adopt the language, attitude and dress of male gangster rap emcees, often expressing misogyny against other women and an exploitative attitude towards men. This chauvinism also sometimes occurs amongst women in the LGBT community, causing some women to work actively against this outcome. In *Female Chauvinist*

Pigs Ariel Levy outlines the danger of women deriding other women: 'Attacking femaleness, deriding "girly stuff" and rolling your eyes at "women's issues" are expressions of internalized sexism. If that's the way you feel about your own sex you'll be doomed to feel inferior no matter what you achieve in life.'[43]

Shock Value

Punk is on the catwalks, Che Guevara t-shirts are everywhere, the Palestinian *keffiyeh* has become 'as ubiquitous as leopard print'[44] and 'Liberty' is a shop not a slogan. Nothing is sacred; everything is up for replication. This precedent was set in the 1800s when African headwraps styled by Jamaican slaves were copied by rich white women as an 'island fashion'.[45]

There is an almost numbing inevitability to co-option. Punk, whilst a genuine movement, was nonetheless propelled by shrewd entrepreneurs who were key to both defining and marketing the Punk look.[46] Vivienne Westwood and Malcolm McLaren (manager of the Sex Pistols) ran the Kings Road shop SEX which stocked Punk and S&M-style clothing. Whilst they did not invent Punk, much of their work captured and commodified the movement. Punk's strategy of refusal was no defence against appropriation, and in the end Punk was both a product and a victim of capitalism. After a few explosive years it was incorporated into the mass market.[47]

Yet its political roots mean there are examples of Punk surviving amongst disaffected youth. In Burma there is an underground Punk scene which exists in dangerous opposition to the oppressive regime. Then there is the Russian Punk scene, made famous by the imprisoned Punk band Pussy Riot. For many, Punk is not a trend or a game.

The incorporation of the Women's Lib aesthetic was more subtle but no less real. Malcolm Bernard notes that the 'make-up-free' look is big business, with 'barely there' products and 'how to get the natural look' articles clogging magazines. It is a look that has become highly commodified, with at least eight cosmetic products needed to get a 'natural' face. The custom of going bra-less, and as a result having visible nipples, which started as a protest against patriarchy and female-specific clothing, has also become highly eroticised.[48] Nor are boilersuits or dungarees now a radical option, with celebrities such as Rihanna and Cheryl Cole photographed wearing sexualised versions of them in the *Daily Mail.*

Before the aesthetic and political values of Punk and Women's Liberation were appropriated, society used them to push the politics of both movements to the fringes of society. This is yet another risk faced by any group refusing fashion: they can become isolated[49] as society dictates: *They look mad, so they must be mad – just ignore them.*

The co-option of a style partly depends on the proximity of a subculture to the fashion industry. New York's gay scene and the city's Black and Latino communities have a close sociological proximity to the New York fashion industry, and have a greater influence on fashion than, say, the farmers of Utah, who are sociologically separated from the fashion industry.[50] One London designer described the process of artistic inspiration: 'You're like a sponge; you draw in anything that is close to you.'[51]

This demonstrates the dialectical relationship of fashion and resistance fashion. As Fred Davis notes in *Fashion, Culture and Identity,* they are interdependent and need each other to evolve. Resistance fashion must necessarily acknowledge and oppose mainstream fashion.[52] The wearing of Yoruba clothing by Nigerian women was empowering *because* they were casting aside the dress of the British authorities which they had been told was the 'civilised' way to dress. Mainstream fashion, on the other hand, financially benefits enormously from the constant flow of rebel fashions that emerge.

Keffiyeh or Topshop Tea Towel?

Fashion was labelled 'capitalism's favourite child' by the fashion academic Valerie Steele.[53] It has the ability to take even the most controversial fashion and make millions from it. The *keffiyeh* is a symbol of Palestinian resistance against Israel, its black-and-white chequered pattern historically seen in newsreels of Yasser Arafat, Leila Khaled and Palestinian resistance fighters. With the Second Intifada and Israel's barbaric Operation Cast Lead in Winter 2008–9, support for the Palestinians grew, and in Europe – and London in particular – *keffiyehs* became fashionable as a symbol of pro-Palestinian and anti-imperialist sentiment. Fast-forward a few months and the *keffiyeh* had transitioned into a 'multi-ethnic desert scarf' available in every shop and stall on the high street, in a wide range of colours. Balenciaga sold *keffiyehs* for $2,000 each.

Fearing the *keffiyeh* had been stripped of political meaning, those campaigning for Palestine were not happy. Tracks by the pro-Palestinian rapper Lowkey, who had been key to popularising the *keffiyeh*, were littered with references like 'I rock a *keffiyeh* not a Topshop tea towel' and 'Before you speak, learn the meaning of that scarf on your neck'. Nor were the pro-Israeli Right happy. One US blogger equated the *keffiyeh* with 'modifying Klan-style hoods in Burberry plaid as the next big thing'.[54] Symbols of Palestinian resistance were suddenly everywhere, causing controversy in Eurostar adverts and around the necks of pop stars. So who benefited most from the *keffiyeh* trend? Was it the pro-Palestinian movement, the pro-Israeli lobby or Topshop?

Sections of the pro-Israeli lobby may have hoped that the mass manufacture of 'desert scarves' would take the sting out of the *keffiyeh*. But this did not happen. No lasting damage was done to the pro-Palestinian movement by its popularisation. Demonstrations and campaigns continued regardless. Throughout the 'trend' it was easy to tell a *keffiyeh* from a Topshop tea towel and conversations about Palestine were sparked across the globe.

Topshop, Primark, Balenciaga and any other brand that brought out an imitation scarf certainly benefited. Whilst these companies could not neutralise the politics behind the print, they used the trend to make money. Companies took the ideas of rebellion and freedom associated with the *keffiyeh* and transferred it wholesale into their brand. The Palestinian cause is, however, big and potent enough to weather a storm-in-a-teacup like the 'desert scarf'. Palestine is remembered for Palestine, not for a fashion trend.

Co-option

There are smaller movements that have not been as lucky. In 1980s New York there was an underground network of young, gay, primarily black men who danced and posed dressed as glamorous cultural icons – an impressionistic dance style that became known as 'Voguing'. One academic described the young men as being deeply oppressed as outsiders, racially, sexually and because they were effeminate and poor. The Vogue Movement both parodied and affirmed the dream of being on the front cover of a magazine.[55] The co-option by Madonna and Warner Brothers that took place with the song 'Vogue' is common knowledge, unlike the back-story of the oppression of the Vogue Movement. Whilst some argued that Madonna had given the Movement a voice, the fact that the original message was 'lost in a sea of hand gestures' implies that what took place was little more than the exploitation of an oppressed minority.[56]

The sad truth is that resistance styles never really threaten the fashion industry. The industry is so capable of not just absorbing shocks and controversy but of benefiting from them, that it is even able to call for its own demise. For Spring/Summer 1990 Moschino ran an advertising campaign entitled *Stop the Fashion System*, which featured vampiric models crossed out in red paint. The designer Franco Moschino once remarked: 'Fashion is full of chic.' He spent much of his time criticising the fashion industry, producing jackets embroidered with the slogan *Expensive Jacket*, belts that read *Waist of Money* and, in 1989, a coat made from teddy bear pelts. Yet Moschino was celebrated by the people he purported to insult: 'He mocked top fashion editors by leaving moo-boxes on their seats, implying they were dull bovines with not an original thought in their heads, but they applauded all the more.'[57]

These 'insults' are actually a sign of extreme confidence. What Moschino was displaying was great self-assurance in both his company and the fashion system. If ever there is something to be wary of, it is the self-effacing brand.[58] This double bluff is a useful example of the industry's ability to commodify revolt. Moschino's attempt to defy and denounce propelled him to the very top of what he hated.[59]

This is also what happens when resistance takes place outside the fashion industry. Whilst Punk was confrontational statement dressing, anti-consumerist Grunge was, as Jean Paul Gaultier noted, 'nothing more than the way we dress when we have no money'.[60]

Bands like Nirvana, with their unwashed hair, plaid shirts and ripped sneakers, were Grunge icons.

Despite the anti-consumerist origins of Grunge, the fashion industry swiftly set to work. Several designers co-opted it. Marc Jacobs was fired from Perry Ellis for a collection so controversial it was never produced. Grunge was not a popular style for the fashion elite. Suzy Menkes led the opposition by handing out *Grunge is Ghastly* badges – an ironic use of the badge which is a staple of the Grunge look.

Thus even the ultimate not-making-a-statement fashion can become a fashion statement. One commentator noted the 'painful irony in social rebels having to view the signs of their rebellion sported in exquisite materials by those they thought they were rebelling against'.[61] The dialectical relationship between the fashion industry and resistance fashion means that resistance is simply absorbed, repackaged and sold back to us.

Resisting Fashion

In the early 1990s Fred Davis envisaged that fashion would soon stop being trend-driven and resistance fashion – what he called anti-fashion – would have nothing to rebel against. Would this, he asked, lead to those engaging in anti-fashion being forced to find less benign ways to express their discontent?[62] Over 20 years later fashion is still trend-driven and the industry has speeded up. The advent of fast-fashion has increased the industry's ability to absorb and resell resistance fashion.[63] Styles are 'trend-spotted' and reproduced within weeks.

Reproduction should not be mistaken for democracy. First, the ability of multinational corporations to reproduce items like the *keffiyeh* and retain all the profits is far from democratic. There is no social equality in this system and no means for people to exercise control over the corporations they buy from (the idea of shopping and 'dollar votes' as democracy is discussed in Chapter 9). This approach also confuses democracy with the so-called free market.[64] What does it matter what is available in the shops when the underlying problems that made people resist in the first place go untouched?

Second, we are far from the tolerant utopia imagined by some postmodernists. In the 12 months that I have been writing this book, 265 people have been murdered simply for being themselves, for being transgender, for wearing the 'wrong' clothes.[65] Authorities react to baggy jeans by expelling children from schools and preventing people from boarding planes. Women are being blamed for being raped if they wear mini-skirts, or sacked, excluded from school and attacked for wearing the *hijab*. A true aesthetic democracy will only be possible once full democracy has been attained, when neither the ownership of beauty nor society's means of production are in the hands of the few, and when racism, sexism and class are no more.

The movements showcased in this chapter have been resisting more than just fashion, but they have used clothes to make their point. Many resistance fashion movements have achieved important outcomes as part of the battles waged by progressive forces. As a means for challenging capitalism, however, the conclusion must be that resistance fashion alone does not mount a serious challenge to capitalism. It was best explained by the outspoken environmentalist fashion designer Katharine Hamnett as 'a combination of a threat and a Fortnum's hamper'.[66]

Resistance both challenges and fuels fashion. Dress is most useful serving as a tool to keep resistance alive, to maintain cultural identity in the face of oppression and to inspire people towards a new dawn. As with African slaves in Jamaica, rebellious cultural practices have been described by the feminist academic bell hooks as nourishing the capacity to resist.[67]

We have not reached a point where people can dress in a gender-free style, for example, but imagining what that might look like could cause the imaginations of an entire generation to soar. The role of art in prompting imagination is essential, since without the ability to imagine new worlds, we have little hope of building one.

Encouraging freedom of expression for individuals can also lead people to see that fashion and beauty ideals are just ideologies put in place to benefit the ruling class. This is part of bringing capitalism into focus rather than it being too close to the lens to be objectified. Once capitalism is visible, it can be challenged.

Resistance fashion's primary characteristic is that it is not an organised response to capitalism. It is disparate rather than united, its participants rarely have stated aims and it occurs haphazardly. What then would happen if those who want out of the fashion system came up with an organised purpose and tried to unite? This is the subject of Chapter 9, which examines movements that aim to act collectively in their fashion choices.

CHAPTER NINE

Reforming Fashion

Join us in rejecting the ti(red) notion that shopping
is a reasonable response to human suffering.
Buylesscrap.com

Of all the tragic and disturbing issues discussed in this book, it is the subject matter in this chapter that has so far proved the most provocative. To reform capitalism or to overthrow it, that is the question. These positions are sometimes incorrectly paraphrased: stick plasters over gaping wounds and try to save a few souls while millions are condemned to barbarism, or wait hopelessly for an almighty change that may never come.

The setting for this chapter is not a factory in China or a mall in New York but rather the family kitchen of some good friends of mine in the North of England, where I went to stay part-way through writing this book. Spotting a brochure for an Indian clothing co-operative on the kitchen table, I (unhelpfully) offered to tell my stressed-out, overworked friend everything that was wrong with both the company and the premise of 'ethical fashion'. Since my friend had ordered clothes for her children from the catalogue, it is unsurprising that a heated argument ensued. She yelled that waiting for a revolution before doing anything was immoral and I yelled back that trying to reform capitalism was a naïve and damaging distraction from reality.

Eventually, we agreed that we had the same outcome in mind, but were suggesting different means of getting there. Arguments about the politics of clothing, like arguments about the politics of food, become heated very quickly because they feel so personal. Clothing is presented to us as a question of individual choice. On the surface the choice seems simple: 'good clothes' or 'evil clothes'. If you choose the 'good' clothing you are virtuous; if you pick the 'evil' clothing you are 'evil'. Whilst it makes sense to buy the least harmful option when purchasing any product, what about the myriad factors that determine 'choice'? Class is the primary factor. You buy what you can afford. If you cannot afford £16 for a pair of knickers, then it does not matter that they are handcrafted in Britain from organic cotton; you will have to buy five pairs for £3 from Primark – and will probably feel guilty and ashamed for doing so.

It is no coincidence that we have been steered into the dead-end of viewing clothing as an individual issue. This goes right to the very heart of neoliberalism – a system that teaches us that empowerment comes from acting individually (not collectively), that freedom means variety in what we consume, and that we should trust in the system and shop (not fight) our way to a new world.

There is no way out of sweatshop labour or environmental devastation via an individual route. You cannot shop workers in China to freedom. You cannot shop the Aral Sea back to life. The neoliberal mindset that permeates the fashion industry must be shaken off because it is dangerous nonsense. Rather, we must confront the issues in this book critically and with a collectivist anti-capitalist attitude. We do have agency on an individual level but we must confront the challenges ahead collectively and with a realistic assessment of the barriers that people face. Marx defined this contradiction: 'Men and women make their own history, but they do not make it as they please; they do not make it under self-selected circumstances, but under circumstances existing already, given and transmitted from the past.'

That is why constructive argument over the issues contained in this chapter is important. We must recognise who the real enemies are, and all those wanting change must learn to work together on their common ground. The differences in opinion between people wanting change are tiny when compared to the gulf between us and that of, say, Kansas oil barons like the Koch brothers. Angela Davis quoted a Betsy Rose song on this point: 'We may have come here on different ships, but we're in the same boat now.'[1]

Contention arises in the last three chapters of this book because they represent the starting point for action. Once you decide you want to change the world, you then have to decide how to go about it and there will naturally be differences in opinion. Realistic assessment and debate over what works and what does not is the only way forward. In this chapter I look at several methods for organised reform of the fashion industry: people organising collectively as consumers, shopping differently to change the world; government-led reform; the increasing trend for 'reform' amongst multinational corporations; and finally trade union-led worker reform.[2]

An Early Challenge

The fashion industry has long caused revulsion. In 1889, horror at the sweatshops of newly industrialised North America prompted the social reformers Jane Addams and Ellen Starr to found Hull House in Chicago, a community of reformers who worked on education and healthcare projects. One Hull House resident was Florence Kelley, a social reformer and friend of Engels.[3] Kelley conducted fieldwork in the square mile surrounding Hull House and found children as young as three working in tenement sweatshops.[4] She later attained the unprecedented position of being appointed as the state's first factory inspector by newly elected Governor John P. Altgeld. Her research led to the state of Illinois prohibiting the employment of children under the age of 14 and limiting women and children to a maximum eight-hour day. In 1895, however, the Illinois Association of Manufacturers had the law declared unconstitutional.

Alice Woodbridge, another campaigner and secretary of the Working Women's Society, carried out detailed research into the working conditions of women in the New York retail sector. Her reports prompted the social reformer Josephine Shaw Lowell to found the New York Consumers League in 1890. The League researched and publicised the plight of exploited women and children and sought to protect consumers from overpricing and poor-quality goods. One of the first investigations carried out by the League was into working conditions for those making cotton underwear.[5] The League emphasised the ability of consumers to bring about change by buying only from companies who treated their workers with respect.[6] It published a White List advising shoppers which companies paid fair wages and had reasonable hours and sanitary conditions. As other cities established Consumer Leagues, in 1899 Josephine Shaw Lowell and Jane Addams chartered the National Consumers League (NCL) and invited Florence Kelley to New York to become its general secretary.

Kelley's pioneering programmes included the issuing of a 'White Label' that could be used by certified companies to prove that their products had been made under fair working conditions and without child labour. She organised consumers to boycott sweatshop-produced clothing, stating: 'To live means to buy, to buy means to have power, to have power means to have responsibility.'[7] As a committed socialist, she taught that real change would not come until the roots of social ills were addressed, rather than just its symptoms.

Ethical Calculus

Our wardrobes are today the meeting point for two premises – that the fashion industry is responsible for widespread devastation and misery and that it is our behaviour as consumers that is to blame. Many small businesses now offer 'ethical fashion' as a solution. Ethical fashion has become a catch-all phrase encompassing issues such as environmental toxicity, labour rights, air miles, animal cruelty and product sustainability. After 20 or so years and despite some innovative initiatives, it holds an 'exceptionally low market share' at just over 1 per cent of the overall apparel market.[8]

An abundance of books advise on ethical fashion. Many share recurring themes which limit their ability to provide a satisfactory solution to fashion's problems. A central dilemma for ethical fashion is how to prioritise all the issues thrown up by the industry. One book explains that there is no 'simple list of moral ticks and crosses' with which to decide which is most important.[9] Is it better to buy a dress sewn in a co-op in India which uses thousands of freight miles or a locally manufactured dress from a company that uses fur trim? Is it better to buy organic cotton jeans from a retailer who shuns workplace safety regulations, or conventional pesticide ridden jeans from a regulated retailer? How about a recycled polyester fleece which sheds synthetic lint fibres and contaminates oceans, beaches and marine life?[10] Is it better to buy vegetarian shoes made in a Chinese sweatshop or leather from a designer who says fat people are ugly?

The unhelpful solution proffered by ethical fashion books is for consumers to try an 'ethical calculus' to figure out which issues matter most.[11] This inability to provide a decent answer stems from not wanting to name capitalism as the cause of the problem. The founder of a sustainable fashion label did provide a sensible answer from a design point of view: 'When approaching sustainability, concentrate your efforts on the area where you can make the biggest difference.'[12] This still leaves consumers with what one ethical fashion guide called 'the knotty question of which ethical standards matter the most'.[13] By not recognising the capitalist system as being responsible for the ills of the industry, these books seek other sources of blame, like consumer apathy or human greed.

Because they do not name capitalism as the problem, ethical fashion books are forced to look to unlikely sources for salvation. As well as urging people to buy less, most ethical fashion books read like a shopping list, with brands and products advertised on every page. Readers will often be surprised to read positive reviews of the very companies that made them concerned enough to pick up the book in the first place. *Green is the New Black* lists Nike, Sainsbury's, Tesco and Topshop amongst its 'high street heroes'. *Heart On Your Sleeve*, an Oxfam publication, also lists Topshop as a place to find ethical clothes, along with M&S and Gap. Predicting that these lists might appear contradictory, *Green is the New Black* states: 'If you have a problem with big corporations, remember that they are the ones with power, and if they change, it creates big waves that really make a difference. Even if it is all a big PR promotion, what does it matter?'[14]

It matters both because this is a neoliberal mindset and because PR promotions obscure the reality of corporate practices. In June 2011 the Institute for Global Labour and Human Rights published its investigation into the huge Classic Fashion factory in Jordan. Clothes made at Classic Fashion enter the United States duty-free under the US–Jordan Free Trade Agreement. The investigation found that the all-female workforce, mostly migrants from South Asia, had undergone beatings, forced labour and systematic sexual abuse and rape. Five major brands in the United States are supplied by Classic Fashion – Hanes, Kohl's, Macy's, Target and Walmart. Their lack of response following the findings prompted the report's author, Charles Kernaghan, to state: 'Walmart and Hanes are not into human rights, but we thought they would draw a line in the sand at these rapes. Instead they've been virtually silent.'[15]

At the same time as the women making their clothes were being beaten and raped, these companies were announcing 'ethical initiatives' on their social policy websites: 'We are committed to doing our part in keeping the world a healthy and safe place worth living in' (Hanes). 'Macy's, Inc. has had a stringent Vendor and Supplier Code of Conduct designed to protect workers in this country and abroad' (Macy's). 'By using our unique size and scale, we are empowering women around the world' (Walmart). This is the difference between a PR promotion and real change, illustrating why many people have a very big problem with corporations. Since these horrors were exposed, conditions have yet to improve at Classic Fashion. It has emerged that in the last two years, at least 25 women have disappeared from the factory, with their fellow workers reporting: 'We believe that those kidnapped women were raped and killed.'[16]

'Causumerism'

There are more general problems with the idea of causumerism. Purchase or dollar votes are cast in direct accordance to how many dollars you have.[17] How can you influence De Beers if you cannot buy diamonds? How can you influence the labour practices of Chanel if you cannot afford a £100 bottle of perfume let alone a £1,500 handbag? Dollar votes entrench the position that to have power in society you must have money.

Causumerism shifts blame for the world's ills from capitalism onto individuals. As discussed, products considered 'ethical' are often the most expensive on the market, so ethical consumption is unfortunately deeply class-based. It is wrong to blame those with the least individual power in society for the destruction of the planet or the existence of sweatshops. Why is it not the case that all products have been ethically made? Why does responsibility not lie further up the chain? Yva Alexandrova of the ethical label Yvian commented: 'I don't think you should put all the blame on the consumer. I think people should buy beautiful clothes and I think it's the designer's responsibility to make sure that these clothes are also beautifully made.'[18]

Ethical consumerism can cement people's identity as passive consumers rather than as active citizens. Life is about more than just retail and we must not allow all major functions of society to be subordinated to the task of shopping.[19]

Sit Back and Wait?

People who argue against reform only are often accused of being unwilling to act in the here and now, but this is a misrepresentation of their political stance. Why would those who most want change be content to sit back and wait for it? 'They cannot and dare not wait, in a fatalist fashion, with folded arms for the advent of the "revolutionary situation",'[20] declared the revolutionary Rosa Luxemburg. It is not a simple choice between reform and revolution; rather, they condition and complement each other.[21]

There is a long, radical history of people gaining rights for themselves and for others by acting as political consumers. The Russian Revolution began with women's protests over bread prices. The Montgomery Bus Boycott of the American Civil Rights struggle (*Walk in dignity not ride in humiliation*) was so widespread that it ended racial segregation on buses after 13 months. The Harlem Housewives League carried out a *Don't buy where you can't work* campaign to force shops to hire black employees. There have been rent strikes, Gandhi's boycott of imported Lancashire cotton and the global consumer boycott of South African goods.

What links these campaigns is that consumerism was a means to an end, not an end in itself. The Russian Revolution began with women's protests over bread prices, but the end was not cheap bread. Political consumerism, as opposed to 'causumerism', works with the knowledge that capitalism cannot be reformed. It uses consumption to bring about a specific change, it does not make a different type of consumption the end game.

The following questions distinguish causumer campaigns from political consumption campaigns: Is the campaign being organised by a corporation? Is a corporation making money from the campaign? Does the campaign see itself as an end in itself or does it challenge capitalism? Does the campaign empower people to do more than just shop? Who or what does the campaign blame for exploitation?

I do not take the view that people should never engage in consumer campaigns. Indeed, it makes sense to buy the least harmful products possible and many consumer campaigns have been successful in raising awareness about issues like climate change and sweatshops. What I am saying is that action must not stop at the checkout.

Regulation?

None of the crises facing the world, such as climate change, are confined within state borders.[22] New, internationalist solutions such as boycotts can enhance traditional forms of politics. One worthy aim of some consumer campaigns is to get governments to legislate in favour of better labour practices or environmental protection. But governments are unwilling to legislate to control corporations because, as Luxemburg wrote 100 years ago: 'State control is penetrated with the exclusive interests of the ruling class.'[23]

The approach of the British government with regard to protecting garment workers and the environment is to trust in voluntary corporate social responsibility (CSR) schemes by corporations. Happily for corporations this is precisely the approach they favour as it means they can avoid legal regulations. The primary voluntary CSR organisation in the United Kingdom is the Ethical Trading Initiative, an umbrella organisation made up of corporations, trade unions and NGOs. Whilst its aims are worthy, the Ethical Trading Initiative is constantly ignored and trampled upon by a corporate membership that includes Asda, Tesco and Primark.

In Britain, a large obstacle landed in the path of legislative reform when the owner of the Arcadia retail conglomerate Philip Green was appointed as a government advisor by David Cameron. Green has not signed up to the Ethical Trading Initiative. When a journalist asked why, he told her that he had already threatened to punch her colleague 'on the nose and throw him out of the window'.[24] In 2002, Green sold Arcadia to his wife Tina, who lives in the tax haven of Monaco; hundreds of millions of pounds of taxes were thereby 'not due' to be paid in the United Kingdom. Legislation of the sort that would make it illegal for UK retailers to use overseas sweatshop labour is extremely unlikely for the time being. Globalisation has resulted in a global 'race to the bottom'. As international capitalist competition grows stronger, the likelihood of state regulation drops even further.

The US equivalent of the Ethical Trading Initiative is the Fair Labour Association. Another organisation that has proved weak and ineffective, the Association has caused controversy by praising Foxconn, the inhumane iPad contractor. The United States exemplifies a neoliberal trend that has eroded workers' rights by deregulation and the cutting and privatising of labour law enforcement. In 1983 government-employed wage and hour investigators were responsible for inspecting 5,700 workplaces each; by 1996 this had risen to 8,700. After Clinton privatised Labour Standards Enforcement, more jobs were cut and each investigator became responsible for 140,652 workers (up from 40,000 in 1957). This impossible situation has been described as 'heaven' for sweatshop owners.[25] Continual cuts to labour law enforcement have left workers open to flagrant abuse, showing the deep class bias in Washington's legislative system.[26]

Philanthro-capitalism

The upsurge in public interest in ethical consumption has resulted in a distinct move on the part of multinationals to embrace the language and appearance of ethical consumer campaigns. This signifies a deliberate shift in the way brands seek to engage with people. Many brands now attempt to engage with customers and give them a more personalised experience, to shift consumer loyalty from being simply price-based to involving a sense of ownership through participation. Companies have 'conversation departments' to engage with customers online, and a growing number of companies offer customised products. Several brands offer trainers with personalised embroidered slogans, though Nike will not as yet embroider the word 'sweatshop'.

People are more concerned than ever about climate change and sweatshop conditions. Scandal after scandal has eroded trust in politicians, the media, banks and corporations. People want change and multinationals face the challenge of moving with the times and inculcating themselves into this movement – *If you can't beat 'em, join em.*

High-fashion houses have yet to begin seriously marketing themselves as ethical – they need not make such overtures to reform because their audience is unconcerned. This is not the case for brands catering to the mass market. They must reform their image to appear part of the solution not just part of the problem.

TOMS, therefore, offers eye operations; Armani tackles HIV/AIDS; M&S established a 'shwopping' campaign; Nike becomes a champion of women ('Make it Count') and a champion of workers (Nike Makers: 'makers of the world, unite'); Reebok have a Human Rights Award; and H&M pledges to use more organic cotton. As Naomi Klein explains: 'every company with a powerful brand is attempting to develop a relationship with consumers that resonates so completely with their sense of self.'[27]

The language, images, emblems and rhetoric of each of these brand campaigns are empathetic and convincing because they are lifted directly from social movements. Levi's produced a stirring advert based on Charles Bukowski's poem 'The Laughing Heart', which masquerades as a call to arms for young people to resist authority. It featured enough 'youth vs. police' footage to get it banned in the United Kingdom during the 'riot summer' of 2011. This advert exemplifies the commodification of our beliefs and our need for real change. Levi's sold us back our ideas devoid of original meaning and used them as a screen for human rights and environmental abuses. Corporate causumerism is a direct opponent of progressive social movements.

Marx noted in the rules of the First International: 'the emancipation of the working classes must be conquered by the working classes themselves'.[28] Corporations do not intend to free us, nor are they able to. Freedom can only come from within.

TOMS

TOMS is a US-based shoe company founded in 2006 by Blake Mycoskie. Its unique selling point is BOGO (Buy One Give One). Each time a pair of TOMS shoes is sold, the company donates a second pair to a child in one of over 20 countries. By 2013 it had given away over two million pairs of shoes. The company has also founded TOMS Eyewear, which intends to provide eye surgery for every pair of sunglasses purchased.

Customers are entered into a 'Giving Trip' prize draw to win the chance to visit a poverty-stricken village and hand over shoes. According to the company's website: 'Compassionate young people are getting involved with TOMS like no other brand.' TOMS talks of turning 'customers into benefactors' and of 'customer-philanthropists'. Mycoskie's job title is 'Chief Shoe Giver' and there is a TOMS shoe printed with Gandhi's message: *Become the change you want to see happen.*

The TOMS BOGO policy has been listed as one of the worst aid ideas of all time.[29] It involves dumping shoes in economies that would be better served by the establishment of local industries. As one blog noted: 'Things like jobs help poverty. Jobs making things like shoes.'[30] Schemes like TOMS' BOGO ignore the fact that shoelessness is a symptom of poverty, not its cause. Rather than address the causes of poverty, TOMS tackles shoelessness and in the process *causes* poverty.

Experts criticise companies for destroying the ability of villages to produce goods on an industrial scale, while celebrating flooding the market with cheap overseas goods. Africa has been labelled 'the biggest dumping ground on the planet'.[31] For Africa's apparel industry, 40 per cent of the decline in production and 50 per cent of the decline in employment over the period 1981–2000 is attributed to used clothing imports and imposed Structural Adjustment Programs.[32] One African think-tank described charitable imports as 'poison coated with sugar'.[33]

The impoverished 'beneficiary' children do not receive the TOMS shoes that retail in the shops. TOMS' retail shoes cost between $3.50 and $5.00 to make in Chinese factories. They sell for between $44 and $98. The give-away shoes are cheap plimsolls made in Ethiopia. By turning poverty into a marketing ploy, TOMS makes more money from making two pairs of shoes and giving one away than it would if it only produced one pair of shoes and marketed them differently. This approach is summed up by the title of a keynote speech Mycoskie offers through the Lanvin Agency: 'Conscious Capitalism and the Future of Business. Why is philanthropy your best competitive advantage? How do you make money and do good simultaneously?'[34]

TOMS is a prime example of the shift from charity to commerce charity. In previous times people like the hated union-buster Andrew Carnegie would give donations to charity that were separate from their business assets.[35] This has now shifted to a model which relies on the simultaneous generation of charitable donations and profit. The notion that supporting a multinational corporation by buying its products will help solve poverty and reduce inequality is an extremely clever pretence that fundamentally alters the perception of corporations and lets them appear interactive, inclusive and charitable. It is fundamentally contradictory. Poverty is the result of an exploitative system of global capitalism, of which multinational corporations are key exponents and beneficiaries. What is actually occurring with charity commerce is the maximisation of corporate profits through the exploitative marketing of human misery.

The (RED) Manifesto

The Davos Summit of 2006 saw the launch of the (RED) brand by U2 front-man Bono. Its premise seems simple: buy specially branded (RED) products from brands like Giorgio Armani, Gap, Converse and American Express and an undisclosed portion of the cost will be donated to the Global Fund which provides HIV/AIDS medicine in Africa. The (RED) website asks: 'Has there ever been a better reason to shop?'[36] A critical appraisal of (RED) can be found in Lisa Ann Richey and Stefano Ponte's *Brand Aid – Shopping Well to Save the World*. (RED) has been charged with allowing corporations to raise their CSR profile without having to make any progressive changes to their business model. Like TOMS, (RED) focuses solely on the symptoms of disease and poverty rather than their causes.

(RED) even has its own 'manifesto', but there is nothing in it about the social conditions that underpin poverty, inequality and disease. There is no mention of the exploited workers who make (RED) products, often in Chinese factories. Nor is there any mention of the environmental impact of the products. Instead, HIV/AIDS is presented as an emergency that justifies ignoring race, gender and global inequalities.[37] When pressed about this, Bono did his own 'ethical calculus' and responded: 'Labour issues are very, very serious, but six and a half thousand Africans dying is more serious.'[38]

Far from asking people to consume less or to consume differently, (RED) advises: 'You can look chic enough in Armani, hip enough in Converse, pay for your goods with American Express, and feel good about yourself ethically.' The 'conscious consumer' is replaced with the unthinking 'compassionate consumer'[39] who trusts multinationals to do good and find a cure for AIDS. This is a deliberate attempt to undercut gains made by ethical consumerism campaigns and social movements which have encouraged people to become conscious and critical. It is the deflection of attention away from the causes of crises like the AIDS epidemic.[40]

For a campaign designed to alleviate the HIV/AIDS pandemic in Africa, critics have pointed out that there is no African agency in the campaign. The special (RED) edition of *The Independent* disgracefully featured Kate Moss blacked up on its cover. Many (RED) products are not even available in Africa.[41] Instead, in the same manner as TOMS, suffering Africans are used to market designer products.[42] *Brand Aid* recounts the story of the talk-show host Oprah Winfrey wearing a GAP inspi(RED) t-shirt on her show ('the most important t-shirt I've ever worn in my life'). Oprah gave each audience member a t-shirt, explaining that half the profits from the audience's t-shirts would provide medicine for 14,000 pregnant women. At face value this is compelling, but what Oprah did not explain is that buying a GAP t-shirt provides just two weeks worth of medicine. It would take 27 t-shirts to care for one person for a year and countless numbers for a lifetime of medication.[43]

AIDS medicine should be globally provided to everyone who needs it as a matter of course rather than being a side-line for multinational corporations. Health care should not rely on the free market. The economic crisis and the resulting downturn in consumer spending make the vulnerability of these campaigns particularly pertinent. What happens when HIV/AIDS medication no longer generates profits for multinational corporations? It is not enough to give the poor medicine; we must ask why they do not have it in the first place.

The amount donated by (RED) in its first five years is tiny: 1 per cent of the Global Fund's donations.[44] (RED)'s primary aim, however, is the rehabilitation of global commerce as a force for good. Multinational fashion corporations are more scrutinised than ever. Campaigns like (RED) provide a safe way for them to repair their image and move from talk of sweatshops to talk of curing HIV/AIDS in Africa. Sweatshops, environmental devastation and the increasing concentration of wealth and power in the hands of the rich are all hidden behind a veneer of beneficent, life-giving corporations. Giorgio Armani stated of his participation in (RED): 'Commerce will no longer have a negative connotation.'[45]

Bono also founded the fashion label Edun with his wife, Ali Hewson. Edun's stated aim was to revitalise apparel manufacture in Sub-Saharan Africa. What Edun ignored however is the fact that per capita growth grew respectably in Africa during the 1960s and 70s, but collapsed in the 1980s when the World Bank and the IMF forced Sub-Saharan African countries to adopt free-market, free-trade policies which destroyed domestic manufacturing.[46] In 2010 the company committed what the *Wall Street Journal* called a 'big about-face'. With the company failing and holding launch parties in the dark to hide the poor manufacture of its clothes, Edun sold a 49 per cent stake in the company to LVMH. The first thing LVMH did was to move 70 per cent of the company's production to China and 15 per cent to Peru, leaving just 15 per cent in Africa. Producing clothing in Africa has dropped to a principle that the company intends to achieve 'over time'.[47]

Sweatshop Warriors

The term 'international labour movement' here encompasses traditional trade unions around the world; migrant worker 'guerrilla groups' and migrant worker centres like Fuerza Unida,[48] anti-corporate campaigns like UK Uncut and the anti-sweatshop campaigns of Labour Behind the Label, United Students Against Sweatshops, Clean Clothes Campaign, War on Want, and many, many others. Political moments such as the giant protests against the WTO in Seattle (1999) and against the G8 in Genoa (2001) have provided new opportunities for building cross-class, cross-sector, multiracial fronts involving the radical labour movement, youth, intellectuals and professionals.[49]

It is out of this movement that the real gains for garment workers have been made. What this movement demonstrates is that the way we change the world is as people, as citizens, as workers. This is the power we have over governments and companies. They need us more than we need them.

A key element in this movement is solidarity. Big gains were made, for example, when Honduran trade unionists worked with United Students Against Sweatshops to implement the biggest ever collegiate boycott of a single company. Fruit of the Loom is the largest private employer in Honduras, over 100 universities cut ties with the company until it was forced to enter into an agreement with the union.

Recognising that sweatshop workers are not mere victims led United Students Against Sweatshops to adopt a quote from an Australian Aboriginal activist as its motto: 'If you have come to help me, you are wasting your time. But if you've come because your liberation is bound up with mine, then let us work together.'[50]

Amirul Haque Amir, president of the National Garment Workers Federation in Bangladesh, is adamant that solidarity does not just mean a flow of money and support from North to South. He described Bangladeshi garment workers holding protests in Dhaka to support British trade unions facing austerity and unemployment. 'It really matters what is meant by international solidarity,' he explains. 'This is not just help from North to South. Multinationals are exploiting us globally – textile and garment workers, transport workers, retail workers, and consumers. We must work together.'[51]

Miriam Ching Yoon Louie's anthology *Sweatshop Warriors* is, amongst other things, an effective anthology of garment workers' struggles against neoliberal policies in the United States. One case study details the Asian Immigrant Women's Advocates' (AIWA) early watershed struggle to expose the inequalities of the fashion industry and make manufacturers take responsibility for their subcontractors. The campaign was initiated to try to get back-pay for 12 Chinese workers after one manufacturer, Jessica McClintock, pulled a contract and their sweatshop closed. Jessica McClintock denied any responsibility for the Chinese workers, but after a campaign of consumer boycotts, pickets, media exposure and political pressure, the company was forced to negotiate.

In 1996, after a four-year struggle, the immigrant women workers won an undisclosed cash settlement, an education fund for garment workers to learn about their rights, a scholarship fund for workers and their children, a bilingual hotline for workers to report any violations of their rights in shops contracted with McClintock, and an agreement from both sides to work to improve conditions within the industry.[52] The case discredited the idea that manufacturers were not responsible for the abuse suffered by workers in sweatshops.

In 2000, the golfer Tiger Woods was ambushed in a luxury Bangkok hotel by 30 Thai garment workers dressed in black. Led by Junya Yimprasert of the Thai Labour Campaign, the workers informed Woods that it would take a Thai Nike worker 72,000 years to earn the equivalent of Wood's latest Nike sponsorship.[53] The ambush received world-wide coverage. Such examples show the labour movement to be *the* critical element in the journey towards a fair society where no one is enslaved by poverty.

Yet despite the efforts of the international labour movement, this is how campaigners describe the fashion industry, as summarised by Liesbeth Sluiter in *Clean Clothes*:

> Overall, wages in the garment-producing sector in developing countries are stagnant or falling. The rights to freedom of association and collective bargaining have to be won again and again, and many battles are lost. Relocations within the industry are still rampant, leading to an informalisation of economies that undermines workers lives, including the capacity to fight for a better one. Governments, adhering to the dogmas of export-led growth, neoliberal deregulation, and global competition, fail to enact or enforce labour laws.[54]

History is not a linear march towards progress; rather, it is struggle between two sides – the working class and the ruling class. Gains for one represent a loss for the other; the myth of Sisyphus was an apt analogy for Rosa Luxemburg to make about the struggle for reform. Trade union work becomes increasingly difficult during periods of economic crises when shrinking numbers of jobs and falling rates of pay sometimes divide workers and lower their confidence. When this is the case, trade union work can be reduced, at best, to trying to defend the few rights that you still have.[55]

Is a Just Capitalism Possible?

One of the richest men in Europe has bought Edun. How do we build an Eden that is not for sale? Arguments in favour of reform often (accidentally or not) turn into pro-capitalist arguments. The economic crisis means that the notion of an unstable 'casino capitalism' is widely accepted, yet there remains the myth of a 'just capitalism'.[56] This implies that capitalism can be fair. It recommends trusting in the neoliberal values of the free market.

The idea of 'just capitalism' is an illusion that promises fundamental change without the need to alter the balance of power.[57] Even worse, it proffers the same economic system that has wreaked such havoc as the solution to the problems it has generated.[58]

In a system racked with exploitation and environmental destruction, surface modifications are not enough. 'The quixotic quest to construct a capitalism that might be ethical and just will have to be abandoned,' wrote David Harvey. 'At the end of the day it matters not one whit whether we are well intentioned and ethically inclined or self-indulgently greedy and competitively destructive. The logic of endless capitalist accumulation and of endless growth is always with us.'[59] The problem, therefore, is not that I do not believe in a 'just capitalism', the problem is that it does not exist.

Some of the methods for organised reform discussed in this chapter are fragments of a blueprint for an ideal society. The international labour movement and solidarity campaigns have vital parts to play in changing the world and fashioning a new one. Organised campaigns can unite, engage, educate and inspire people. What they cannot do is produce clothes that are free of exploitation or environmental degradation. This is impossible under capitalism. As disappointing as it may be to hear this, there are no ethical clothes for sale. Temporary disappointment is, however, a small price to pay for taking part in the biggest challenge ever faced by humanity – the overthrow of capitalism.

CHAPTER TEN

Revolutionising Fashion

Dress suitably in short skirts and strong boots,
leave your jewels in the bank, and buy a revolver.
Fashion advice from the Irish revolutionary
Countess Constance Markievicz

Aim high, very high.
Anna Wintour, editor-in-chief, *Vogue*

Revolution

The word revolution signifies two things. First, it captures the scale of the problems facing humanity today, problems that only revolution can answer. Second, it represents the spirit of people fighting injustice in pursuit of a better world.[1] This chapter imagines a post-capitalist society where capitalism has been overthrown and the world is in a state of permanent revolution. Whilst this might seem a distant possibility, it is important that this chapter be set in a revolutionary future because the problem with raising only partial demands is that partial demands face a pre-established framework and the limitations set by capitalism.[2] To reach revolution and create a new world requires the liberation of the imagination and hope. This is in contrast to an overall social climate that promotes disillusionment and despair.[3] That is why this chapter has permission to envision and dream.

Marxism is not a blueprint for a future society, nor is it a set of rules or a creed by which to live. Rather, it is a demand for recognition that a new form of society *can* exist. How can we imagine an epoch that we have not experienced? Trotsky noted that what this society will look like is unwritten because 'the development of art is the highest test of the vitality and significance of each epoch'.[4] In one sense how things will look is immaterial because what happens under freedom is less important than reaching it. In the film *Lincoln*, which depicts the ending of legal slavery, one former slave, Mrs Keckley, tells Lincoln: 'Negroes have been fighting and dying for freedom since the first of us was a slave. I never heard any ask what freedom will bring. Freedom's first.'[5]

Whilst the main task is to achieve freedom rather than worry about what happens next, I want to use this chapter to showcase some of the countless ideas for the creation of a fair society, to show that we have a world brimming over with ideas for attaining justice and equality. I have also sought to answer some of the questions about revolutionising fashion that repeatedly arise, the primary one being: *Will we all have to wear Maoist smocks?*

I begin by investigating the impact of commerce on art, and the work of the Bolshevik fashion designers Liubov Popova and Varvara Stepanova. I then look at production and discuss how it might be transformed by applying a new economic model. Would there be factories? Who would work in them? Who would decide what to make? Finally, I discuss how the removal of issues such as class, race, gender, size and private property might transform the visual aspects of society. What would happen to culture without capitalism? Would there be monotony or unimaginable variety?

There is nothing inevitable about progress and nothing in this chapter is 'destined' to come true. What I discuss in this chapter are possibilities. Whether they become realities depends entirely on what we do.

The Vast Storehouse of Potential

> However sugarcoated and ambiguous, every form of authoritarianism must start with a belief in some group's greater right to power.
>
> Gloria Steinem

Art plays a hugely important role in society. It has the power to make life beautiful, to make us dream, to challenge us and to lift our gaze above the horizon to picture a better future. This includes clothing. Yet art and fashion are tangled in a web of commerce, competition and exclusivity. A few years ago, whilst admiring the Central St. Martin's graduate collections, a friend quipped: 'Don't worry, this time next year they'll all be broke and unemployed so you can buy up their collections for peanuts.' She spoke from bitter experience.

Even designers graduating at the top of their class face the prospect of unpaid internships, unemployment or 'succumbing' to employment by a brand they neither like nor respect. A designer's fate, like that of our common cultural heritage, is determined by a relatively small number of private financial and industrial institutions which are completely unaccountable to the public. These corporations hold the power to block and control which narratives will emerge in society.[6]

Corporate power is ideologically bolstered by the Romantic idea that the famous fashion designer is a God-like figure capable of summoning their ideas out of thin air.[7] This idea of art was critiqued by Bertolt Brecht and Walter Benjamin as an individualistic and mystified concept which omits the artist as a worker rooted in a particular history with specific materials at their disposal. Fashion designers do not make the materials with which they work. The constant recycling or reinvention of ideas in the industry shows that just as car assembly-plant workers use already processed materials to make cars, so too do fashion's forms, myths, symbols and ideologies come already worked on.[8] In *The Style Engine*, one curator described how 'the core function of most creative people in an information glutted age is not innovation but rearrangement'.[9]

Artistic work should not be oversimplified. Clothing design is a skilled art-form which does differ from machine work.[10] Yet the idea of the designer as 're-arranger' is an antidote to the elitism and deification that is rife in the fashion industry, showing instead that all the materials and skills that produce great works are socially produced. Mészáros points out that even the greatest pianist needs a socially produced piano to perform on.[11] The most lauded designer also needs socially produced pencils and paper, materials, a set of skills learned from teachers, and a history both to follow and to rebel against – not to mention huge assistance in the form of design teams, administrators, financiers and domestic staff. Yet with power so concentrated in the industry, people sycophantically flock around key figures in the hope of gaining their share.

Nor is design a level playing-field where talent automatically wins over hardship. Fashion can appear an egalitarian industry with a significant number of designers being female, working class or from the LGBT community. Yet it is still the case that class limitations combine with race and gender barriers to exclude many people from creative work. Student selection processes at art colleges have been found to be openly racist, replicating the inequalities found in wider society.[12] The economics of aesthetic production (buying materials and having spare time) also limit opportunities.[13] The risk involved in becoming an impoverished creative producer is far less for those who know, for example, that they will inherit a house from their parents.[14] This is replicated to a greater extent on a world-wide scale: how many Schiaparellis or Balenciagas have lived and died in cotton fields and sweatshops?

Society sharply and criminally limits human potential. There exists at present a gross underuse of talent. This probably means that the cure for cancer is trapped in a slum-dweller's cortex somewhere in India. It undoubtedly also has a profound impact on our creative and fashion worlds. The public is 'barred' from participating in the process of artistic fashion creation. We are allowed to make purchases and to style ourselves, but that is it. People create marvellous beauty with their limited purchases, often in dire circumstances. Does this offer a glimpse of what might be possible in terms of design creation? The Marxist professor Bertell Ollman asks that we imagine a society where everyone is free to be creative, when for each person 'the vast storehouse of their potentialities is at last emptied'.[15] What, then, might we see in terms of clothing design?

A major problem facing designers is that, due to the confines of the market, creativity comes second to what can be sold to produce maximum profit. The Bolshevik designer Varvara Stepanova (of whom more later) despised the influence of commerce on art, saying that it kept an artist bogged down in mediocre bourgeois taste.[16] The *Guardian* made the same point about the *haute couture* industry: 'When haute couture had no customers but was a laboratory of no-holds-barred creativity, it might have been commercially irrelevant but the frocks were fabulous. Now that it has found women to sell to, haute couture designers are making the clothes of their customers' dreams, not their own.'[17]

A designer's work is not art for art's sake, but art for profit's sake – an alienated means to an end that hampers creativity and potential.

What is needed is to sever the link between design and money, to reach the point where art and design are not stepping stones in a career but have been set free.

But what, some might ask, if there was suddenly an excess of designs, an outpouring of creativity and ideas? How would we decide which was the best? An excess of art is surely the point. In an ideal society the floodgates will open and everyone will be unrestricted. After the Russian Revolution, art led a feverish existence.[18] It would be the same in the world that this chapter envisages: a tidal wave of new influences and inspiration. Everything would come alive and everyone would be an artist: 'above the ridge new peaks will rise'.[19]

Attempting to restrict or contain art is capitalism's habit whereby art is a commodity rather than a social good. The Parisian couturiers fought tooth and nail to keep fashion for the rich. If this elitism ended, an excess of designs would not matter. We might at last see the freedom of choice that capitalism pretends to give us. Competition and elitism are concerns only under capitalism, as John Berger notes: 'The arranging of artists into a hierarchy of merit is an idle and essentially dilettante process. What matters are the needs which art answers.'[20]

Young designers graduate to discover that their friends and peers are now competing for the same few jobs. What if, instead of promoting individualised entrepreneurship and competitive achievement, society valued collaboration, mutual recognition, solidarity and compassion?[21] Were society's productive resources to fall under collective control, there would be a material abundance that would allow for universal creativity. In today's industry, a few individuals decide who works in fashion; in an ideal society there would be unlimited creative space.

Passive consumption means people are presented with ready-made products they have had no hand in creating.[22] This passivity mystifies clothes and lands us in a visual world that we did not make for ourselves.[23] The consequences are alienation and a tendency not to value the clothes we possess. Imagine how much more we would value and care for our clothes, let alone our world, if we played a meaningful creative role. If we reach the point where clothing has become a true social production, we will have transcended competition, cultural privatisation and greed, and will experience art as a true public good.

Revolutionary Fashion

For a few years before and after the Russian Revolution of 1917, art in Russia experienced a movement that remains unique in the history of modern art in terms of its creativity and powerful, relevant engagement with everyday life. In *Art and Revolution*, Berger describes how this process evolved. The liberation of the serfs in 1861 allowed for the development of capitalism and a small urban proletariat which swiftly became the most militant and revolutionary in Europe, and directly opposed to absolutist and undemocratic Tsarist rule.

Russia's avant-garde artists, as part of the intelligentsia, were deeply concerned with the political and spiritual future of their country. The cultural backwardness of Russia and the absence of bourgeois patrons left them somewhat out on a limb: 'Instead of a present they had a past and a future. Instead of compromises they had extremes. Instead of limited possibilities they had open prophecies.'[24] Russia's avant-garde saw themselves representing a liberated future. It was an art scene where women were considered equal to men,[25] and there was a common belief in art having a social role that was affirmative rather than critical.[26] Thus after the revolution there were several years during which artists freely chose to serve their state and the revolution.[27]

Until Liubov Popova and Varvara Stepanova were invited to work as designers at the First Moscow Textile Printing Factory in 1923, all designs there had been Western imports. The two women worked at the factory for a year, producing 150 textile designs, of which about two dozen were put into mass production.[28] They were artists designing for mass factory production and their work was celebrated as the first implementation of the slogan 'art into production'.[29] Whilst only a small proportion of their designs were mass-produced, they were hugely influential. They made prints achieve the level of 'real art' and were described by art critics as having 'brought the rich colours and intense ornament of contemporary art to the cities'.[30]

Originally from a wealthy background, Liubov Popova, who died prematurely in 1924, regarded her artistic work as a duty and a social obligation.[31] Yet her art is not dogmatic. Instead it is full of 'vital creativity itself', having embodied the spirit of creative progress, renewal and inquiry.[32] Displaying an attitude unimaginable in her European contemporaries, Popova once said: 'No single artistic success gave me such profound satisfaction as the sight of a peasant woman buying a piece of my fabric for a dress.'[33]

The designs of these two women are rich, graphic, complex, colourful and well ahead of their time, certainly in terms of fashion design. But in a sense, like many Russian artists, Popova and Stepanova were too dynamic for the social and economic realities of the period[34] and their designs were often seen as too 'fashion forward'. 'There is always the danger that the relative freedom of art can render it meaningless,' argues Berger. 'Yet it is this same freedom which allows art, and art alone, to express and preserve the profoundest expectations of a period'[35] – comments highly applicable to Popova and Stepanova.

Simply placing fashion designs by Popova and Stepanova alongside designs by their European contemporaries speaks volumes. Their prints encapsulate the hope, audacity and dreams of the Russian Revolution. Across the rest of the world, fashion was the plaything of the rich. This was a time when working people were supposed to be no more than drab factory and cannon fodder, yet Popova and Stepanova saw them clothed in light and colour. Their designs speak of a new world, bright, beautiful and defiantly shining forth the phrase the Russian working class was throwing at its adversary: 'I am nothing and I should be everything.'[36]

Production

Stepanova was against an artificial divide between clothing designers and producers. A textile designer, she believed, should discover what happened to fabric once it left the factory gates.[37] With the Design Council reporting that 80 per cent of a product's environmental impact is decided at the design stage,[38] and with the United Kingdom putting 1.4 million tonnes of textiles into landfill each year, this approach is more important than ever. The question of waste reduction must be paramount in design and specialist knowledge must not be separated from decision-making. Designers should participate fully in society's production decisions rather than being passive.[39]

Another false divide that should be scrapped is that of consumers and producers. Roland Barthes wrote that capitalism needs consumers who do not calculate the real cost of their purchases: 'If clothing producers and consumers had the same consciousness, clothing would be bought (and produced) only at the very slow rate of its dilapidation.'[40] If people helped to make their clothes they would undoubtedly consume less, respect more and lose the alienated need for so many possessions.

Before fashion was mass-produced in factories it was produced by households and there was much less of it. For thousands of years it was commonplace for people to have just one outfit and stay in bed when it was being washed.[41] Some argue that making your own clothes is a more sustainable method of production. At the start of the economic crisis in 2008 there were countless high-fashion magazine articles with such make-do-and-mend tips as *how to make a belt from a curtain tie*. These articles were, of course, aimed solely at women.

The Russian Revolutionary leader Alexandra Kollontai wrote in *Communism and the Family* that the danger of seeing households as units of production is that the burden falls on 'the active fingers of the wife'.[42] On top of work and domestic duties she must now make clothes. Women have fought to free themselves from the domestic yoke; an ideal society would not send them back to it. Home-alone knitting is neither the most efficient nor enjoyable way to make socks. It represents the triumph of individualism over collectivity.

Nor are we aiming for a society of scarcity. In 2012 I visited a 'social grocery' in Athens. Run by a big supermarket chain, customers need a poverty card to shop there. Inside it was a free marketeer's nightmare projection of communism – the shelves were full, but there were only about 20 products in the entire shop. All variety had been lost, replaced by a few scant products. Of course, the grocery provides a far better alternative than starvation, but the month after month choice of single-brand bread, margarine, sausages and washing powder clearly takes a serious toll on people's spirits. The polar opposite of supermarkets stocking 40 different brands of shampoo, the social grocery was not a product of communism, but of free-market capitalism, as orchestrated by the IMF. This lack of variety and democracy is not what we are aiming for.

Humans differ from animals in that we free ourselves from need through production. It is important for culture that we are not in a position of scarcity because, as Trotsky explained: 'Culture feeds on the sap of economics, and a material surplus is necessary, so that culture may grow. Art needs comfort, even abundance.'[43] Whilst it is essential to free ourselves from scarcity through production, there is no reason for life to be segmented and compartmentalised.[44]

Sweatshops and compartmentalised Taylorist methods of production compound alienation. They turn highly skilled, autonomous artisans like the silk-weavers of Lyon into workers on assembly lines passing objects or parts of objects in front of them during 12-hour shifts.[45] This oppressive and meaningless work damages society's artistic potential by limiting individual potential. Ending this work is key to letting society experience an unprecedented, and to some extent unimaginable, liberation of the imagination.

Social Production[46]

The workers of Rana Plaza in Bangladesh died because they had no control whatsoever over the factory they worked in. They were coerced into entering a building they knew was unsafe by fear of violence, destitution and starvation. This was possible because the factory, and thus the lives of the workers, were controlled by one extremely rich businessman, enthralled to the needs of multinationals.

But what if the means of production – in this case the Rana Plaza factory – were collectively owned? What if every clothing factory, cotton field, technology developer and the *Chambre Syndicale de la Haute Couture* in Paris were under collective ownership? What if instead of operating to produce profits for the few, they were run for the benefit of humanity and the planet? For Rana Plaza this would have meant that no illegal extra floors would have been built, no workers would have been sent into an unsafe workspace, no hazardous generators would have been installed (as electricity production would also be under collective control), and hours and conditions would be collectively agreed.

This would have several immediate effects. First, social production organised by workers would end unsafe working practices because no one is going to vote to work in a death trap. The former owner of Rana Plaza would be working in the factory like everyone else and so it would also be his life at risk from criminal practices. This levelling of society would end other dangerous and polluting practices like sanding jeans, the dust from which causes silicosis. If everyone took turns working in factories, no one would sanction such deadly and unnecessary practices.

Socially organised production would end over-production because no one not reliant on wages is going to vote to work 15-hour days seven days a week on an assembly line to produce 20 billion pieces of clothing. The only people that need such vast quantities of clothing are the people that sell them at a profit; under collective ownership their role would have ceased.

The end of the drive to make a profit would bring about a return of use-value over exchange value because people would make things to use them (and enjoy them) rather than to sell them. Happily, socially organised production would also result in fewer work hours and far more leisure time. Rather than working five, six or seven days a week, if production was collectively managed people could work for just two or three days.

Job diversification – everyone taking turns at certain forms of labour – could mean that everyone played a part in clothing production, which would end the separation of consciousness between consumers and producers and prevent any one person or group becoming stuck in one job.[47] Under capitalism, people choose, or are assigned, a certain trade and more or less stick to it to avoid starvation.

In an ideal society people would be able to spend some of their time designing or making clothes without being pigeon-holed as a designer or factory worker. Currently, reserving art and design for the few is inseparable from its suppression in the masses.[48] Opening up art and design to everyone would reverse this situation.

Most importantly perhaps, common ownership would end the present scenario where people do a full day of back-breaking labour yet still go hungry:

> What he produces for himself is not the silk that he weaves, not the gold that he draws up the mining shaft, not the palace that he builds. What he produces for himself is wages; and the silk, the gold, and the palace are resolved for him into a certain quantity of necessaries of life, perhaps into a cotton jacket, into copper coins, and into a basement dwelling.[49] (Karl Marx)

Associate producer communities are not the same as present-day cooperatives, since unfortunately under capitalism, workers in cooperatives have to become the capitalist entrepreneur. They have to discipline themselves, cut their own wages and potentially fire each other.[50]

Genuine collective ownership of all the world's resources would sever the link between appearance and the ability to work. It would end the obligation to keep up with fashion. Severing the link between commerce and fashion and beauty would end the constant messages that women must diet, get cosmetic surgery, buy clothes and feel bad about themselves.

Freed from capitalism's alienation people would once again see themselves as part of nature not separate from it. Rather than seeing ourselves as the owners of nature, we would instead participate in the social use of nature. This would bring an end to fashion's unjustifiable reliance on water pollution, chemical production and mono-crop cultures. It would also end the industrial slaughter of animals.

Collective production is the most efficient form of production, and clothes would undoubtedly, for the most part, be made in factories collectively owned by communities of associated producers.[51] But how would these communities decide what to make? The communities of associated producers (the parts) would function democratically as part of society (the whole). Currently, fashion operates in a top-down structure whereby there is a perverse centrality which destroys any chance of collectivity. Think, for example, of companies like LVMH or Inditex which undemocratically determine production. Post-capitalism, the whole and its parts would work together in a non-adversarial manner. Substantive democratic decision-making would occur within the parts. At the same time, conscious planning and coordination of the parts by the whole – for example, ensuring that all society's clothing needs are being met – would ensure the parts functioned democratically as part of the whole.[52]

There is a need to satisfy communal requirements on a global scale. Satisfying these needs means that an abundance of food, housing, sanitation, clean air, water, health care, education and socially owned transport takes precedence over clothing production.[53] For a country like Haiti this would mean shutting down fashion factories and growing food again. Because we live on an 'island planet'[54] the idea of communal needs must work on a global scale until economic inequality becomes a historical memory. These communal needs include the planet itself, which would mean planning how to live in harmony with nature and ensuring production had no lasting adverse consequences for biodiversity or the planet.

Worker control produces the possibility for far more variety and innovation than under capitalism.[55] The 1976 Lucas Aerospace Plan contained 150 worker-devised schemes for socially useful goods that could have been made instead of military hardware. Hope thrives on reason and experience, and we have all the skills we need to refashion society, a truth kept secret by the present system. Current ideas for fashion technology include: digital body scans which produce tailored clothes that actually fit so you need fewer of them, and materials engineered for durability, sustainability, warmth and sensual pleasure.

Appearance

In some ways it is easier to imagine the impact of these post-capitalist changes on a world-wide scale than to envisage their impact at street level. How would these changes affect the visual world that we each inhabit? Would daily life change? And what would people look like? Again, it is important to reiterate that we cannot know how people would dress in a post-capitalist world. Art, and fashion, resonate with people because they mirror and represent the world they are living in.[56] Fashion thus changes over time because it arises in different social environments. A post-revolutionary society would have unimaginable consequences for clothing.

We can, however, try to imagine whether 'fashion' would still exist. Fashion has been defined in this book as *changing styles of dress and appearance adopted by groups of people*, a definition that aims to keep fashion in the material not the ethereal world. Fashion has the ability to sum up an epoch, to evoke the spirit of the times, which is why Varvara Stepanova wrote: 'It would be a mistake to think that fashion can be abolished, or that it is haphazard or unnecessary. Fashion gives us the lines and shapes to suit a particular time.'[57]

Art is not static any more than life is static, and it would be odd to argue that there is an ultimate way of dressing (or doing anything) that should remain unchanged for all of time. But whilst fashion as a concept of change may exist after the revolution, fashion as an industry would be unrecognisably different. Clothing is consolidated into fashion via a series of social constructs.[58] Like a solid gold picture frame, it is everything that goes *round* clothes that makes them fashion – the catwalks, the media prestige and hype, the elaborate shops and ideology all combine to produce a false religiosity.[59] This false religiosity both celebrates wealth and ownership and cements it. As Kanye West said: 'They made us hate ourself and love their wealth.'[60]

False religiosity exists to help the fashion system produce maximum profits for corporations. Commodities like bags and shoes are placed on pedestals for worship. Worship is the flipside of the industry. Fashion is needed to produce money for corporations, but it is certainly *wanted* by its consumers. On closer inspection the pleasure that fashion brings to people (myself included) does not actually afford an escape from the very things that make us seek pleasure in the first place.[61] Fashion is worshipped because life is alienated and mundane for most people: 'The more monotonous the present, the more the imagination must seize upon the future,'[62] Berger argued. Fashion's startling ability to make people believe in 'the heady possibility of making a new start'[63] keeps people coming back for more. It is wanted because it is linked to the ability to get a job, a partner or social standing.

What if life was on the whole joyful and stimulating? What if you were assured of prosperity and a meaningful existence? What if private property and competition were not enshrined? What if work, love and standing in the community were not based on appearance? This would result in people not being compelled to worship at the altar of fashion, praying for success. Some people might still want to partake in studied dress but gone would be the barbarity of fashion and cosmetics that stems from their obligatory nature.[64] We might reach a situation where the only chastisement given to a woman who does not paint her face is that given to someone who decides not to paint a watercolour – none.[65] A society without capitalism would necessarily be a society without the fashion industry as we know it.

Mao Suits?

The Cultural Revolution, which took place between 1966 and 1976, aimed to rid China of 'old' thinking and culture. For the authorities, this new society had no middle ground – everything and everyone was either revolutionary or reactionary.[66] To be labelled reactionary had dire consequences, fear of which led people to speak, act and dress as inconspicuously as possible. As a result the *zhongshan zhuang* ('Mao suit) became the prevailing fashion of the time.

Interestingly, as Juan Juan Wu outlines in *Chinese Fashion, from Mao to Now*, there was no government decree *ordering* people to wear the *zhongshan zhuang*; rather its prevalence was the result of an atmosphere of conformity, fear and revolutionary fervour.[67] Given, however, the banning of items like Western suits and the threat of death for being reactionary, the government's role in this style should not be underestimated. The ubiquitous drab blue or grey Mao suits could also be taken as a sign of the government's professed allegiance to working people and the need to clothe nearly a billion people at a time of great scarcity.

What the Mao suit was *not* was the end of fashion. Quite the contrary, in fact, due to a perverse twist of fate that saw people become 'aware of dress and appearance to an unprecedented degree' for during the

Cultural Revolution a fashion *faux pas* could mean death. This meant that people studied 'prevailing fashions down to the minutest detail with a singular intensity'. Juan Juan Wu explains that rather than exterminate fashion, the Cultural Revolution produced one of the most fashion-conscious (to the point of paranoia) nations in history. One simply could not *not* care about fashion.[68]

In the same vein, strict uniforms are adopted by certain political groupings who purport not to care about fashion, for example Europe's anarchists. Amongst such groups the parameters of the accepted uniform are strictly policed so everyone wears the same thing. This indifference to fashion is so studied, and such care is taken not to step outside the lines, that the obsessional and self-policing nature of fashion becomes clear.

The fashion academic Ulrich Lehmann has rightly argued that uniforms are not always a joyless way to dress; he points to the joy people get from wearing identical football shirts.[69] Yet just as we are not aiming for a society of economic scarcity, nor are we aiming for one of cultural uniformity brought about through repression. A fully post-capitalist society which was democratically structured through associated communities of producers rather than ruled in a top-down manner would not need, want or be able to repress people in this manner. Instead it would enshrine democracy and freedom of expression for individuals.

Gender, Race and Class

That it is 'ideological' is an accusation commonly thrown at the art of those on the Left as if the work of Johannes Vermeer, Paul Gauguin or Christian Dior was not ideological and as if free marketeers were somehow neutral. As bell hooks explains, there is no art that is politically neutral.[70] This includes fashion. The way people dress today is defined by prevailing ideologies. So what might the impact on fashion be in a post-capitalist society where ideological constructs like gender, race and class have been renounced?

The likelihood is that some obvious gender fashion rules will be cast aside as relics of an old oppressive order: pink for girls, blue for boys, trousers for men, dresses for women. But what of items such as high heels and corsets? Heels have long been rejected as the antithesis of the ideals of feminism.[71] So would they be banned post-revolution? The same question can be asked about items like the *hijab*, which sections of the French feminist Left campaigned to have outlawed. The short answer is no, items would not be banned. It was a huge mistake to ban the *hijab* in France just as outlawing high heels or mini-skirts would be a mistake. Liberation is not, as some French feminists mistakenly believe, about the substitution of rules for more rules. You do not seek to free women from what you consider to be a cage by placing them in a bigger cage. Self-emancipation is the only route to freedom. Anti-hijab legislation covering schools or workplaces risks what one cultural commentator described as: 'creating a geography where Muslim women's bodies are not welcome in certain places, and policing where they can and cannot venture.'[72]

The debate about the *hijab* has raged for centuries, with women's voices generally excluded. One Egyptian woman commented in 1890 that the male legislator was being 'as despotic about liberating us as he has been about our enslavement. We are weary of his despotism.'[73]

The key with clothing for women is choice. It will be acceptable to wear heels, but also not wear them – ever. Under neoliberalism heels have been rebranded as a symbol of power and liberation for women despite them not empowering women in any meaningful way.[74] Instead under capitalism choices shrink: 'A tawdry, tarty, cartoon like version of female sexuality has become so ubiquitous [that] it no longer seems particular. What we once regarded as a kind of sexual expression we now view as sexuality.'[75]

A single vision of anything, let along sexuality, is not freedom of choice. The fashion industry's loss of power would also mean an end to the exclusion of bodies that do not 'measure up'. Body insecurity would be replaced by the loving acceptance and celebration of all kinds of beauty. Women must have the freedom to be whatever they want and not be subject to negative or critical messages if they decide not to give two hoots about their appearance. The struggle for emancipation is 'nourished by the image of enslaved ancestors rather than that of liberated grandchildren,' argued Walter Benjamin.[76] Certainly, this is how I feel about women's clothing. It is the spectre of past restrictions on life-roles and dress, encapsulated by 1950s dress, that make me work for change.

Under capitalism, racism in the fashion industry manifests itself in the exclusion of models of colour and by the exclusion *and* appropriation of culture. If those powerful elements in society who depend on excluding people to secure their own power were removed then there would be no need to exclude people. The ending of race as a means of exclusion would end for good the idea of beauty having one colour. It would also end shame and oppression in dress, allowing people to wear their own cultural dress without becoming targets for abuse.[77] Currently, dominant societies want a minority's culture but not the immigration of its people: there is a disparity between 'how black culture is consumed versus how black people are treated'.[78] Equality in society would end this form of racism.

Commodification and cultural co-option occur because art is viewed as something to be bought or sold rather than celebrated. What is needed are ways to fulfil our humanity that go beyond possession.[79] This would end cultural appropriation as a means to fill up the monotonous nature of modern life with escapist fantasy.[80] Rather than alienation, a post-capitalist society would be one of fulfilment and creativity.

Under capitalism the definitive factor in fashion is class, with people branded by their net worth. Ancient Egyptians had different coloured robes for different ranks. Thousands of years later, Britain had cloth caps, bowler hats or top hats – 'the higher the crown, the higher the social ranking'.[81] The same divisions are replicated in dress for leisure time. If you want to display your wealth, simply attach expensive objects to your body.

An end to a hierarchical society would mean an end to people fighting to keep their place at the top of society. Currently fashion underpins the power of a particular social class.[82] If there was no class, there would be no fashion as we know it because there would be no need to signify wealth through clothing, to own commodities in order to prove your difference from those who cannot afford what you have and to express class power through clothing. Instead, there would be freedom of expression for individuals and an equality that would not separate the makers from the wearers of beautiful clothes.

Myriad of Possibilities

Capitalism should be regarded as a failed system.[83] It cannot provide the people of this world with adequate food, shelter, clothing, health care or education. Its impact on the planet is devastating and may well lead to planetary catastrophe unless we act. Its impact on people is to cripple them physically, mentally, spiritually and artistically. Riven with contradictions, capitalism will only ever bring crisis, war and devastation. For every advance made there are a thousand more locked away in denied potential.

The production of fashion exemplifies this state of affairs by devastating the planet, maiming its workers and rigidly implementing the idea that there is only one way to look and to live. Fashion will never be free without an end to capitalism. And yet fashion can contribute to the remaking of the world. It has the ability to replace the old with the new, to make us hope and dream. That is why for every division in clothing that must be torn down, there is a myriad of possibilities that could spring up. This will be the adventure experienced by the new society. The Russian poet Alexander Blok described the task ahead: 'To redo everything. To arrange things so that everything becomes new; so that the false, the dirty, dull ugly life which is ours becomes just life, pure, gay, beautiful.'[84]

* * *

When I interviewed Isham Sardouk, senior trend-forecaster at Stylesight, it suddenly occurred to me that I was sitting opposite someone who has an uncanny knack of predicting the future. He had after all predicted the Arab Uprisings of 2011 in a trend-forecast called Raw Energy. It became impossible not to ask him what he thought the future holds. Time was short, so rather than dig for fashion secrets, I asked whether he predicted any more uprisings. He replied that the inequalities of the world, 'of people who have so much and people who don't have anything, is going to become a big trend at some point where things will have to balance out'.

Let us see if we can make him right.

Notes

Introduction

1. Ridley Scott, director, *Robin Hood*, Universal Studios, 2010.
2. Ingrid Loscheck, *When Clothes Become Fashion: Design and Innovation Systems*. Berg, 2009, p. 135.
3. Colin Gale and Jasbin Kaur, *Fashion & Textiles*. Berg, 2004, p. 20.
4. Dana Thomas, *Deluxe*. Penguin, 2007. The entire book investigates this question.
5. István Mészáros, *Marx's Theory of Alienation*. Merlin, 2006, p. 175. Virtuoso piano players need socially produced pianos.
6. Kaisik Wong's work, copied by Nicolas Ghesquière for Balenciaga: www. businessoffashion.com/2013/03/op-ed-who-watches-the-watchmen. html?utm_source=Subscribers&utm_campaign=5d6286da05-&utm_ medium=email. Dior, Prada and Celine were caught copying historic designs: www.fashionista.com/2013/04/raf-simons-miuccia-prada-called-out-for-copying-historic-designs.
7. I agree with the approach taken in Linda Welters and Abby Lillethun (eds.), *The Fashion Reader*, 2nd edition. Bloomsbury, 2007, pp. xxv–xxix. See Sandra Niessen and Jennifer Craik's chapters for more on this argument.
8. Radu Stern, *Aganist Fashion: Clothing as Art 1850–1930*. MIT Press, 2004, p. 2.
9. Valerie Steele, *Paris Fashion*. Berg, 1988, p. 18.
10. Jean Allman (ed.), *Fashioning Africa: Power and the Politics of Dress*. Indiana University Press, 2004, p. 2. 'The people without history' is a quote from Eric Wolf which was adapted by Allman to 'The people without fashion'.
11. John Berger, *Art and Revolution*. Writers & Readers, 1969, p. 157.
12. Thanks to SPARC (Society for the Promotion of Area Resource Centers), an Indian NGO partnered with the National Slum Dwellers Federation.
13. Terry Eagleton, *Marxism and Literary Criticism*. Methuen, 1985, p. 59. Eagleton makes this point about writers, books and publishing houses.
14. Giannino Malossi (ed.), *The Style Engine*. Monacelli Press, 1998, p. 30.
15. Jean Rostard, quoted in Rachel Carson, *Silent Spring*. Houghton Mifflin, 1987, p. 13.
16. www.businessoffashion.com/2012/10/springsummer-2013-the-season-that-was.html#more-37507.
17. Jeanette A. Jarrow and Beatrice Judelle (eds.), *Inside the Fashion Business*. John Wiley & Sons, 1966, p. vii.

18. R. T. Naylor, *Crass Struggle*. McGill-Queen's University Press, 2011, p. 26.
19. See Chapter 4 for more on this point; and Jason Hickle, www.fpif.org/articles/rethinking_sweatshop_economics.
20. Manfred B. Steger and Ravi K. Roy, *Neoliberalism: A Very Short Introduction*. Oxford University Press, 2010, p. 53.
21. Naylor, *Crass Struggle*, p. 5.
22. *Ibid.*, p. 372.
23. *Ibid.*, p. 5.
24. Malossi, *The Style Engine*, p. 68.
25. www.fashion.telegraph.co.uk/news-features/TMG4841479/Financial-crunch-bites-as-Milan-Fashion-Week-opens.html.
26. CEO Johann Rupert, www.businessinsider.com/how-the-10-biggest-luxury-brands-came-to-dominate-the-world-2012-6?op=1#ixzz2M6Yl6Yhk.
27. Terry Eagleton lecture, Counterfire Conference, London, 5 November 2011.
28. James C. Scott, *Weapons of the Weak: Everyday Forms of Peasant Resistance*. Yale University Press, 1985, p. 301.
29. Eagleton, *Marxism and Literary Criticism*, p. viii.
30. Neil Faulkner, *A Marxist History of the World: From Neanderthals to Neoliberals*. Pluto Press, 2013, p. 152.
31. *Ibid.*, p. ix.
32. Eagleton, *Marxism and Literary Criticism*, p. 5.
33. John Berger, *Ways of Seeing*, documentary, part 1.
34. Eagleton, *Marxism and Literary Criticism*, p. 5.
35. Malcolm Barnard, *Fashion as Communication*. Routledge, 1996, p. 145 and chapter 1.
36. Interview with Neil Faulkner, 26 February 2013.
37. Terry Eagleton, *After Theory*. Allen Lane, 2003, p. 100.
38. Louis Althusser, quoted in Eagleton, *Marxism and Literary Criticism*, p. 18.
39. Bertolt Brecht, quoted in *ibid.*, p. 49.
40. *Ibid.*, p. viii.
41. South End Press (ed.), *Talking About a Revolution*. South End Press, 1998, p. 7.
42. Terry Eagleton lecture.

Chapter 1

1. www.independent.co.uk/life-style/fashion/news/21-workers-die-in-fire-at-hm-factory-1914292.html.
2. Friedrich Engels, *The Condition of the Working Class in England 1844*, 'The Great Towns'.
3. Eric M. Sigsworth, *Montague Burton: The Tailor of Taste*. Manchester University Press, 1990, p. vii.
4. *Ibid.*, p. 28.

5. Diana de Marly, *Working Dress*. Holmes & Meier, 1986.
6. *Ibid.*, p. 145.
7. Sigsworth, *Montague Burton*, p. 42.
8. *Wadsworth Review of Economic Studies*, quoted in Christopher Sladen, *The Conscription of Fashion*. Scholar Press, 1995, p. 11.
9. *Ibid.*, p. 18.
10. *Ibid.*, p. 23.
11. *Ibid.*, p. 37.
12. *Ibid.*, p. 39.
13. Alison Settle, *English Fashion*. Collins, 1959, p. 47.
14. J. Anderson Black and Madge Garland, *A History of Fashion*. McDonald (Black Cat imprint), 1990, p. 245.
15. Valerie Steele, *Paris Fashion*. Berg, 1988, p. 263.
16. *Ibid.*, p. 269.
17. www.designmuseum.org/design/christian-dior.
18. Steele, *Paris Fashion*, p. 270.
19. *Harper's Bazaar*, February 2012.
20. Lindsey German, *Sex Class and Socialism*. Bookmarks, 1998, p. 105.
21. Steele, *Paris Fashion*, p. 274.
22. www.designmuseum.org/design/christian-dior.
23. Sladen, *The Conscription of Fashion*, p. 76.
24. *Ibid.*, p. 76.
25. Kurt Lang and Gladys Engel Lang, 'The Power of Fashion', in Linda Welters and Abby Lillethun (eds.), *The Fashion Reader*. Bloomsbury Academic, 2007, p. 84.
26. Sladen, *The Conscription of Fashion*, p. 54.
27. George Orwell, *The Road to Wigan Pier*. Victor Gollancz, 1937, chapter 8.
28. Sladen, *The Conscription of Fashion*, p. 104.
29. Faulkner, *A Marxist History of the World*, p. 255.
30. *Ibid.*, p. 253.
31. German, *Sex Class and Socialism*, p. 106.
32. Steele, *Paris Fashion*, p. 279.
33. Colin McDowell, *The Designer Scam*. Hutchinson and Random House, 1994, p. 20.
34. Tobé Coller Davis, 25th Annual Boston Conference on Distribution, 1953. Quoted in Jarrow and Judelle, *Inside the Fashion Business*, p. 246.
35. Jarrow and Judelle, *Inside the Fashion Business*, pp. 158, 160.
36. *Ibid.*, p. 246.
37. Steele, *Paris Fashion*, p. 282.
38. Enrique Badia, *Zara and her Sisters*. Palgrave Macmillan, 2009, p. 69.
39. http://tinyurl.com/cu8gdwx.
40. www.forbes.com/billionaires/#page:1_sort:0_direction:asc_search:_filter:All%20industries_filter:All%20countries_filter:All%20states.

41. Lucy Siegle, *To Die For: Is Fast Fashion Wearing out the World?* Fourth Estate, 2011, p. 15.

42. *Ibid.*, pp. 29–30.

43. www.dailymail.co.uk/news/article-2269427/Supermarket-chic-How-clothes-sales-superstores-grown-double-rate-High-Street-chains-cash-strapped-Britons-cut-spending.html#ixzz2M0IPo8RO.

44. ASOS CEO, quoted in Primark and ASOS Show the Way with Storming Figures, *The Independent*, 20 January 2012.

45. www.vfc.com/about.

46. Sigsworth. *Montague Burton*, p. 98.

47. Naylor, *Crass Struggle*, p. 12.

48. Ethical Consumer's Corporate Critic database, July 2011.

49. Bernard Arnault, quoted in LVMH Net Boosted by Louis Vuitton, WWD Issue, 13 September 2003.

50. Thomas, *Deluxe*, p. 18.

51. www.forbes.com/profile/bernard-arnault.

52. *Libération.* www.wwd.com/business-news/business-features/newsmaker-of-the-year-nominees-6506060?page=2.

53. www.fashion.telegraph.co.uk/article/TMG9965759/Bernard-Arnault-Knighted-by-Prince-Charles.html.

54. Interview with Pierre Mallevays, Savigny Partners, Business of Fashion website, 18 November 2009.

55. The Prada Group owns Prada, miu miu, Church's and Car Shoes. Miuccia Prada's 2012 net worth is $12.4 billion as of March 2013.

56. The shoe company Jimmy Choo was founded in 1996 by the businesswoman Tamara Mellon and Jimmy Choo, a little-known shoemaker. Jimmy Choo left his namesake company and name in 2001, but was reportedly trying to buy them back with help from the Malaysian government in 2011 when Mellon sold to Labelux for over £500 million.

57. The Two Faces of Burberry, *Guardian*, 15 April 2004.

58. www.businessoffashion.com/2013/04/lets-show-the-world-that-fashion-is-serious-business.html?utm_source=Subscribers&utm_campaign=cc02b5cb0b-&utm_medium=email.

59. www.thesundaytimes.co.uk/sto/news/uk_news/National/article 1027406.ece.

60. Quentin Bell, *On Human Finery*. Hogarth Press, 1947, p. 22.

61. www.businessoffashion.com/2013/09/chanels-wertheimers-found-11-billion-richer-selling-no-5.html.

62. McDowell, *The Designer Scam*, p. 5.

63. Thomas, *Deluxe*, p. 163.

64. *Ibid.*, p. 168.

65. Thomas Maier, quoted in www.newyorker.com/reporting/2011/01/03/110103fa_fact_colapinto. The bag designer Luella Bartley also called It Bags 'the beginning of the end of culture in general'. Vogue.co.uk.

66. Thomas, *Deluxe*, p. 168.
67. *Ibid.*, p. 168.
68. *Ibid.*, p. 203.
69. Faulkner, *Marxist History of the World*, p. 279.
70. www.europe.chinadaily.com.cn/china/2013-02/08/content_16214640.htm.
71. *Ibid.*
72. Forbes, *Master of the Brand: Bernard Arnault*, 11 April 2010.
73. Richemont CEO Johann Rupert, www.businessinsider.com/how-the-10-biggest-luxury-brands-came-to-dominate-the-world-2012-6?op=1#ixzz2M6Y16Yhk.
74. Vanessa Friedman, Fung Brands to Buy Most of Sonia Rykiel, *Financial Times* blog, 26 January 2012.
75. Paris Group Plans Expansion for Gianfranco Ferré, *Financial Times*, 25 February 2011.
76. McDowell, *The Designer Scam*, p. 6.

Chapter 2

1. Interview with Jackie Newcombe, Managing Director of IPC Southbank, 16 May 2012.
2. Interview with Natalie Singh, Head of Denim & Street at WGSN, April 2012.
3. Cynthia L. White, *Women's Magazines 1693–1968*. Michael Joseph, 1970.
4. Jenny McKay, *The Magazines Handbook*. Routledge, 2006.
5. Caroline Seebohm, *The Man Who Was Vogue*. Weidenfeld & Nicolson, 1982, p. 38.
6. *Ibid.*, p. 80, Condé Nast's underlining.
7. www.ft.com/cms/s/2/40071460-8315-11e1-929f-00144feab49a.html#axzz2M0sHzSXm.
8. www.nypost.com/p/news/national/item_IasvwQTyblLkQMoraHzx3H#ixzz1uCYBOpfu.
9. In 1997, *Tatler*'s editor Jane Procture described it as a magazine about 'being incredibly rich, and consuming and having lots of fun'. Anna Gough Yates, *Women's Magazines*. Routledge, 2003.
10. Gavin Waddell, *How Fashion Works*. Blackwell, 2007, p. 157.
11. David Croteau and William Hoynes, *The Business of Media*. Pine Forge Press, 2001, p. 4.
12. In 2012 Hearst also published *Redbook*, *Oprah*, *Company*, *Cosmopolitan* (63 international editions) and *Seventeen* which has 13 million readers a month. Hearst Digital Media publishes 28 websites, multiple mobile sites and Hearst Books.
13. The concept of synergy is from Croteau and Hoynes, *The Business of Media*, pp. 74–81.

14. Newcombe interview.
15. *Ibid.*
16. Croteau and Hoynes, *The Business of Media*, p. 4.
17. Benjamin M. Compaine and Douglas Gomary, *Who Owns the Media?* Lawrence Erlbaum, 2000, p. 151.
18. Newcombe interview.
19. *Ibid.*
20. *Financial Times*, 17 April 2012.
21. BBC3 *Secrets of the Super Brands – Fashion.*
22. Dallas Walker Smythe, *Dependency Road: Communications, Capitalism and Canada.* Ablex, 1982, p. 37.
23. McKay, *The Magazine Handbook*, p. 200.
24. Olivia Whitehorne, *Cosmo Woman*, Crescent Moon, 2007, p. 82.
25. Croteau and Hoynes *The Business of Media*, p. 179.
26. Eric Clark, *The Want Makers*, Hodder & Stoughton, 1988, p. 350.
27. Robert Merton, *Paul Lazarfeld*, 1948, quoted in Smythe, *Dependency Road*, p. 18.
28. Gloria Steinham, *Moving Beyond Words: Age, Rage, Sex, Power, Money, Muscles: Breaking the Boundaries of Gender.* Touchstone, 1994.
29. Richard Shortway, quoted in McKay, *The Magazine Handbook*, p. 200.
30. Myrna Blythe, *Spin Sisters*. St. Martin's Press, 2004, p. 104.
31. McKay, *The Magazine Handbook.*
32. McDowell, *The Designer Scam*, p. 48.
33. Nick Knight, www.businessoffashion.com/2012/10/springsummer-2013-the-season-that-was.html#more-37507.
34 Fashion Week: The beleaguered art of fashion criticism. *Toronto Star*, 7 March 2012.
35. *Ibid.*
36. Hadley Freeman, Gaultier's Gleeful Savagery. *Guardian*, 8 July 2006.
37. www.nytimes.com/2008/03/13/fashion/shows/13banned.html?page wanted=all&_r=0
38. Simone Werle, *Style Diaries: World Fashion from Berlin to Tokyo*. Prestel, 2010, Introduction.
39. David Klein and Dan Burstein, *Blog!* CDS Books, 2005, p. xvii.
40. The Pulitzer Prize-winning fashion critic Robin Givhan, quoted in Fashion Week: The beleaguered art of fashion criticism. *Toronto Star*, 7 March 2012.
41. Reuters, Designers Embrace Power of Fashion's Blogging Crowd, 23 February 2012.
42. Daniel Albertazzi and Paul Cobley, *The Media: An Introduction.* Pearson Education, 2009, p. 161.
43. William Higham, *The Next Big Thing.* Kogan Page, 2009, p. 20.
44. www.signature9.com/style-99 On other blog rating sites the order is often slightly different but the contenders basically the same.

45. A book by blogger Yuli Ziv.
46. Valentine Uhovski, quoted by Fashionista.com, 18 April 2012.
47. www.businessinsider.com/the-fashion-blogs-who-are-beating-vogue-at-online-influence-2011-17.
48. www.mediabistro.com/fishbowlny/the-sartorialist-inks-cond-nast-deal_b5501.
49. Schuman interview, *Business of Fashion*, 3 October 2011. Advertisers have included Tiffany, Coach and Ferragamo, American Apparel, Net-a-porter.
50. Fashionista.com, 15 May 2012.
51. Tavi Gevinson interview, *Business of Fashion*, April 2012.
52. Christian Fuchs, The Internet: Serving the revolution? Counterfire.org, 2010.
53. Bloggers are required by the US Federal Trade Commission to disclose any gifts they receive.
54. Fuchs, *The Internet*.
55. *Ibid.*
56. A UK trend forecasting agency.
57. *St. Petersburg Times*, 27 December 1962.
58. Higham, *The Next Big Thing*, p. 44.
59. Chris Sanderson, *The Future Laboratory*, quoted in Martin Raymond, *The Trend Forecasters Handbook*. Lawrence King, 2010, p. 125.
60. Singh interview.
61. Interview with a Topshop product specialist, who asked to remain anonymous.
62. Jayne Sheridan, *Fashion Media Promotion: The New Black Magic*. Wiley Blackwell, 2010, p. 14.
63. Frank Bober, Stylesight CEO, interview by Telegraph.co.uk.
64. Interview with Isham Sardouk, senior vice president of Trend Forecasting at Stylesight, 15 April 2012.
65. Interview with Jaana Jatyri, founder of Trendstop, 20 April 2012.
66. Sardouk interview.
67. Sharon Graubard, chief trend analyst at Stylesight, *The Telegraph*.
68. Singh interview.
69. *Ibid.*

Chapter 3

1. Hardy Amies, *Just So Far*, Collins, 1954. Book dedication.
2. Anne Fogarty, *The Art of Being a Well-Dressed Wife*, 1959. Reprinted V & A Enterprises, 2011.
3. www.independent.co.uk/voices/commentators/camila-batmanghelidjh-caring-costs-ndash-but-so-do-riots-2333991.html.

4. www.social-europe.eu/2011/08/the-london-riots-on-consumerism-coming-home-to-roost.
5. www.guardian.co.uk/uk/2011/sep/05/riot-jail-sentences-crown-courts. www.telegraph.co.uk/news/uknews/crime/8695988/London-riots-Lidl-water-thief-jailed-for-six-months.html.
6. www.social-europe.eu/2011/08/the-london-riots-on-consumerism-coming-home-to-roost.
7. Naylor, *Crass Struggle*, p. 372.
8. Juliet B. Schor, Why Do We Consume So Much? p. 3, www.csbsju.edu/Academics/Lecture-Series/Clemens-Lecture-Series/Past-Lectures/Schor.htm.
9. Simonetta Falasca-Zamponi, *Waste and Consumption*, Routledge, 2007, p. 16.
10. www.rt.com/usa/half-poor-america-poverty-909.
11. Alan Tomlinson (ed.), *Consumption, Identity and Style: Marketing, Meanings and the Packaging of Pleasure*. Routledge, 1991, p. 13.
12. www.thesartorialist.com/photos/not-giving-up-nyc.
13. www.threadbared.blogspot.co.uk/2009/09/tramp-chic-and-photograph.html. Founded by academics Minh-Ha T. Pham and Mimi Thi Nguyen.
14. Engels, *The Conditions of the Working Class*, 'The Great Towns'.
15. Barnard, *Fashion as Communication*, pp. 107, 145, and chapter 1.
16. An eighteenth-century commentator, quoted in *ibid.*, p. 107.
17. Tamsin Blanchard, *Green is the New Black*. Hodder & Stoughton, 2007, p. xi.
18. Juliet Schor, In Defence of Consumer Critique: Revisiting the consumption debates of the twentieth century, *Annals of the American Academy of Political and Social Science*, 2007.
19. Elizabeth Wilson, *Adorned in Dreams*. Virago, 1985, p. 17.
20. Karl Marx, *The Poverty of Philosophy*, pp. 41–2.
21. Suj Jhally, *The Codes of Advertising*. Routledge, 1990, p. 2.
22. Nicholas Barbon, *A Discourse of Trade*, 1690. Quoted by Ulrich Lehmann in his Fashion and Materialism, Marxism in Culture lecture, Senate House, 15 June 2012.
23. Karl Marx, *Outline of the Critique of Political Economy* (*Grundrisse*) www.marxists.org/archive/marx/works/1857/grundrisse/ch01.htm.
24. Ingrid Loschek, *When Clothes Become Fashion: Design and Innovation Systems*. Berg, 2009, p. 135.
25. John Bellamy Foster, Brett Clark and Richard York, *The Ecological Rift: Capitalism's War on the Earth*. Monthly Review Press, 2010, p. 392.
26. *Ibid.*, p. 394.
27. *Ibid.*

28. www.dailymail.co.uk/news/article-2075509/Britain-spends-1-5-million-minute-busiest-shopping-days-year-takings-10-year.html#ixzz1x1dauTGT.

29. *Fashion NYC 2020*. New York City Economic Development Corporation, p. 11.

30. www.businessoffashion.com/2013/04/lets-show-the-world-that-fashion-is-serious-business.html?utm_source=Subscribers&utm_campaign=cc02b5cb0b-&utm_medium=email.

31. Jhally, *The Codes of Advertising*, p. 2.

32. Croteau and Hoynes, *The Business of Media*, p. 180.

33. István Mészáros, *Marx's Theory of Alienation*, Merlin, 2005, p. 145, quoting Marx.

34. Singh interview.

35. Ashley Mears, *Pricing Beauty*, University of California Press, 2011, p. 75.

36. British *Vogue*, November 2011, p. 111.

37 *Times* Online, Style Article 3304394.

38. Newcombe interview.

39. www.vogue.co.uk/news/2009/07/17/the-truth-about-fashion-in-a-recession.

40. Berger, *Ways of Seeing*.

41. *Stylist*, Issue 100, 2 November 2011.

42. www.dressforsuccess.org/whatwedo_suits.aspx.

43. Joseph Hansen and Evelyn Reed, *Cosmetics, Fashions, and the Exploitation of Women*, Pathfinder Press, 1986, p. 51.

44. *Ibid.*, p. 39.

45. Sandra Lee Bartky, *Femininity and Domination*, Routledge, 1990, p. 75.

46. *Ibid.*, p. 71.

47. G. K. Chesterton, *The New Jerusalem* [1920], 2012, chapter 4.

48. Bellamy Foster, Clark and York, *Ecological Rift*, pp. 393–4.

49. John O'Toole, *The Trouble with Advertising*, quoted in Clark, *The Want Makers*, p. 17.

50. David Norman and Guy Shrubsole, *Think of Me as Evil?* WWF and the Public Interest Research Centre Report, 2011, p. 18.

51. Mészáros, *Marx's Theory of Alienation*, p. 144.

52. Faulkner interview.

53. Berger, *Ways of Seeing*, p. 125.

54. *Ibid.*, p. 143.

55. www.cbsoutdoor.co.uk.

56. Jarrow and Judelle, *Inside the Fashion Business*, p. 256.

57. Joel Waldfogel, *Scroogenomics*. Princeton University Press, 2009, p. 81.

58. www.online.wsj.com/article/SB10001424052970203710704577052373900992432.html?mod=wsj_share_tweet.

59. As debt levels rise and the cost of debt becomes unsustainable, crises inevitably arise.

60. Larry Elliott and Dan Atkinson, *The Gods that Failed*. The Bodley Head, 2008, p. 164.
61. *Ibid.*, p. 176.
62. Previously known as Consumer Credit Counselling Service.
63. Ring-a-Ding-Ding, *Sex and the City*, episode 64, season 4.
64. www.telegraph.co.uk/finance/personalfinance/borrowing/credit cards/8907992/Discount-ban-could-kill-off-store-cards.html.
65. Interview with Una Farrell, Step Change press officer, Spring 2013.
66. www.telegraph.co.uk/finance/personalfinance/borrowing/8194968/ Store-card-holders-to-face-charges-if-they-dont-spend.html.
67. Jarrow and Judelle, *Inside the Fashion Business*, p. 168.
68. Matt Haig, *Brand Success: How the World's Top 100 Brands Thrive and Survive*, 2nd edition. Kogan Page, 2011, p. 117.
69. Jhally, *The Codes of Advertising*, pp. 53–4.
70. *Grazia*, issue 353; *Stylist*, issue 111.
71. Friedrich Engels, *Outlines of a Critique of Political Economy* in Mészáros, *Marx's Theory of Alienation*, p. 158.
72. *Ibid.*, p. 204.
73. Berger, *Ways of Seeing*, part 4.
74. Marx, in Mészáros. *Marx's Theory of Alienation*, p. 130.
75. Opening lines of Patrick Hamilton's novel *Slaves of Solitude*, Constable, 2006.
76. Thomas, *Deluxe*, pp. 224–5.
77. Marx, in Mészáros, *Marx's Theory of Alienation*, p. 145.
78. Phillip Brown, Hugh Lauder and David Ashton, *The Global Auction: The Broken Promises of Education, Jobs, and Incomes*. Oxford University Press, 2011.
79. www.guardian.co.uk/commentisfree/2011/feb/28/education-jobs-middle-class-decline.
80. Marx, in Mészáros, *Marx's Theory of Alienation*, p. 158.
81 Raymond Williams, in Bellamy Foster, Clark and York, *Ecological Rift*, p. 393.
82. John Bellamy Foster, *Marx's Ecology*. Monthly Review Press, p. 2.
83. Mears, *Pricing Beauty*, p. 25.
84. An Appeal to Walt Disney, in Andrew Ross (ed.), *No Sweat: Fashion, Free Trade and the Rights of Workers*. Verso, 1997, p. 101.
85. Thomas. *Deluxe*, p. 197. The entire book investigates this question.
86. www.social-europe.eu/2011/08/the-london-riots-on-consumerism-coming-home-to-roost.
87. Ben Fine, *The World of Consumption: The Material and Cultural Revisited*. Routledge, 2002, p. 66.
88. Mészáros, *Marx's Theory of Alienation*, p. 156.
89. www.robertmontgomery.org.

Chapter 4

1. www.playfair2008.org, in Liesbeth Sluiter, *Clean Clothes*. Pluto Press, 2009, p. 76.
2. Gary Gereffi and Stacey Frederick, The Global Apparel Value Chain, Trade & the Crisis: Challenges and opportunities for developing countries, in Olivier Cattaneo, Gary Gereffi and Cornelia Staritz (eds.), *Global Value Chains in a Post-Crisis World*. The World Bank, 2010, chapter 5, p. 157.
3. Zara, www.telegraph.co.uk/finance/newsbysector/retailandconsumer/9552298/Zara-owner-Inditex-grows-market-share-and-profits.html. LVMH, www.bbc.co.uk/news/business-16863923.
4. Interview with James Meadway, NEF senior economist, 16 October 2012.
5. www.nosweat.org.uk.
6. Sluiter, *Clean Clothes*, p. 200.
7. Andrew Ross, *No Sweat: Fashion Free Trade and the Rights of Garment Workers*. Verso, 1997, in Laura Hapke, *Sweatshop: The History of an American Idea*. Rutgers University Press, 2004, p. 2.
8. Faulkner, *A Marxist History of the World*, pp. 145–6.
9. Definition from Gerard P. Cachon and Robert Swinney, The Value of Fast Fashion: Quick response, enhanced design, and strategic consumer behaviour, *Management Science*, Vol. 57, No. 4, April 2011, pp. 778–95.
10. Ross, *Slaves to Fashion*, p. 132.
11. www.metmuseum.org/toah/works-of-art/156.4J23.
12. Engels, *The Condition of the Working Class in England*.
13. www.radicalmanchester.wordpress.com.
14. Karen Tranberg Hansen, *Salaula: The World of Second Hand Clothing and Zambia*. University of Chicago Press, 2000, p. 24.
15. *Ibid.*, p. 9.
16. Engels, *The Condition of the Working Class in England*.
17. Ross, *Slaves to Fashion*, p. 18.
18. www.simpletoremember.com/articles/a/jewish_life_in_america.
19. Hapke, *Sweatshop*, p. 7.
20. Lisa Featherstone and USAS, *Students against Sweatshops*. Verso, 2000, p. 71.
21. *Ibid.*, p. 70.
22. Jewish Women's Archive: www.jwa.org/encyclopedia/article/shavelson-clara-lemlich. American Postal Workers Union archive: www.apwu.org/join/women/lbportraits/portraits-labor-triangle.htm. PBS archive: www.pbs.org/wgbh/americanexperience/features/biography/triangle-lemlich.
23. Ross, *Slaves to Fashion*, p. 64.
24. *Ibid.*, p. 54.
25. www.spiegel.de/international/world/criticism-over-damages-offered-by-german-discounter-for-pakistani-dead-a-862918.html.

26. *Ibid.*
27. www.guardian.co.uk/commentisfree/2012/sep/14/karachi-factory-fire-pakistan-health-safety.
28. Inspectors Certified Pakistani Factory as Safe Before Disaster, *New York Times*, 19 September 2012.
29. Inside Story Americas, 22 September 2012, www.aljazeera.com/programmes/insidestoryamericas/2012/09/2012922111531866568.html.
30. *Ibid.*
31. Inspectors Certified Pakistani Factory as Safe before Disaster, *New York Times*, 19 September 2012.
32. www.waronwant.org/news/press-releases/17982-retailers-attacked-on-rana-plaza-snub.
33. Interview with Philip Jennings 10 September 2013.
34. www.guardian.co.uk/commentisfree/2013/apr/30/bangladesh-workers-need-more-than-boycotts.
35. Interview with Amirul Haque Amir 9 September 2013.
36. www.nytimes.com/2012/09/10/world/asia/killing-of-bangladesh-labor-leader-spotlights-grievances-of-workers.html?pagewanted=all&_r=1&.
37. Ross, *Slaves to Fashion*, p. 69.
38. *Ibid.*, p. 69.
39. *Ibid.*, p. 96.
40. *Ibid.*, p. 103. The term 'global scanning' is from Raymond Vernon 1979; global scanning is also used to search for sales sites.
41. *Ibid.*, pp. 103, 122.
42. www.aabri.com/manuscripts/10615.pdf.
43. Attributed to Karl Marx.
44. Samantha Smith, The Multi Fibre Arrangement – A Thread of Protectionism, www.tcd.ie/Economics/SER/pasti.php?y=98.
45. Yongzheng Yang, The Impact of MFA Phasing out on World Clothing and Textile Markets, *Journal of Development Studies*, Vol. 30, Issue 4, 1994.
46. Cattaneo, Gereffi and Staritz, *Global Value Chains in a Post-Crisis World*, p. 159.
47. Ross, *Slaves to Fashion*, pp. 140–3. In January 2004, 30,000 Saipan garment workers won a landmark $20 million settlement after 26 US retailers and 23 Saipan factories were sued by labour rights organisations for human rights violations. Retailers included Gap, which was responsible for $200 million of production in Saipan, a fifth of the island's output.
48. www.current.com/shows/vanguard/89785807_battle-of-saipan.htm.
49. www.guardian.co.uk/business/2005/sep/06/politics.europeanunion.
50. Cattaneo, Gereffi and Staritz, *Global Value Chains in a Post-Crisis World*, p. 183.
51. *Ibid.*, p. 198, Table.

52. *Ibid.*

53. *Ibid.*, p. 165.

54. Stacey Frederick and Gary Gereffi, Upgrading and Restructuring in the Global Apparel Value Chain: Why China and Asia are outperforming Mexico and Central America, *International Journal of Technological Learning, Innovation and Development*,Vol. 4, Nos. 1/2/3, 2011.

55. Cattaneo, Gereffi and Staritz, *Global Value Chains in a Post-Crisis World*, p. 165.

56. Manufacturing: The end of cheap China, www.economist.com/node/21549956.

57. *Ibid.*

58. Cattaneo, Gereffi and Staritz, *Global Value Chains in a Post-Crisis World*, p. 174.

59. *Ibid.*, p. 165.

60. *Ibid.*, p. 174.

61. *Ibid.*

62. Frederick and Gereffi, Upgrading and Restructuring, p. 7.

63. Cattaneo, Gereffi and Staritz, *Global Value Chains in a Post-Crisis World*, p. 175.

64. *Ibid.*, p. 183.

65. *Ibid.*, p, 178, Table.

66. Chris Harman, *Economics of the Madhouse*. Bookmarks, 1995, p. 18.

67. Ben Fine and Alfredo Saad-Filho, *Marx's 'Capital'*, 5th edition. Pluto Press, 2010, pp. 71–2. Intrasectoral competition is examined in *Capital*. Volume 1; intersectoral competition in Volume 3.

68. www.fpif.org/articles/rethinking_sweatshop_economics.

69. *Ibid.*

70. Faulkner interview. The concept is from Karl Marx, *Capital*, Volume 1, chapter 25.

71. Ross, *Slaves to Fashion*, p. 5.

72. Nicholas D. Kristof and Sheryl Wudunn, Two Cheers for Sweatshops, *New York Times*, 24 September 2000.

73. Hapke, *Sweatshop*, p. 1.

74. Ross, *Slaves to Fashion*, p. 177.

75. *Ibid.*, p. 324.

76. www.thenation.com/article/161057/wikileaks-haiti-let-them-live-3-day.

77. *Ibid.*

78. Meadway interview.

79. www.burmacampaign.org.uk/index.php/news-and-reports/news-stories/Clothing-Retailers-told-to-Come-Clean-on-Burma/3. Companies named and shamed for refusing to disclose their policy include Harrods, Bay Trading, By Design, Benetton, Ciro Citteri, Elle, Etam, Intersport, Karen Millen, Liberty, TCS, Animal, Naf Naf, Jo Bloggs, Jeffrey Rogers, Pied-à-Terre, Savoy Tailors Guild, Shellys, Calvin Klein, La Coste,

Young Fashion, Great Universal Stores, Argos, Claire's Accessories, MK One, Shoe Box, First Sport, Lillywhites, Hawkshead, Urban Outfitters, Mambo, Mexx, Paul Smith, Reiss, Hobbs, Jane Norman, Miss Sixty, Boxfresh and L. K. Bennett.

80. www.ft.com/cms/s/0/7dcbdd92-3c63-11e1-8d3800144feabdc0.html#ixzz2AgyDaDRq.
81. www.opendemocracy.net/matt-kennard/haiti-and-shock-doctrine.
82. *Ibid.*
83. www.cje.oxfordjournals.org/content/28/2/153.abstract.
84. www.senate.columbia.edu/committees_dan/external/wrc1105.pdf.
85. www.dailymail.co.uk/news/article-1391673/Kates-dazzling-dress-Romanian-sweatshop-women-just-99p-hour.html?ito=feeds-newsxml.
86. Meadway interview.
87. www.dailymail.co.uk/news/article-1391673/Kates-dazzling-dress-Romanian-sweatshop-women-just-99p-hour.html#ixzz2M6jcUClg.
88. Ross, *Slaves to Fashion*, p. 72.

Chapter 5

1. Environmental Justice Foundation, http://archive.is/QRrp.
2. IPE, *Cleaning up the Fashion Industry*, www.ipe.org.cn.
3. www.blogs.ei.columbia.edu/2011/05/05/how-china-is-dealing-with-its-water-crisis.
4. IPE, *Cleaning up the Fashion Industry*.
5. www.theaustralian.com.au/news/breaking-news/croc-farmer-decries-carbon-tax-impost/story-fn3dxiwe-1226462688596.
6. www.independent.co.uk/environment/crocodile-farms-is-it-cruel-to-keep-these-wild-creatures-captive-418794.html.
7. Bhopal Medical Appeal, 1994, www.studentsforbhopal.org/node/18.
8. Mészáros, *Beyond Capital*. Capital 'inevitably brings a bitter harvest'.
9. www.ejfoundation.org/cotton/white-gold.
10. *Ibid.*
11. *Guardian,* www.guardian.co.uk/world/us-embassy-cables-documents/40515.
12. To Reduce Poverty and Pollution, China Needs More Billionaires Like This, www.forbes.com, 9 July 2012.
13. IPE, *Cleaning up the Fashion Industry*
14. *Ibid.*
15. *Ibid.*
16. *Ibid.*
17. *Ibid.*
18. www.independent.co.uk/environment/crocodile-farms-is-it-cruel-to-keep-these-wild-creatures-captive-418794.html.
19. www.scientificamerican.com/article.cfm?id=croc-unlocked-a-gene-map.

20. www.dailymail.co.uk/femail/article-1198947/Crocs-gold-Why-stars-like-Victoria-Beckham-flaunt-designer-bags-exploit-brutal-trade-crocodile-skin.html.

21. www.bbc.co.uk/news/business-17479818.

22. www.toxipedia.org/display/toxipedia/Aldicarb.

23. National Research Council, *The Use and Storage of Methyl Isocyanate (MIC) at Bayer CropScience.* Washington, DC: The National Academies Press, 2012.

24. Over half a million people were injured in the disaster and the area remains contaminated. Not until 2010 was anyone convicted of a criminal offence, when eight Indian Union Carbide executives received two-year prison sentences and fines of $2,100. Warren Anderson, CEO of Union Carbide, has not been prosecuted despite attempts to extradite him to India. http://bhopal.net.

25. www.bhopal.org/what-happened.

26. Carson, *Silent Spring*, p. 16.

27. www.toxipedia.org/display/toxipedia/Aldicarb.

28. www.cotton.org/econ/cropinfo/cropdata/rankings.cfm.

29. www.environmentalhealthnews.org/ehs/news/aldicarb-phaseout.

30. *Ibid.*

31. www.nytimes.com/1985/11/28/us/union-carbide-says-it-plans-to-resume-making-aldicarb.html.

32. www.environmentalhealthnews.org/ehs/news/aldicarb-phaseout.

33. www.cbgnetwork.org/2877.html.

34. www.environmentalhealthnews.org/ehs/news/aldicarb-phaseout.

35. Interview with Dilys Williams, director of the Center for Sustainable Fashion, 23 November 2012.

36. John Bellamy Foster, *Ecology Against Capitalism.* Monthly Review Press, 2002, p. 80.

37. Bellamy Foster, Clark and York, *The Ecological Rift*, p. 78.

38. David Harvey, quoted in Fred Magdoff and John Bellamy Foster, *What Every Environmentalist Needs to Know about Capitalism.* Monthly Review Press, 2011, p. 97.

39. The environmental ecologist K. William Kapp, quoted in Bellamy Foster, *Ecology Against Capitalism*, p. 57.

40. Siegle, *To Die For*, p. 105.

41. *Ibid.*, pp. 105–6.

42. Bellamy Foster, Clark and York, *The Ecological Rift*, p. 394.

43. *Ibid.*, p. 39.

44. *Ibid.*, p. 64.

45. www.dailymail.co.uk/femail/article-482849/Pythons-skinned-left-die-The-shocking-reality-fashions-new-obsession.html.

46. Siegle, *To Die For*, pp. 193–4. Chapter 9 refutes 'fur is ethical/warm/vintage/ sustainable' arguments.

47. *Ibid.*, p. 197.
48. Magdoff and Bellamy Foster, *What Every Environmentalist Needs to Know about Capitalism*, p. 101.
49. Bellamy Foster, *Ecology Against Capitalism*, p. 55.
50. Magdoff and Bellamy Foster, *What Every Environmentalist Needs to Know about Capitalism*, p. 101.
51. Bertell Ollman, *Alienation: Marx's Conception of Man in Capitalist Society*. Cambridge University Press, 1976, p. 135.
52. Bellamy Foster, *Ecology Against Capitalism*, p. 81.
53. John Bellamy Foster, Marx's Ecology and its Historical Significance, in Michael R. Redclift and Graham Woodgate (eds.), *The International Handbook of Environmental Sociology*, 2nd edition. Edward Elgar, 2000, p. 106.
54. www.wrap.org.uk/content/time-unlock-value-household-textile-waste-says-wrap.
55. Blanchard, *Green is the New Black*, p. 22.
56. Gloria Steinem.
57. Thomas, *Deluxe*, p. 197.
58. Cattaneo, Gereffi and Staritz, *Global Value Chains in a Post-Crisis World*, p. 198, Table.
59. Magdoff and Bellamy Foster, *What Every Environmentalist Needs to Know about Capitalism*, p. 32.
60. *Ibid.*, p. 34.
61. Bellamy Foster, Clark and York, *The Ecological Rift*, p. 8.
62. Karl Marx, *The Poverty of Philosophy*, pp. 41–2, quoted in *ibid.*, p. 383.
63. Bartky, *Femininity and Domination*, p. 72.
64. Falasca-Zamponi, *Waste and Consumption*, p. 48.
65. James Gustave Speth, quoted in Magdoff and Bellamy Foster, *What Every Environmentalist Needs to Know about Capitalism*, p. 29.
66. Bellamy Foster, Clark and York, *The Ecological Rift*, p. 101.
67. *Ibid.*, Preface.
68. *Ibid.*, p. 101.
69. Magdoff and Bellamy Foster *What Every Environmentalist Needs to Know about Capitalism*, p. 106.
70. www.ran.org/guccis-luxury-packaging-gets-greener-makeover-0#ixzz27OGWIw6t.
71. Bellamy Foster, Clark and York, *The Ecological Rift*, p. 389.
72. www.textiletoolbox.com/posts/design-to-reduce-the-need-to-consume.
73. Greenpeace, *Dirty Laundry*, http://tinyurl.com/avy7jmy; *Dirty Laundry 2: Hung out to Dry*. http://tinyurl.com/aslsmew.
74. H&M 2011 annual report part 1: http://tinyurl.com/agrnqps.
75. Lucy Siegle, Is H&M the New Home of Ethical Fashion? *Guardian*, 7 April 2012.

76. www.guardian.co.uk/environment/2008/oct/23/ethicalbusiness-consumeraffairs.

77. Albert Einstein, Why socialism? *Monthly Review*, 1949, www.monthlyreview.org/2009/05/01/why-socialism.

78. Bellamy Foster, Clark and York *The Ecological Rift*, p. 80.

79. István Mészáros, *The Structural Crisis of Capitalism*. Monthly Review Press, 2010, p. 66.

80. Williams interview. Chapter 11 of Lucy Siegle's book examines what happens to clothes in charity shops, textile banks, recycling plants and salaula markets in Africa.

81. www.corpwatch.org/article.php?id=2328.

82. *Ibid.*

83. *Ibid*

84. www.smithsonianmag.com/science-nature/plastic.html.

85. Matilda Lee, *Eco Chic*. Octopus, 2007, chapter 3.

86. www.guardian.co.uk/environment/2008/oct/23/ethicalbusiness-consumeraffairs.

87. www.anothermag.com/current/view/1991/Biomaterials.

88. Sluiter, *Clean Clothes*, p. 76.

89. Bellamy Foster, *Ecology Against Capitalism*, p. 25.

Chapter 6

1. Susie Orbach, *Bodies*. Profile Books, 2010, p. 92.

2. www.iheartthreadbared.wordpress.com/2013/01/07/ashion-and-americas-culture-of-violence.

3. Orbach, *Bodies*, p. 7.

4. www.guardian.co.uk/theguardian/2012/feb/04/jo-swinson-interview.

5. www.mind.org.uk/help/research_and_policy/statistics_1_how_common_is_mental_distress#_edn15.

6. www.any-body.org. Orbach, speech to the UN Commission on the Status of Women, 6 March 2012.

7. Orbach, *Bodies*, p. 137.

8. *Ibid.*, p. 89.

9. *Ibid.*, p. 81.

10. Jean Kilbourne documentary, *Killing Us Softly*.

11. Bartky, *Femininity and Domination*, p. 72.

12. www.businessoffashion.com/2013/04/10-of-londons-top-young-fashion-creatives.html#comment-770561.

13. www.thelocal.se/37770/20111206/ Norwegian website – Bildbluffen.

14. www.newyorker.com/reporting/2008/05/12/080512fa_fact_collins.

15. *Ibid.*

16. Mears, *Pricing Beauty*, p. 35.

17. www.modelalliance.org/introductory-note.

18. www.spiegel.de/international/spiegel/spiegel-interview-with-plus-size-model-i-was-asking-how-many-calories-chewing-gum-had-a-653745.html.
19. www.proud2bme.org/node/159.
20. www.medicalnewstoday.com/articles/259412.php.
21. Mears, *Pricing Beauty*, pp. 182–3.
22. www.independent.co.uk/news/the-model-agencies-say-one-of-these-girls-is-the-proper-shape-and-the-other-is-too-fat-are-they-right-1312076.html.
23. Mears, *Pricing Beauty*, p. 183.
24. www.abcnews.go.com/blogs/headlines/2012/01/most-models-meet-criteria-for-anorexia-size-6-is-plus-size-magazine.
25. Interview with Dunja Knezevic, president of The Models Union, 17 September 2012.
26. Mears, *Pricing Beauty*, p. 183.
27. www.spiegel.de/international/spiegel/spiegel-interview-with-plus-size-model-i-was-asking-how-many-calories-chewing-gum-had-a-653745.html.
28. Knezevic interview.
29. The World Health Organisation considers anyone with a body mass index (BMI) of 16 or less to be starving. Luisel Ramos's BMI was 14.5 and Ana Carolina Reston's 13.4. Controversy remains around the usefulness of BMI in assessing health.
30. www.dailymail.co.uk/femail/article-433829/Size-zero-hysteria-London-Fashion-Week.html#ixzz22qoh8xHZ.
31. Knezevic interview.
32. www.vanityfair.com/online/daily/2012/10/kate-moss-years-of-crying-johnny-depp.
33. Mears, *Pricing Beauty*, p. 204.
34. Little and Large Are Both Losers, *Huffington Post*, 22 September 2011.
35. 'Too Thin' Topshop Model Codie Young Hits Back, *Daily Telegraph*, 19 July 2011.
36. www.fashionista.com/2012/07/is-kate-upton-too-fat-too-skinny-why-kate-upton-just-cant-win.
37. Mears, *Pricing Beauty*, p. 182.
38. *Ibid.*, p. 190.
39. *Ibid.*, p. 203.
40. Knezevic interview.
41. Ollman, *Alienation*, p. 166.
42. Karl Marx, *Economic and Philosophical Manuscripts of 1844*.
43. Marx *Capital*, Volume 1.
44. Eagleton, *After Theory*, p. 42.
45. Knezevic interview.
46. Bellamy Foster, Clark and York, *The Ecological Rift*, p. 392.
47. Knezevic interview.
48. *Ibid.*

49. Linda Evangalista.

50. Knezevic interview.

51. Ross, *Slaves to Fashion*, pp. 21–3.

52. Bartky, *Femininity and Domination*, p. 73.

53. Orbach, *Bodies*, p. 94.

54. Susie Orbach, Ad Men Today Are Wrong on Body, *Size* www.any-body. org.

55. Orbach, *Bodies*, p. 94.

56. *Ibid.*, p. 89.

57. *Ibid.*, p. 12.

58. Karl Lagerfeld. CNN interview. www.ellecanada.com/living/culture/can-using-different-types-of-models-benefit-brands/a/58327.

59. www.ellecanada.com/living/culture/can-using-different-types-of-models-benefit-brands/a/58327.

60. Ollman, *Alienation*, p. 135.

61. Magdoff and Bellamy Foster, *What Every Environmentalist Needs to Know about* Capitalism, p. 101.

62. Ruth Frankenburg (ed.), *Displacing Whiteness*, Duke University Press, 1997, p. 13.

63. Naomi Wolf, *The Beauty Myth*, Vintage, Random House, 1991, p. 185.

64. *Ibid.*

65. Ann Hollander, *Seeing Through Clothes*, p. 151, quoted *ibid.*, p. 184.

66. *Ibid.*, p. 185.

67. Bartky, *Femininity and Domination*, p. 65.

68. *Ibid.*, p. 79.

69. www.dictionaryblog.cambridge.org/category/new-words.

70. www.hup.harvard.edu/catalog.php?isbn=9780674049307.

71. www.iheartthreadbared.wordpress.com/2013/01/07/ashion-and-americas-culture-of-violence.

72. Eagleton, *After Theory*, p. 67.

73. www.ellecanada.com/living/culture/can-using-different-types-of-models-benefit-brands/a/58327.

74. *Ibid.*

75. www.youtube.com/watch?v=nP-LSSxj3UU Interview with Victoria Keon-Cohen.

76. Knezevic interview.

77. *Ibid.*

78. www.reuters.com/article/2012/02/07/usa-fashion-rights-idUSL2E8D 70B320120207.

79. www.huffingtonpost.com/jean-fain-licsw-msw/body-image_b_1583322. html.

80. www.athickgirlscloset.tumblr.com.

81. www.jezebel.com/5547247/american-apparel-is-not-interested-in-your-plus+size-dollars.

82. www.extrawiggleroom.tumblr.com/page/2.

83. www.guardian.co.uk/lifeandstyle/2012/jan/17/slimming-clubs-straitjackets-susie-orbach.

84. www.guardian.co.uk/theguardian/2012/feb/04/jo-swinson-interview.

85. *Ibid.*

86. Rosalind Gill, *Media, Empowerment and the 'Sexualization of Culture' Debates*, 5 January 2012, Feminist Forum # Springer Science+Business Media, LLC 2012.

87. *Ibid.*

88. Joan Costa-Font and Mireia Jofre-Bonet, *Anorexia, Body Image and Peer Effects: Evidence from a Sample of European Women.* Centre for Economic Performance, Discussion Paper No. 1098, November 2011.

89. Knezevic interview.

90. www.anybody.squarespace.com/anybody_vent/2012/3/6/susie-orbach-speaks-at-the-un-commission-on-the-status-of-wo.html.

Chapter 7

1. www.youtube.com/watch?v=6L8uOk9fvXQ&feature=relmfu.

2. Allman, *Fashioning Africa*, p. 2.

3. I have selected the term 'models of colour' for this chapter rather than the political term 'black' in an attempt to show that I am writing inclusively about a multitude of ethnicities who are targets of racism, including Afro-Caribbean, Latina, Asian, South East Asian and Native American people.

4. www.nymag.com/fashion/11/fall/china-machado.

5. Is Fashion Racist? US *Vogue*, July 2008.

6. www.dailykos.com/story/2009/04/04/716393/–Whites-Only-Designers-Reap-What-They-Sew-w-Mrs-O-POLL.

7. www.independent.co.uk/news/uk/home-news/fashion-is-racist-insider-lifts-lid-on-ethnic-exclusion-782974.html.

8. Knezevic interview.

9. The Colour of Beauty, www.nfb.ca/film/colour_of_beauty.

10. www.independent.co.uk/news/uk/home-news/fashion-is-racist-insider-lifts-lid-on-ethnic-exclusion-782974.html.

11. Janell Hobson, *Venus in the Dark: Blackness and Beauty in Popular Culture*, Routledge, 2005, p. 114.

12. www.nytimes.com/2008/09/01/business/worldbusiness/01vogue.html.

13. Frankenburg, *Displacing Whiteness*, p. 12.

14. Mears, *Pricing Beauty*, p. 194.

15. Alek Wek, *Alek*, HarperCollins' Amistad, 2007.

16. James Smalls, Slavery is a Woman: Race, Gender, and Visuality in Marie Benoist's Portrait d'une négresse (1800), www.arthistoryarchive.com/arthistory/Slavery-is-a-Woman.htm.

17. *Ibid.*

18. *Ibid.*, quoting Coco Fusco, *The Bodies That Were Not Ours and Other Writings*, London and New York: Routledge, 2001, p. 6.

19. *Ibid.*

20. Ill Doctrine, Ugly Shoes and Good Intentions, http://vimeo.com/44343389.

21. www.thehindu.com/todays-paper/tp-international/paris-fashion-denies-racism-charge/article5158820.ece.

22. Eduardo Bonilla-Silva, *Racism without Racists*, Rowman & Littlefield, 2010, p. 8.

23. Ruth Frankenberg *White Women, Race Matters: The Social Construction of Whiteness*. University of Minnesota Press, 1993, p. 11.

24. Leila Ahmed, *A Quiet Revolution.* Yale University Press, 2011, p. 23.

25. *Ibid.*, p. 24.

26. Maxine Leeds Craig, *Ain't I A Beauty Queen?* Oxford University Press, 2002, p. 9.

27. www.independent.co.uk/life-style/fashion/features/wrap-superstar-designer-diane-von-furstenberg-tells-her-story-801189.html.

28. Leeds Craig, *Ain't I A Beauty Queen?* chapter 1.

29. *Ibid.*, p. 6.

30. *Ibid.*, p. 25.

31. Hobson, *Venus in the Dark*, p. 7.

32. Leeds Craig, *Ain't I A Beauty Queen?* p. 37.

33. www.iheartthreadbared.wordpress.com/2011/05/05/whats-missing-in-vogue-italias-tribute-to-black-beauties.

34. Shevelle Rhule, Pride, www.guardian.co.uk/world/2009/oct/14/french-vogue-blacking-up.

35. Carine Roitfeld to Depart French *Vogue,* WWD 17 December 2010.

36. Leeds Craig, *Ain't I A Beauty Queen?* p. 14.

37. Christopher Boulton, Rebranding Diversity: Colourblind Racism within the US Advertising Industry, www.vimeo.com/44500667.

38. Penny Jane Burke and Jackie McManus, Art for a Few: Exclusions and misrecognitions in higher education admissions practices, *Discourse: Studies in the Cultural Politics of Education*, vol. 32, issue 5, 2011, pp. 699–712.

39. Oliver Wang interview, *Yellow Apparel: When the Coolie Becomes Cool*, 2000.

40. An Uneasy Cultural Exchange, *New York Times*, 14 March 2012.

41. The Turbulent Life of John Galliano, British *Vogue*, September 2011, p. 384.

42. Native Americans Know that Cultural Misappropriation is a Land of Darkness, Guardian.co.uk, 18 May 2012.

43. Richard Fung, Working Through Appropriation, www.richardfung.ca/index.php?/articles/working-through-appropriation-1993.

44. *Ibid.*

45. www.racialicious.com/2011/10/10/an-open-letter-to-urban-outfitters-on-columbus-day.

46. www.alagarconniere.blogspot.co.uk/2010/04/critical-fashion-lovers-basic-guide-to.html.

47. Erving Goffman, *The Presentation of Self in Everyday Life*. Allen Lane, Penguin, 1969, p. 53.

48. www.apihtawikosisan.tumblr.com/post/24815044400/cultural-appropriation-the-longer-article.

49. Prospect, What's in a Name? http://prospect.org/article/whats-name-3.

50. www.washingtonpost.com/blogs/arts-post/post/un-expert-offended-by-rodarte-aboriginal-print-fashion/2012/03/16/gIQAr0nNGS_blog.html.

51. Prospect, What's in a name?

52. Raahi Reddy interview, *Yellow Apparel: When the Coolie Becomes Cool*, 2000.

53. www.apihtawikosisan.tumblr.com/post/24815044400/cultural-appropriation-the-longer-article.

54. Native Americans Know that Cultural Misappropriation is a Land of Darkness, Guardian.co.uk.

55. Larry Elliott, and Dan Atkinson, *The Gods that Failed*. Bodley Head (2008), p. 180.

56. www.telegraph.co.uk/finance/china-business/9900009/Asia-has-more-billionaires-than-North-America.html.

57. www.guardian.co.uk/commentisfree/2011/feb/28/education-jobs-middle-class-decline.

58. Nicola White, *Reconstructing Italian Fashion: America and the Development of the Italian Fashion Industry*. Berg, 2000.

59. www.businessoffashion.com/2011/01/bof-exclusive-chinas-oprah-hung-huang-picks-her-top-5-chinese-fashion-talents.html.

60. Singh interview.

61. Cattaneo, Gereffi and Staritz, *Global Value Chains in a Post-Crisis World*, p. 183.

62. Chinoiserie Query, *Pigeons & Peacocks*, Issue 4.

63. Edward W. Said, *Culture & Imperialism*. Vintage, 1994, p. xiii.

64. Accenture Report, *Five Lessons for the Chinese Fashion Industry from the French*, January 2012.

65. www.economist.com/node/10962707.

66. Catherine Dior was a noted French Resistance member; Christian Dior's niece Françoise a notorious fascist.

67. www.nytimes.com/2011/09/04/books/review/sleeping-with-the-enemy-coco-chanels-secret-war-by-hal-vaughan-book-review.html?_r=1.

68. www.businessoffashion.com/2013/09/chanels-wertheimers-found-11-billion-richer-selling-no-5.html.

69. Louis Vuitton's Links with Vichy Regime Exposed, *Guardian* online, 3 June 2004.

70. www.vogue.com/voguepedia/Cristobal_Balenciaga.

71. Paul N. Siegel (ed.), *Leon Trotsky on Literature and Art*, Pathfinder Press, 1970, p. 77.

72. Faulkner interview.

73. *Ibid.*

74. Wilson, *Adorned in Dreams*, p. 44.

75. *Ibid.*, p. 204.

76. Said, *Culture and Imperialism*, p. xxx.

77. Frankenburg, *Displacing Whiteness*, p. 13.

Chapter 8

1. Fred Davis, *Fashion, Culture and Identity*. University of Chicago Press, 1992, p. 162.

2. Ulrich Lehmann, Fashion and Materialism lecture, 2012.

3. www.scribd.com/doc/38260/Harajuku-Rebels-on-the-Bridge.

4. Davis, *Fashion, Culture and Identity*, p. 168.

5. Malossi, *The Style Engine*, p. 59.

6. Barnard, *Fashion as Communication*, p. 43.

7. Karl Marx, *The German Ideology*, Part I: Feuerbach. Opposition of the Materialist and Idealist Outlook B. The Illusion of the Epoch.

8. Barnard, *Fashion as Communication*, p. 39.

9. Steele, *Paris Fashion*, p. 18.

10. Barnard, *Fashion As Communication*, p. 41.

11. *Ibid.*

12. Wilson, *Adorned in Dreams*, p. 198.

13. Davis, *Fashion, Culture and Identity*, p. 166.

14. James C. Scott, *Weapons of the Weak – Everyday Forms of Peasant Resistance*. Yale University Press, 1985, p. 292.

15. *Ibid.*, p. 293.

16. *Ibid.*, p. 296.

17. Joy James (ed.), *The Angela Y. Davis Reader*. Wiley Blackwell, 1998, p. 277.

18. Steeve O. Buckridge, *The Language of Dress: Resistance and Accommodation in Jamaica 1760–1890*. University of West Indies Press, 2004, p. 95.

19. *Ibid.*

20. Allman, *Fashioning Africa*, p. 37. Example of Funmilayo Ransome-Kuti of the Abeokuta Women's Union.

21. Kirstin Knox. *Culture to Catwalk – How World Cultures Influence Fashion*. A. & C. Black, 2011, p. 86. Gauze, the super-fine silk, got its name from

Gaza (*gazzatum*) having been produced there from the thirteenth century for export to Europe.

22. Barnard, *Fashion as Communication*, p. 144.
23. *Ibid.*, p. 123
24. *Ibid.*, p. 130, quoting Dick Hebdige.
25. *Ibid.*, p. 132.
26. Davis, *Fashion, Culture and Identity*, p. 168.
27. Ahmed, *A Quiet Revolution*, p. 305.
28. *Ibid.*, p. 222. Whilst trying to crush women's movements in both Britain and Egypt, Cromer feigned concern for women's rights in Egypt to further imperialism.
29. *Ibid.*, p. 209.
30. *Ibid.*, p. 210. For an interesting discussion of the difference between resistance dressing and the attire of, for example, Hassidic Jews, who are less interested in challenging society than in preserving their way of life, see Davis, *Fashion, Culture and Identity*, p. 181.
31. Alain Badiou, Behind The Scarfed Law There is Fear, Islam.Online.net, 3 March 2004.
32. Joëlle Jolivet, *The Colossal Book of Costumes Dressing up Around the World*. Thames & Hudson, 2008.
33. Gayle V. Fischer, *Pantaloons and Power*. Kent State University Press, 2001, p. 4.
34. *Ibid.*, p. 4.
35. *Ibid.*, pp. 30, 169.
36. *Ibid.*, p. 175. Harem skirt collection shown by French designers Drecoll and Bechoff-David.
37. *Ibid.*, p. 176.
38. www.telegraph.co.uk/news/worldnews/africaandindianocean/sudan/5956721/Whip-me-if-you-dare-says-Lubna-Hussein-Sudans-defiant-trouser-woman.html.
39. www.guardian.co.uk/world/2009/aug/02/sudan-women-dress-code.
40. There are notable exceptions: queer fashion labels; Hedi Slimane at Dior Homme selling menswear cut for women; Calvin Klein selling unisex fragrances, etc.
41. Davis, *Fashion, Culture and Identity*, p. 168.
42. Barnard, *Fashion as Communication*, p. 135.
43. Ariel Levy, *Female Chauvinist Pigs: Women and the Rise of Raunch Culture*. Free Press, 2006. See also *Tender Butch Manifesto*, www.autostraddle.com.
44. Description of *keffiyeh* print by *Sex and the City* stylist Patricia Fields.
45. Buckridge, *The Language of Dress*, p. 86.
46. Shannon Price, Vivienne Westwood (born 1941) and the Postmodern Legacy of Punk Style, Essays from The Costume Institute, Metropolitan Museum of Art, www.metmuseum.org/toah/hd/vivw/hd_vivw.htm.
47. *Ibid.*

48. Barnard, *Fashion as Communication*, p. 132.
49. *Ibid.*, p. 132.
50. Davis, *Fashion, Culture and Identity*, p. 181.
51. Interview with Mohsin Ali, menswear designer, 5 October 2012.
52. Davis, *Fashion, Culture and Identity*, p. 161.
53. Valerie Steele, Why People Hate Fashion, in Malossi, *The Style Engine*, p. 68.
54. Knox, *Culture to Catwalk*, p. 87, quoting Michelle Malkin.
55. Tim Edwards, Express Yourself: The politics of dressing up, in Barnard, *Fashion Theory*, p. 195.
56. *Ibid.*
57. www.fashionencyclopedia.com/Ma-Mu/Moschino-Franco.html.
58. Robert Heath, *Seducing the Subconscious: The Psychology of Emotional Influence in Advertising.* John Wiley & Sons, 2012.
59. Steele, *Fashion, Italian Style*, p. 77.
60. www.vogue.com/voguepedia/Grunge.
61. Elizabeth Fox-Genovese, quoted in Barnard, *Fashion as Communication*, p. 123.
62. Davis, *Fashion, Culture and Identity*, p. 187.
63. *Ibid.*, p. 168.
64. Thomas Docherty, *Aesthetic Democracy.* Stanford University Press, 2006, p. xiv.
65. www.transrespect-transphobia.org/en_US/tvt-project/tmm-results/tdor2012.htm.
66. Malossi, *The Style Engine*, p. 244.
67. Buckridge, *The Language of Dress*, p. 86.

Chapter 9

1. James, *The Angela Y. Davis Reader*, p. 244.
2. This chapter is not an examination of small, 'ethical' businesses. There are already numerous books on this subject that readers can find if they are interested. In particular 'Naked Fashion' by People Tree founder Safia Minney.
3. Florence Kelley was a follower of Karl Marx and a friend of Friedrich Engels. Her translation into English of Engels' *The Condition of the Working Class in England* is still used today.
4. www.boisestate.edu/socwork/dhuff/history/extras/kelly.htm.
5. www.rmc.library.cornell.edu/EAD/htmldocs/KCL05307.html.
6. www.socialwelfarehistory.com/people/lowell-josephine-shaw.
7. www.nclnet.org/history.
8. www.source.ethicalfashionforum.com/digital/sustainable-fashion-towards-the-tipping-point.

9. Duncan Clark, *The Rough Guide to Ethical Shopping*. Rough Guides, 2004, p. viii.

10. www.news.sciencemag.org/sciencenow/2011/10/laundry-lint-pollutes-the-worlds.html.

11. Christina Weil, *Heart on Your Sleeve*. Oxfam Activities, 2008, p. 18.

12. Interview with Yva Alexandrova, 4 February 2013.

13. Weil, *Heart on Your Sleeve*, p. 18.

14. Blanchard, *Green is the New Black*, p. 42.

15. Major American Brands Silent on Alleged Rights Abuses at Overseas Factories, *Huffington Post*, 21 July 2011.

16. www.globallabourrights.org/alerts?id=0394.

17. N. Craig Smith, *Morality and the Market*. Routledge, 1990, p. 6.

18. Alexandrova interview.

19. Mészáros, *Marx's Theory of Alienation*, p. 206.

20. Helen Scott (ed.), *The Essential Rosa Luxemburg*. Haymarket Books, 2007, p. 1.

21. *Ibid.*, p. 89.

22. Michele Micheletti, *Political Virtue and Shopping*. Palgrave Macmillan, 2003, pp. 5–6.

23. Scott, *The Essential Rosa Luxemburg*, p. 65.

24. www.independent.co.uk/news/uk/home-news/the-real-cost-of-fashion-a-special-report-400611.html.

25. Ross, *Slaves to Fashion*, pp. 151–5.

26. *Ibid.*, p. 171.

27. Naomi Klein, *No Logo: No Space, No Choice, No Jobs*. Picador, 2001, p. 149.

28. www.marxists.org/archive/draper/1971/xx/emancipation.html.

29. www.matadornetwork.com/change/7-worst-international-aid-ideas.

30. *Ibid.*

31. Bad Charity? (All I Got Was This Lousy T-Shirt!), *Time Magazine* online, 12 May 2010.

32. G. Frazer, Used-Clothing Donations and Apparel Production in Africa, *Economic Journal*, vol. 118, October 2008, pp. 1764–84.

33. Bad Charity? (All I Got Was This Lousy T-Shirt!).

34. www.thelavinagency.com.

35. Lisa Ann Richey and Stefano Ponte, *Brand Aid: Shopping Well to Save the World*. University of Minnesota Press, 2011, p. 16.

36. Richey and Ponte, *Brand Aid*, Preface.

37. *Ibid.*, p. xii.

38. *Ibid.*, p. 187.

39. *Ibid.*, p. 174.

40. *Ibid.*, p. 9.

41. *Ibid.*, p. 152.

42. *Ibid.*, p. 1.

43. *Ibid.*, p. 157.

44. *Ibid.*, p. 3.
45. *Ibid.*, p. 5.
46. Ha-Joon Chang, *23 Things They Don't Tell You About Capitalism.* Penguin Books, 2010, p. 117.
47. Rachel Dodes, Out of Africa, into Asia, *Wall Street Journal,* 9 September 2010. Bono was also criticised by Christian Aid and the Tax Justice Network for tax evasion, when U2 shifted its financial affairs offshore to the Netherlands in 2006.
48. See Ching Yoon Louie, *Sweatshop Warriors* for details of the Fuerza Unida Centre.
49. *Ibid.*, p. 232.
50. Aboriginal Activists Group, Queensland 1970s, popularised by campaigner Lilla Watson. USAS.org.
51. Interview with Amirul Haque Amir 9 September 2013.
52. Ching Yoon Louie, *Sweatshop Warriors*, p. 228.
53. Sluiter, *Clean Clothes*, p. 63.
54. *Ibid.*, p. 181.
55. Scott, *The Essential Rosa Luxemburg*, p. 58.
56. Craig Smith, *Morality and the Market*, p. 40.
57. Magdoff and Bellamy Foster, *What Every Environmentalist Needs to Know about Capitalism*, p. 134.
58. Bellamy Foster, *Ecology Against Capitalism*, p. 25.
59. David Harvey, *The Enigma of Capital and the Crises of Capitalism.* Profile Books, 2011, p. 277.

Chapter 10

1. South End Press (ed.), *Talking about a Revolution* South End Press, 1998, p. v.
2. István Mészáros, *Beyond Capital.* Merlin Press, 1995, p. 812.
3. bell hooks interview, South End Press , *Talking About A Revolution*, p. 52.
4. Leon Trotsky, Literature and Revolution, www.marxists.org/archive/trotsky/1924/lit_revo/intro.htm.
5. From *Lincoln* screenplay, by Tony Kushner. Lines from Gloria Reuben as Mrs Elizabeth Keckley, social activist, close friend of Mrs Lincoln and author of *Behind the Scenes – or Thirty Years a Slave and Four Years in the White House*, 1868.
6. Said, *Culture and Imperialism*, p. xiii.
7. Eagleton, *Marxism and Literary Criticism*, p. 68.
8. *Ibid.*, p. 69. Quote about writers from Pierre Mackerey, based on Louis Althusser.
9. Nicholas Bourriaud, quoted in Malossi, *The Style Engine*, p. 271.
10. John Berger, *Art and Revolution.* Writers & Readers, 1969, p. 43.
11. Mészáros, *Marx's Theory of Alienation*, p. 175.

12. Penny Jane Burke and Jackie McManus, Art for a Few: Exclusions and misrecognitions in higher education admissions practices, *Discourse: Studies in the Cultural Politics of Education*, vol. 32, issue 5, 2011, pp. 699–712.

13. Audre Lorde, *Sister Outsider*, quoted in Hobson, *Venus in the Dark*, p. 143.

14. bell hooks interview, pp. 51–2.

15. Ollman, *Alienation*, p. 92.

16. Varvara Stepanova, *Tasks of the Artist in Textile Production*, p. 190, quoted in Stern, *Against Fashion*, p. 55.

17. www.guardian.co.uk/fashion/2012/jan/25/haute-couture-nice-frocks-no-shocks.

18. Mikhail Guerman, *Art of the October Revolution*, quoted in www.marxist.com/ArtAndLiterature-old/marxism_and_art.html.

19. Leon Trotsky, *Literature and Revolution*, pp. 255-6 Quoted in www.marxist.com/ArtAndLiterature-old/marxism_and_art.html.

20. Berger, *Art and Revolution*, Foreword.

21. Michael R. Redclift and Graham Woodgate (eds.), *The International Handbook of Environmental Sociology*, 2nd edition. Edward Elgar, 2010, p. 208.

22. Mészáros, *Marx's Theory of Alienation*, p. 205.

23. Karl Marx, quoted in Orbach, *Bodies*, p. 138.

24. Berger, *Art and Revolution*, p. 30.

25. John E. Bowlt and Matthew Drutt (eds.), *Amazons of the Avant-garde*. Guggenheim Museum Publications, 1999, p. 109.

26. Berger, *Art and Revolution*, p. 37.

27. There then followed the loss of the Bolshevik Revolution to Stalinism, which 'expressed itself in one of the most devastating assaults on artistic culture ever witnessed in modern history – an assault conducted in the name of a theory and practise of social liberation'. Eagleton, *Marxism and Literary Criticism*, p. 38.

28. Alexander Laurentier, *Varvara Stepanova*. Thames & Hudson, 1988, p. 81.

29. *Ibid.*

30. Art critic D. Aranovich, 1926, quoted in *ibid.*, p. 83.

31. Bowlt and Drutt, *Amazons of the Avant-garde*, p. 190.

32. M. N. Yablonskaya, *Women Artists of Russia's New Age*. Thames & Hudson, 1990, p. 115.

33. www.tate.org.uk/whats-on/tate-modern/exhibition/rodchenko-popova/rodchenko-and-popova-defining-constructivism-9.

34. Stern, *Against Fashion*, p. 55.

35. Berger, *Art and Revolution*, p. 47.

36. P. Walton and A. Gamble, *From Alienation to Surplus Value*. Sheed & Ward, 1972, p. 218.

37. Yablonskaya, *Women Artists of Russia's New Age*, p. 156.

38. Lee, *Eco Chic*, p. 82.

39. Mészáros, *Beyond Capital*, p. 739.

40. Roland Barthes, *The Fashion System*, Jonathan Cape, 1985.

41. de Marly, *Working Dress*, p. 154.

42. Alexandra Kollontai, *Communism and the Family*, 1920.

43. www.marxists.org/archive/trotsky/1924/lit_revo/intro.htm.

44. Walton and Gamble, *From Alienation to Surplus Value*, p. 12.

45. Ulrich Lehmann, Fashion and Materialism lecture, 2012.

46. This section is based on István Mészáros, *Beyond Capital*, which was used by the administration of Venezuelan President Hugo Chavez to develop the concept of an 'elementary triangle of socialism', to which the environmentalist John Bellamy Foster added an ecological element. The three concepts, which must be accorded equal weight, are: 1) social ownership of the means of production and social use, not ownership, of nature; 2) social production organised by workers and the regulation by communities of the relationship between humanity and nature; and 3) the satisfaction of the communal needs of present and future generations and of life itself.

47. Karl Marx, quoted in Mészáros, *Marx's Theory of Alienation*, p. 212.

48. *Ibid.*, p. 211.

49. Karl Marx, *Wage Labour and Capital*.

50. Rosa Luxemberg, *Reform or Revolution*, in Mészáros, *Beyond Capital*, p. 836.

51. Karl Marx, quoted *ibid.*, p. xxv.

52. *Ibid.*, p. 845.

53. Roy Morrison, quoted in John Bellamy Foster, *The Ecological Revolution*, Monthly Review Press, 2009, p. 264.

54. Andrew Simms, *Tescopoly*. Constable, 2007, p. 232.

55. Mike Cooley, *Architect or Bee*. South End Press, 1982.

56. Alan Woods, Marxism and Art, www.marxist.com/ArtAndLiterature-old/marxism_and_art.html.

57. Stepanova, 1928, quoted in Yablonskaya, *Women Artists of Russia's New Age*, p. 156.

58. Loschek, *When Clothes Become Fashion*, p. 2; and Berger, *Ways of Seeing*, Part 1.

59. Berger, *Ways of Seeing*, Part 1.

60. Kanye West, *All Falls Down*, featuring Syleena Johnson, 2004.

61. Anna Gough-Yates, *Women's Magazines*. Routledge, 2003, p. 10.

62. Berger, *Ways of Seeing*, Part 4.

63. McDowell, *The Designer Scam*, p. 28.

64. Hansen and Reed, *Cosmetics, Fashions and the Exploitation of Women*, p. 53.

65. Bartky, *Femininity and Domination*, p. 71.

66. Juan Juan Wu, *Chinese Fashion: from Mao to Now*. Berg, 2009, p. 2.

67. *Ibid.*, p. 8.

68. *Ibid.*, p. 2.
69. Lehmann, *Fashion and Materialism* lecture, 2012.
70 bell hooks interview, p. 50. Attacking 'Left-oriented' art is ideological in itself as an attempt to shut down debate and prevent art from having a social function. People should not have to struggle between their 'political beliefs with their aesthetic and artistic vision'.
71. Debbie Ging, Well-heeled women: Post-feminism and shoe fetishism, webpages.dcu.ie/~gingd/articleslectures.html.
72. Raisa Kabir: www.thefword.org.uk/blog/2013/09/the_veil_debate.
73. Ahmed, *A Quiet Revolution*, p. 34, Comment from Cairo in 1890.
74. Ging, Well-heeled women.
75. Levy, *Female Chauvinist Pigs*.
76. Walter Benjamin, On the Concept of History, www.marxists.org/reference/archive/benjamin/1940/history.htm, 2009.
77. Raahi Reddy interview in *Yellow Apparel*, 2000.
78. Oliver Wang interview in *ibid.*
79. Falasca-Zamponi, *Waste and Consumption*, p. 47.
80. Vijay Prashad interview, *Yellow Apparel*, 2000.
81. www.online.wsj.com/article/SB10001424052970203479104577124613246783618.html.
82. Eagleton, *Marxism and Literary Criticism*, p. 6.
83. Bellamy Foster, Clark and York, *The Ecological Rift*, p. 103.
84. Alexander Blok, *The Intelligensia and the Revolution*, 1918.

Bibliography

Ahmed, Leila, *A Quiet Revolution*. Yale University Press, 2011.

Albertazzi, Daniele and Cobley, Paul, *The Media: An Introduction*. Pearson Education, 2009.

Aldridge, Alan, *Consumption*. Polity Press, 2003.

Allman, Jean (ed.), *Fashioning Africa: Power and the Politics of Dress*. Indiana University Press, 2004.

Amie, Hardy, *Just So Far*. Collins, 1954.

Anderson Black, J. and Garland, Madge, *A History of Fashion*. McDonald (Black Cat imprint), 1990.

Badia, Enrique, *Zara and her Sisters: The Story of the World's Largest Clothing Retailer*, Palgrave Macmillan, 2009.

Barnard, Malcolm, *Fashion As Communication*. Routledge, 1996.

Barnard, Malcolm (ed.), *Fashion Theory: A Reader*. Routledge, 2007.

Barrell, Joan and Braithwaite, Brian, *The Business of Women's Magazines*, Kogan Page, 1988.

Barthes, Roland, *The Fashion System*, Jonathan Cape, 1985.

Bartky, Sandra Lee, *Femininity and Domination*. Routledge, 1990.

Bartlett, Djurdja, *Fashion East – The Specter that Haunted Socialism*. MIT Press, 2010.

Bell, Quentin, *On Human Finery*. Hogarth Press, 1947.

Bellamy Foster, John, *Marx's Ecology*. Monthly Review Press, 2000.

Bellamy Foster, John, *Ecology Against Capitalism*. Monthly Review Press, 2002.

Bellamy Foster, John, *The Ecological Revolution*, Monthly Review Press, 2009.

Bellamy Foster, John, Clark, Brett and York, Richard, *The Ecological Rift: Capitalism's War on the Earth*. Monthly Review Press, 2010.

Berger, John, *Art and Revolution*. Writers and Readers, 1969.

Berger, John, *Ways of Seeing*. Penguin Classics, 2008.

BIS, *Never Leave The House Naked*. BIS Publishers, 2009.

Blanchard, Tamsin, *Green is the New Black*. Hodder & Stoughton, 2007.

Blyth, Myrna, *Spin Sisters*. St. Martin's Press, 2004.

Bonilla-Silva, Eduardo, *Racism without Racists*. Rowman & Littlefield, 2010.

Bowlt, John and Drutt Matthew (eds.), *Amazons of the Avant-garde*. Guggenheim Museum Press, 1999.

Breward, Christopher and Evans, Caroline (eds.), *Fashion and Modernity*. Bloomsbury, 2005.

Buckridge, Steeve O., *The Language of Dress: Resistance and Accommodation in Jamaica 1760–1890*. University of West Indies Press, 2004.

Byrne Smith, Laura, *The Urge to Splurge*. ECW Press, 2003.

Carson, Rachel, *Silent Spring*. Houghton Mifflin, 1987.

Catlaneo, Olivier, Gereffi, Gary and Staritz Cornelia (eds.), *Global Value Chains in a Post-Crisis World*. World Bank, 2010.

Chan Kwok-bun, Cheung Tak-sing and Agnes S. Ku (eds.), *Chinese Capitalisms*. Brill, 2008.

Chang, Ha-Joon, *23 Things They Don't Tell You About Capitalism*. Penguin Books, 2010.

Ching Yoon Louie, Miriam, *Sweatshop Warriors*. South End Press, 2001.

Chow, Gregory C., *China as a Leader of the World Economy*. World Scientific Publishing, 2012.

Ciochetto, Lynne, *Globalisation and Advertising in Emerging Economies Brazil, Russia, India and China*. Routledge, 2011.

Clark, Duncan, *The Rough Guide to Ethical Shopping*. Rough Guides, 2004.

Clark, Eric, *The Want Makers*. Hodder & Stoughton, 1988.

Compaine, Benjamin M. and Gomery, Douglas, *Who Owns the Media?* Lawrence Erlbraum Associates, 2000.

Cooley, Mike, *Architect or Bee*. South End Press, 1982.

Croteau, David and Haynes, William, *The Business of Media*. Pine Forge Press, 2001.

Davis, Fred, *Fashion, Culture and Identity*. University of Chicago Press, 1992.

Docherty, Thomas, *Aesthetic Democracy*. Stanford University Press, 2006.

Eagleton, Terry, *Marxism and Literary Criticism*. Methuen, 1985.

Eagleton, Terry, *Ideology: An Introduction*. Verso, 1991.

Eagleton, Terry, *After Theory*. Allen Lane/Penguin, 2003.

Elkington, John and Hailes, Julia, *The Green Consumer Guide*. Victor Gollancz, 1988.

Elliott, David, *New Worlds: Russian Art and Society 1900–1937*. Thames & Hudson, 1980.

Elliott, Larry and Atkinson, Dan, *The Gods that Failed*. Bodley Head, 2008.

Engels, Friedrich, *The Condition of the Working Class in England*. 1845.

Falasca-Zamponi, Simonetta, *Waste and Consumption*. Routledge, 2011.

Faulkner, Neil, *A Marxist History of the World*. Pluto Press, 2013.

Featherstone, Liza and United Students Against Sweatshops, *Students Against Sweatshops*. Verso, 2002.

Fine, Ben, *The World of Consumption: The Material and Cultural Revisited*. Routledge, 2002.

Fine, Ben and Saad-Filho, Alfredo, *Marx's Capital*, 5th edition. Pluto Press, 2010.

Fischer, Gayle V., *Pantaloons and Power*. Kent State University Press, 2001.

Fogarty, Anne, *The Art of Being a Well-Dressed Wife* [1959]. V & A Enterprises, 2011.

Frankenberg, Ruth, *White Women, Race Matters: The Social Construction of Whiteness*. University of Minnesota Press, 1993.

Frankenberg, Ruth, *Displacing Whiteness*. Duke University Press, 1997.

Gale, Colin and Kaur, Jasbin, *Fashion and Textiles*. Berg, 2004.

German, Lindsey, *Sex, Class and Socialism*. Bookmark, 1998.

German, Lindsey, *How a Century of War Changed the Lives of Women*. Pluto Press, 2013.

Goffman, Erving, *The Presentation of Self in Everyday Life*. Allen Lane/Penguin, 1969.

Gough Yates, Anna, *Women's Magazines*. Routledge, 2003.

Granger, Michele, *Fashion: The Industry and its Careers*. Fairchild Publications, 2007.

Haig, Matt, *Brand Success: How the World's Top 100 Brands Thrive and Survive*, 2nd edition. Kogan Page, 2011.

Hansen, Joseph and Reed, Evelyn, *Cosmetics, Fashions and the Exploitation of Women*. Pathfinder Press, 1986.

Hapke, Laura, *Sweatshop: The History of an American Idea*. Rutgers University Press, 2004.

Harman, Chris, *Economics of the Madhouse*. Bookmark, 1995.

Harvey, David, *The Enigma of Capital and the Crises of Capitalism*, Profile Books, 2011.

Heath, Robert, *Seducing the Subconscious: The Psychology of Emotional Influence in Advertising*. Wiley Blackwell, 2012.

Helen Scott (ed.), *The Essential Rosa Luxemburg*. Haymarket Books, 2008.

Higham, William, *The Next Big Thing*. Kogan Page, 2009.

Hobson, Janell, *Venus in the Dark*. Routledge, 2005.

James, Joy (ed.), *The Angela Y. Davis Reader*. Wiley Blackwell, 1998.

Jarrow, Jeanette A. and Judelle, Beatrice (eds.), *Inside the Fashion Business*. John Wiley & Sons, 1966.

Jhally, Suj, *The Codes of Advertising*. Routledge, 1990.

Klein, David and Burstein, Dan, *Blog!* CDS Books, 2005.

Klein, Naomi, *No Logo*. Picador, 1999.

Knox, Kirstin, *Culture to Catwalk: How World Cultures Influence Fashion*. A. & C. Black, 2011.

Kollontai, Alexandra, *Communism and the Family*. 1920.

Kollontai, Alexandra, *The Autobiography of a Sexually Emancipated Communist Woman*. Herder and Herder, 1971.

Laurentier, Alexander, *Varvara Stepanova*. Thames & Hudson, 1988.

Lee, Matilda, *Eco Chic*. Octopus, 2007.

Leeds Craig, Maxine, *Ain't I a Beauty Queen?* Oxford University Press, 2002.

Levy, Ariel, *Female Chauvinist Pigs: Women and the Rise of Raunch Culture*. Free Press, 2006.

Loschek, Ingrid, *When Clothes Become Fashion*. Berg, 2009.

Lunn, Eugene, *Marxism and Modernism*. University of California Press, 1982.

Magdoff, Fred and Bellamy Foster, John, *What Every Environmentalist Needs To Know About Capitalism*. Monthly Review Press, 2011.

Malossi, Giannino (ed.), *The Style Engine*. Monacelli Press, 1998.

de Marly, Diana, *Working Dress*. Holmes & Meier, 1986.

Marx, Karl, *Wage Labour and Capital* (pamphlet).

Marx, Karl, *Economic and Philosophical Manuscripts of 1844 Antithesis of Capital and Labour. Landed Property and Capital*.

Marx, Karl, *The German Ideology*. 1846.

Marx, Karl, *The Poverty of Philosophy*. 1847.

Marx, Karl, *Outline of the Critique of Political Economy (Grundrisse)*. 1857–61.

Marx, Karl, *Capital*, Volume 1. Progress Press, 1887.

Marx, Karl, *Marx: Later Political Writings* [*The Eighteenth Brumaire of Louis Bonaparte*]. Cambridge University Press, 1996.

McDowell, Colin, *The Designer Scam*. Hutchinson and Random House, 1994.

McKay, Jenny, *The Magazines Handbook*. Routledge, 2006.

Mears, Ashley, *Pricing Beauty*. University of California Press, 2011.

Mészáros, István, *Beyond Capital*. Merlin, 1995.

Mészáros, István, *Marx's Theory of Alienation*. Merlin, 2006.

Mészáros, István, *The Structural Crisis of Capital*. Monthly Review Press, 2010.

Micheletti, Michele, *Political Virtue and Shopping*. Palgrave Macmillan, 2003.

Naylor, R. T., *Crass Struggle*. McGill-Queen's University Press, 2011.

North, Richard D., *Rich is Beautiful*. Social Affairs Unit, 2005.

Nystrom, Paul H., *Economics of Fashion*. Ronald Press, 1928.

Ollman, Bertell, *Alienation: Marx's Conception of Man in Capitalist Society*. Cambridge University Press, 1976.

Orbach, Susie, *Fat is a Feminist Issue*. Arrow Books, 2006.

Orbach, Susie, *Bodies*. Profile Books, 2010.

Orwell, George, *The Road to Wigan Pier*. Victor Gollancz, 1937.

Pankhurst, Sylvia, Communism and its Tactics, *Workers' Dreadnought*. 1921.

Raymond, Martin, *The Trend Forecaster's Handbook*. Lawrence King, 2010.

Redclift, Michael R. and Woodgate Graham (eds.), *The International Handbook of Environmental Sociology*, 2nd edition. Edward Elgar, 2010, chapters 7 and 13.

Rhodes Leara D., Magazines, in Erwin K. Thomas and Brown H. Carpenter (eds.), *Mass Media in 2025*. Greenwood Press, 2001.

Richey, Lisa Ann and Ponte, Stefano, *Brand Aid: Shopping Well to Save the World*. University of Minnesota Press, 2011.

Roberts, Paul Craig, *Alienation and the Soviet Economy*. University of Mexico Press, 1971.

Rosenberg, William G. (ed.), *Bolshevik Visions*. University of Michigan Press, 1990.

Ross, Andrew (ed.), *No Sweat: Fashion, Free Trade and the Rights of Workers*. Verso, 1997.

Ross, Robert J. S., *Slaves to Fashion*. University of Michigan Press, 2004.

Said, Edward W., *Culture and Imperialism*. Vintage, 1994.

Scott, James C., *Weapons of the Weak: Everyday Forms of Peasant Resistance*. Yale University Press, 1985.

Seebohm, Caroline, *The Man Who Was Vogue*. Weidenfeld & Nicolson, 1982.

Settle, Alison, *English Fashion*. Collins, 1959.

Sheridan, Jayne, *Fashion, Media, Promotion: The New Black Magic*. Wiley Blackwell, 2010.

Siegel, Paul N. (ed.), *Leon Trotsky on Literature and Art*. Pathfinder Press, 1970.

Siegle, Lucy, *To Die For: Is Fashion Wearing out the World?* Fourth Estate, 2011.

Sigsworth, Eric M., *Montague Burton: The Tailor of Taste*. Manchester University Press, 1990.

Simms, Andrew, *Tescopoly*. Constable, 2007.

Sladen, Christopher, *The Conscription of Fashion*. Scholar Press, 1995.

Sluiter, Liesbeth, *Clean Clothes*. Pluto Press, 2009.

Smith, N. Craig, *Morality and the Market*. Routledge, 1990.

Smythe, Dallas Walker, *Dependency Road: Communication, Capitalism, Consciousness and Canada*. Ablex, 1982.

South End Press (ed.), *Talking About a Revolution*. South End Press, 1998.

Steele, Valerie, *Paris Fashion*. Berg, 1988.

Steger, Manfred B. and Roy, Ravi K. *Neoliberalism: A Very Short Introduction*. Oxford University Press, 2010.

Steinham, Gloria, *Moving Beyond Words: Age, Rage, Sex, Power, Money, Muscles: Breaking the Boundaries of Gender*. Touchstone, 1994.

Stern, Radu, *Against Fashion: Clothing as Art 1850–1930*. MIT Press, 2004.

Strebbins, Robert A., *Leisure and Consumption: Common Ground/Separate Worlds*. Palgrave Macmillan, 2009.

Thomas, Dana, *Duluxe*. Penguin, 2007.

Tomlinson, Alan (ed.), *Consumption, Identity and Style: Marketing, Meanings and the Packaging of Pleasure*. Routledge, 1991.

Tranberg Hansen, Karen, *Salaula: The World of Secondhand Clothing and Zambia*. University of Chicago Press, 2000.

Tulloch, Carol (ed.), *Black Style*. V & A Publications, 2004.

Turow, Joseph and Tsui, Lohman (eds.), *The Hyperlinked Society*. University of Michigan Press, 2008.

Waddell, Gavin, *How Fashion Works*. Blackwell, 2004.

Waldfogel, Joel, *Scroogenomics: Why You Shouldn't Buy Presents for the Holidays*. Princeton University Press, 2009.

Walton, P. and Gamble, A., *From Alienation to Surplus Value*. Sheed & Ward, 1972.

Weil, Christina, *Heart On Your Sleeve*. Oxfam Activities, 2008.

Welters, Linda and Lillethun, Abby (eds.), *The Fashion Reader*. Bloomsbury, 2007. 2nd edition,. Berg, 2011.

Werle, Simone, *Style Diaries: World Fashion from Berlin to Tokyo*. Prestel, 2010.

White, Cynthia L., *Women's Magazines 1693–1968*. Michael Joseph, 1970.

White, Nicola, *Reconstructing Italian Fashion: America and the Development of the Italian Fashion Industry.* Berg, 2000.

Whitehorne, Olivia, *Cosmo Woman.* Crescent Moon, 2007.

Wilson, Elizabeth, *Adorned in Dreams.* Virago, 1985.

Wolf, Naomi, *The Beauty Myth.* Random House, 1991.

Wu, Juan Juan, *Chinese Fashion: from Mao to Now.* Berg, 2009.

Yablowskaya, M. N., *Women Artists of Russia's New Age.* Thames & Hudson, 1990.

Acknowledgements

First, I would like to thank John Berger, with whom I was lucky enough to discuss this project in its early days. He summed up his advice in one word. I pass it on, as you never know when you too will need it: Courage.

To my family for a lifetime of love and support and for always telling me: 'You can do it.'

Thank you to everyone at Counterfire for motivating political discussion. To Clare Solomon for all your support; to John Rees for early chapter readings and for constant encouragement over the last decade; to Lindsey German, James Meadway and Season Butler for reading the finished text and making helpful suggestions.

To Neil Faulkner for polishing this book from a rough diamond to something I wanted everyone to read. For patience, guidance and letting me phone you at all hours to discuss topics ranging from Chanel to use-value.

To Laura Harvey for sharing the really great times as well as the bad, and for arguing over obscure bits of feminist theory.

To Kate Hudson, a hundred thanks for your tireless encouragement. To my friends at CND and the Islam Channel, thank you for your support. To everyone who wanted to talk endlessly about fashion and sent me articles and tip-offs – it all helped make this process a real pleasure. Thank you to all the interviewees in this book, who gave up their valuable time to speak with me; and to Ben Quinn for hints and tips on interviewing.

To Dragon Tiger, KO, Singdayt, Kiatphontip and Oz Osmaston for teaching me discipline, heart and humility. To Kosol Soisangwan for arranging and translating the visit to Beam Design.

Thank you to Pluto Press – Jonathan Maunder, Joana Ramiro, Robert Webb, Melanie Patrick, Jon Wheatley, and Ruth Willats. Thanks also to Dave and Sue Stanford for typesetting and proofreading and Sue Carlton for compiling the index. An especially big thank you to my endlessly patient, yet frank editor David Castle, thank you for understanding what I wanted to do and for helping me to do it. Thank you also 'anonymous reviewers', I properly fell in love with this project when I had to defend it against your comments.

Thank you to the incredible Jade Pilgrom for being my art collaborator. The minute I saw your work I knew you were 'the one'. It has been an honour to work with you, thank you for your magic. Nor would this book look how it does without you Ilanga Preuss – thank you for all your ideas and creativity.

I would like also to give heart-felt thanks to the Lipman Miliband Trust for their generous funding of the illustrations, thank you for your understanding of this project and for your vital support.

To Angela, thank you for helping me find the road and for keeping me on it. That this book exists is in a large part thanks to you.

To all the writers whose work is contained in this book, thank you for letting me stand on the shoulders of giants. Whilst the internet has been important, this is a book of books written at LSE, University of the Arts, Bishopsgate Institute and the public libraries in Hackney and Southwark. I hope our libraries will forever be protected to allow people free access to our cultural heritage.

'Dyslexics of the world – Untie!' Thank you to my dyslexia for making my brain what it is, and to whoever invented the spell-checker.

This book chronicles the lives of millions of people on the sharp end of capitalist exploitation. I wrote it to draw attention to their stories and to answer some of the questions I had about the world. If you have more questions or want to put into practice the ideas in this book, then the movement for change is waiting for you. Come find us.

About the Illustrator

Jade Pilgrom is a freelancing illustrator raised and currently working from Birmingham, Alabama. Her education includes a Visual Arts diploma from The Alabama School of Fine Arts and she received a BFA from Ringling College of Art and Design in 2011. She recently won an Award of Excellence in the 33rd Annual Society for News Design. Her work is primarily vector, with occasional jumps into traditional painting and drawing.

For updates, feedback, employment, and commission inquiries, please contact her at:

www.jadepilgrom.com
www.gezzitjade.tumblr.com
shutupjade@gmail.com

Index

Compiled by Sue Carlton